EMPLOYMENT CONTRACTS, PSYCHOLOGICAL CONTRACTS, AND EMPLOYEE WELL-BEING

Employment Contracts, Psychological Contracts, and Employee Well-Being

An International Study

Edited by

DAVID E. GUEST, KERSTIN ISAKSSON,
AND HANS DE WITTE

OXFORD
UNIVERSITY PRESS

OXFORD
UNIVERSITY PRESS

Great Clarendon Street, Oxford OX2 6DP

Oxford University Press is a department of the University of Oxford.
It furthers the University's objective of excellence in research, scholarship,
and education by publishing worldwide in

Oxford New York

Auckland Cape Town Dar es Salaam Hong Kong Karachi
Kuala Lumpur Madrid Melbourne Mexico City Nairobi
New Delhi Shanghai Taipei Toronto

With offices in

Argentina Austria Brazil Chile Czech Republic France Greece
Guatemala Hungary Italy Japan Poland Portugal Singapore
South Korea Switzerland Thailand Turkey Ukraine Vietnam

Oxford is a registered trade mark of Oxford University Press
in the UK and in certain other countries

Published in the United States
by Oxford University Press Inc., New York

© Oxford University Press, 2010

British Library Cataloguing in Publication Data

Data available

Library of Congress Cataloging in Publication Data

Data available

Typeset by SPI Publisher Services, Pondicherry, India
Printed in Great Britain
on acid-free paper by
MPG Books Group, Bodmin and King's Lynn

ISBN 978–0–19–954269–7

1 3 5 7 9 10 8 6 4 2

Preface

This book has had a long gestation. Its origins can be traced to a workshop held in 2000 at the European Foundation for the Improvement of Living and Working Conditions in Dublin in advance of Sweden's presidency of the European Union. This was one of a series of workshops sponsored by the Swedish government to highlight issues that it might wish to profile during its presidency. The subject of the workshop was flexible employment and in particular temporary employment. One of the outcomes was an acceptance that the evidence base for policy makers was limited and inconsistent and would benefit greatly from stronger comparative research. Some members of the group at the workshop agreed to seek an opportunity to undertake such research.

Initial support for the project was provided by SALTSA, a cooperation between the (then) Swedish National Institute for Working Life and the Swedish Trade Unions, and a team was gathered to undertake an extended pilot study. The countries involved reflected the workshop participants who wanted to pursue the research, although Spain and East Germany were added to ensure a broader European representation. The results of the pilot, conducted in 2002, were presented in a report to SALTSA (Isaksson et al., 2003*a*).

Based on the pilot work and the report to SALTSA, and with strong support from SALTSA, funding for a three year research programme was provided by the European Union for what was termed the PSYCONES (PSYchological CONtracts across Employment Situations) project. The project was coordinated by Kerstin Isaksson and her team in Sweden. The work started in 2003 and was completed in 2006.

The research has been a joint effort by eight teams from seven countries (there were two teams from Belgium working on different aspects of the research). Inevitably, working in different countries, with different research traditions and different mother tongues presents challenges and requires time. But it also reaps considerable rewards and greatly enriches the research experience. We are particularly pleased that the project served as a valuable development experience for the younger researchers on the main national teams most of whom completed their doctoral theses largely through work related to the Psycones research. We held meetings on a regular basis in each of the European countries participating in the study and set up a web page for the project (www.uv.es/~psycon). As a result, there is joint responsibility for the content of the questionnaires that formed the basis for the data collection, although each country team was responsible for collecting its own data. The core analysis was conducted by the UK team and provided the basis for the final report to the European Commission. Additional analysis for the chapters in this book was undertaken by the authors of each chapter. Where this occurred, every effort was made to ensure consistency of method and choice of control variables.

This book draws together the core findings from the study. It is complemented by a large number of articles in academic journals that focus more narrowly on specific aspects of the research or analyse national subsamples of the data. The book has been edited by three members of the research team and they have also been involved as co-authors of most of the chapters. However, the book reflects the research of the Psycones group as a whole.

Contents

List of Figures

List of Tables

List of Contributors

Claudia Bernhard-Oettel is a Post-Doctoral Research Fellow at the Department of Psychology, Stockholm University, Sweden.

Michael Clinton is a Lecturer in Work Psychology and Human Resource Management in the Department of Management at King's College, London, UK.

Amparo Caballer is Associate Professor in the Department of Social Psychology at the University of Valencia, Spain.

Rita Claes is a Professor in the Department of Personnel Management, Work and Organizational Psychology, University of Gent, Belgium

Nele De Cuyper is Assistant Professor in Personnel Psychology in the Research Group on Work, Organizational and Personnel Psychology (WOPP) in the Department of Psychology, K. U. Leuven, Belgium.

Jeroen de Jong is Assistant Professor of Organizational Behaviour in the Department of Organizational Studies at Tilburg University, Holland

Hans De Witte is Full Professor of Work Psychology in the Research Group on Work, Organizational and Personnel Psychology (WOPP), in the Department of Psychology, K. U. Leuven, Belgium.

Francisco Gracia is Associate Professor in the Department of Social Psychology at Valencia University, Spain.

David Guest is Professor of Organizational Psychology and Human Resource Management in the Department of Management at King's College, London.

Kerstin Isaksson is Professor of Psychology in the Department of Psychology, Malardalen University in Vasteras, Sweden.

Moshe Krausz is Emeritus Professor in the Department of Psychology, Bar-Ilan University, Israel.

Gisela Mohr is Professor of Work and Organizational Psychology at the University of Leipzig, Germany.

José Maria Peiró is Professor of Social and Organizational Psychology, at the University of Valencia, Spain.

José Ramos is a Lecturer in Work and Organizational Psychology in the Department of Social Psychology, University of Valencia, Spain.

Thomas Rigotti is a Researcher in Work and Organizational Psychology at the University of Leipzig.

René Schalk is Professor of Policy and Ageing in the Department of Human Resource Studies at Tilburg University, Holland.

Abbreviations

AGFI	Adjusted Goodness of Fit Index
ANCOVA	Analysis of Covariance
CFI	Comparative Fit Index
ISCED	International Standard Classification of Education
NUEWO	New Understanding of European Work Organization
OCB	Organizational Citizenship Behaviour
PCA	Principal Component Analysis
POS	Perceived Organizational Support
PSYCONES	Psychological Contracts across Employment Situations
RMSEA	Root Mean Square Error of Approximation
SALTSA	Samarbetsprogram mellan Arbetslivsinstitutet
SWING	Survey Werk-thuis Interferentie-Nijmegen

1

Introduction

David E. Guest, Kerstin Isaksson, and Hans De Witte

The continuing search for competitive advantage, the opportunities offered by information technologies, and the need to operate in a context of rapid and continuous change have led firms to seek new ways of organizing work and employment (Pfeffer and Baron, 1988). One manifestation of this has been the growth in employment flexibility. Recent decades have seen a steady increase in part-time working, in subcontracting, and in various forms of temporary employment in most advanced industrial countries (OECD, 2002). While much of this growth has been driven by employers and the growth of the service economy, it has also suited some workers. For example, with more women in the workforce and an increasing interest in work–life balance, the opportunity to work part-time has often been welcomed (Barling and Gallagher, 1996; Conway and Briner, 2002a). The growth of knowledge work has meant that some people value the independence that contract work offers, so that a temporary employment contract can become the contract of choice (Barley and Kunda, 2004).

Despite a growing acceptance that flexible employment is likely to be a persisting and significant feature of contemporary work, we have no clear idea about how it affects the satisfaction and well-being of workers. The traditional assumption, still held by some policy-makers in Europe, is that workers experiencing flexible employment are a disadvantaged minority who need protection. This contrasts with the growing literature about those who have been described as 'free workers' (Knell, 2000) and 'boundaryless workers' (Arthur and Rousseau, 1996), whose loyalty is to themselves and their knowledge, and those who value the independence of flexible employment. It is possible that as flexible employment becomes more commonplace, it becomes more acceptable to workers. On the other hand, there is the fear that as it becomes more prevalent, it opens the door to greater exploitation of workers by unscrupulous employers. Such fears have led to action at a European level to control fixed-term employment and to calls, reflected in the Temporary (Agency) Workers Directive, for greater employment rights for those working for temporary agencies.

With so many uncertainties, untested assumptions, and unresolved questions about how workers respond to, and are affected by, flexible employment, there is a need for a stronger evidence base around which to build policy and practice. This book sets out to explore how workers in different countries and different employment sectors are affected by flexible employment and more specifically by the various forms of temporary employment. From a worker's perspective, temporary employment, with its implied uncertainties about continuity of employment, is perhaps the most precarious form of employment flexibility and is therefore the most likely to have an impact upon workers' well-being. By comparing developments and experiences across a number of countries and sectors, we can gain a better idea of the nature, pervasiveness, and impact of temporary employment.

Analysis of employment experiences requires a clear conceptual and analytic framework. For this study, we use as a core organizing framework the employment relationship explored through the lens of the psychological contract (Rousseau, 1995, 2005; Guest, 2004b). This recognizes that employment involves an exchange that is partly captured in the formal employment contract but that inevitably goes further to cover more informal and implicit issues and understandings. There is good reason to believe that these will differ for temporary and permanent workers. We therefore need to compare their experiences of the employment relationship and to explore the causes and consequences of any differences. Since flexible employment and the use of temporary contracts is usually initiated by employers and popularly considered to benefit them, possibly at the expense of temporary workers, it will be particularly important to consider the consequences for the well-being of those in temporary employment. The well-being of temporary workers, broadly defined to cover aspects of their experience at work as well as outside work, and reflected partly in their physical and psychological health, is therefore one of the central themes of this book.

The notion of the employment relationship and of an exchange implies that there are two parties to the contract; it will be important to consider the psychological contract and the 'deal' it implies from the perspective of both the worker and the employer, since the employer's assumptions about temporary workers will have a bearing on how these workers are treated. We therefore explore the psychological contract from the perspective of both employer and worker and consider the promises and obligations of each. Since it is still relatively rare for studies of the psychological contract to explore issues from the perspectives of both parties, this book will make a contribution by broadening and deepening our understanding of psychological contracts.

A preliminary analysis reveals that the growth of flexible employment, and temporary employment in particular, has been uneven across advanced industrial countries (De Cuyper, Isaksson, and De Witte, 2005). While there is a general assumption that temporary employment has been growing, even within Europe this is not a consistent trend across all countries. Furthermore, the form that temporary employment takes, such as the use of agency workers or fixed-term contracts, also varies considerably (Koene, Pauuwe, and Groenewegen, 2004). National institutional factors including employment legislation, labour markets, education systems, and family and cultural traditions are likely to play a part in shaping the nature of flexible employment. A central feature of this study is therefore a comparative analysis across a number of countries that seeks to take account of national institutional factors in explaining variations in practices and in their consequences for worker well-being.

This opening chapter sets the context for the study. The following section outlines the reasons for the growth of interest in flexible employment and in temporary contracts in particular, and describes the presence of temporary employment in different countries. Further sections present the core analytic framework that informs the book, based on the psychological contract, and introduce the concept of worker well-being which, we argue, is an important outcome of the employment relationship. The final section outlines the logic and content of the book.

The growth of flexible employment and temporary contracts

Peter Cappelli, at the start of his influential book *The New Deal at Work*, asserts that

Most observers of the corporate world believe that the traditional relationship between employer and employee is gone, but that there is little understanding of why it ended and even less about what is replacing that relationship. (Cappelli, 1999, p. 1)

While some of us would not agree that in all work settings the traditional relationship has gone, we can acknowledge that it is under considerable pressure. Furthermore, Cappelli and others (see e.g. De Cuyper, Isaksson, and De Witte, 2005) provide a consistent set of clues about why the relationship has been changing.

Most observers will cite the growth of international trade and competition and the impact of new technology as key factors affecting changes in the traditional employment relationship. These developments have put pressure on costs and in particular on labour as a fixed cost. To place themselves in a more favourable position in the competitive market, firms will seek to reduce the fixed cost of labour by introducing various forms of flexible employment. Recent years have also witnessed an expansion of the international labour market and Europe has been experiencing a massive increase in labour migration, mainly from east to west, following the accession of a number of East European countries to the European community. Much of this migration is short term, and both encourages and facilitates the use of temporary employment. It is also deeply susceptible to the rapid changes in the global economic climate that occurred abruptly in 2008.

Further pressure on costs and, in turn, on the traditional employment relationship has come from the growing power of shareholders and financial markets that has contributed to the rising number of mergers and takeovers. One consequence is that in a world where even successful organizations become susceptible to takeover, traditional job security can easily be eroded. The dramatic economic downturn that started in 2008 provides further evidence of the transient nature of job security.

If competitive pressures create a need for employment flexibility, new technologies create the means to put it into practice by facilitating forms of flexibility such as subcontracting and distanced working. The opportunities created by new information technologies for global communication and for more effective and timely monitoring and control of performance have greatly contributed to the opportunity to pursue flexible employment. One of the more obvious examples of this has been the growth of call centres located where there is suitable and available cheap labour (Deery and Kinnie, 2004). Another is the opportunity to work from home or in remote offices. Communication technologies enable employers to monitor, control, and maintain contact with workers, irrespective of their location and employment status.

New technology is closely associated with the growth of the knowledge worker. Knowledge work shares qualities with traditional professional work in so far as the primary allegiance of knowledge workers will often be to their specialist knowledge rather than to the organization in which it is applied. This has helped to advance the concept of the boundaryless worker who possesses transportable knowledge and expertise that is nevertheless likely to be in demand by organizations (Arthur and Rousseau, 1996). An organization may seek this expertise for only short periods, for example, because they have only occasional need for legal, project management, or counselling expertise; and the knowledge worker may prefer the independence of choosing where and when to work. There may therefore be advantages for both parties in using fixed-term or temporary employment arrangements.

Temporary employment arrangements wherein workers deliberately opt for this type of employment have been glamorized through the concept of the 'free worker' (Knell, 2000) and the operation of distinctive high-technology labour markets such as Silicon Valley in California (Saxenian, 1990). Barley and Kunda (2004) have provided a vivid picture of the experiences of a group of technical workers engaged in this type of employment. While most of those they studied had adjusted to and come to see the benefits of their employment circumstances, very few had actively sought it. In other words, temporary employment or self-employment had often been forced upon them and at the time when they embarked upon it, it was rarely their contract of choice. A UK study (Guest and Sturges, 2007) found that workers who displayed a preference for a boundaryless career and adopted a boundaryless career pattern of employment were nevertheless typically rather restless and relatively less satisfied than those with more traditional career patterns and preferences. The emerging picture of the experiences of boundaryless knowledge workers and the consequences of such work for satisfaction and well-being is therefore mixed.

Another key change in the workforce has been the growing proportion of women and of those such as students or the semi-retired who by choice are not seeking permanent employment. The need to attract staff, particularly in parts of the service sector that operate on or close to a 24/7 basis, has meant that firms need to accommodate to the needs of both the market and the workforce by developing complex part-time and shift arrangements, sometimes using on-call and agency workers to staff the peaks in demand. Retail stores, with their weekend opening and extra demand around times such as the lead up to Christmas and the sales periods, are examples of organizations that can only survive through the use of flexible employment patterns.

In summary, there are competitive pressures that create a need for organizations to engage in employment flexibility; technology has made it more feasible to engage in employment flexibility; and the changing nature of work and the workforce has created a demand among some employees for flexible employment. For many organizations, flexible employment is just one part of a process of what has become more or less permanent change. Peters (1987), in his depiction of permanent revolution in the workplace and 'a world turned upside down', has described circumstances that are increasingly familiar. Beyond the pressures from and the unpredictability of the market, employers also have to deal with a growth in regulation and allied initiatives from governments. All this reinforces the need for flexibility and the capacity to adjust rapidly to changing circumstances.

Views about the consequences of the growth of flexible employment for organizations and for individuals have been very mixed. Atkinson (1984), using a model of the flexible firm, supported by Handy (1989) and others, has presented flexibility as an opportunity for firms and has outlined the characteristics of the flexible firm with a core of key permanent staff and a periphery of more loosely attached workers. Williamson and others (Williamson, 1975; Boxall and Purcell, 2008), using transaction cost economics, have argued that generic and easily replaceable skills and infrequently required skills might be more efficiently managed through external contracts rather than permanent employment. Building on this perspective but incorporating elements of human capital theory, Lepak and Snell (1999) have developed a more sophisticated contingency model that advocates four kinds of employment relationship, including one that emphasizes contingent work, and they view their framework as an opportunity for more effective workforce management. A preliminary test of this model reported by Peel and Boxall (2005) provided some support for it but implied a need to give more weight to the frequency of skill use and to the need for financial flexibility in understanding reasons for the use of contracting and temporary employment. Cappelli (1999) cautions that under flexible employment conditions, firms face potentially daunting new challenges in dealing with issues of skill enhancement, commitment, and retention, while Purcell (1999) notes the problems firms face in defining what is core or peripheral activity. As with so many other developments, flexible employment provides employers with both new opportunities and new challenges.

From a worker's perspective, optimists such as Handy (1989) and Bridges (1995), perhaps focusing on professional and knowledge workers in particular, believe that we are seeing the emergence of new networks of independent and 'free' workers who can engage in multiple roles while maintaining an appropriate degree of autonomy. In contrast, Pollert (1991), among many others, has been concerned that flexibility reduces the bargaining power of workers and their unions. Burchell, Lapido, and Wilkinson (2002) and De Witte (2005) are among those who have voiced concerns that employment flexibility enhances job insecurity. Drawing on a broader canvas, Beck (2000) has presented a depressing scenario in which flexible employment will sharpen the divide between the 'haves' and the 'have-nots'; and there is evidence from the growing disparity in the incomes of the rich and poor in the United States, the United Kingdom, and some other European countries to support his case. Beck's analysis also highlights how temporary employment, in particular, shifts the risk from the employer to the worker, altering the balance of the exchange in the employment relationship.

In Europe, the social partners have been concerned about the growth of flexible employment. Although for many years the level of unemployment in Europe has been a major concern, the Lisbon Declaration of 2000 signalled a shift towards a focus on the content of jobs when it called for 'more and better jobs'. At the same time, the permanent full-time job appears to have remained as the template for the ideal model of employment. It is with this in mind that legislation has been enacted at a European level to restrict working hours and to limit the duration of fixed-term contracts. Further legislation in the form of the Temporary (Agency) Workers Directive should help to ensure that temporary agency workers receive the same basic employment conditions comparable to permanent workers. An illustration of a step in this direction can be found in Sweden where for some time most agency workers have a permanent contract with their agency. While there is always a powerful case for ensuring the protection of potentially vulnerable workers, the pressures outlined above make the retention of the permanent full-time job as the template for the ideal form of employment less feasible.

There are signs of some new policy initiatives in Europe designed to address the growth of flexible working by seeking to meet the needs of industry, workers, and society. This is being increasingly described as 'flexicurity'. It consists of a set of policies intended to combine flexible labour markets and working arrangements with greater employment security as well as financial security for those on the margins of employment. A key characteristic of 'flexicurity' is that it recognizes that flexible working, including temporary employment, is likely to be a long-standing feature of the labour market.

Analysing flexible employment

Flexibility at work can take a variety of forms. Since we are mainly interested in flexible employment and more specifically in flexible employment contracts, we will not be addressing issues of flexible reward systems or flexibility in the design and allocation of work. We will also not be discussing the increasingly important issue of subcontracted work. There has been a growing body of research exploring the impact of subcontracting of call centre work to countries such as India (Deery and Kinnie, 2004). However most call centre workers are as likely as any others to have permanent contracts and the key issues of concern in the exploration of call centre working have focused on job design, systems of monitoring and control, and off-shoring of work.

Flexible employment can be described along the dimensions of hours, contract, and location. Flexible hours include part-time working, overtime and other forms of extended hours, varying shift and on-call patterns of work, and arrangements that provide for annual hours and some flexibility about when these hours are worked. The geographical dimension concerns where the work takes place. There has been much interest in home-working, although the major growth may be in the opportunity to do some work from home rather than being permanently home-based. There are also likely to be major variations, particularly for sales and service staff, in the time spent away from their main office base. Contract flexibility draws the main contrast between those on permanent and temporary contracts and we develop this in more detail below. One issue that needs to be taken into account is the increasing scope for contractual and legally supported rights to time off work for permanent employees such as maternity leave and, increasingly, sabbaticals and other types of break from work. Allied to this, we are likely to see a growing interest in flexible retirement patterns, long established in the United States and more recently facilitated in pan-European legislation.

Our major concern in this book is with temporary employment. There are a number of reasons for this. Firstly, it appears to have been an increasingly common pattern of employment in a number of advanced industrial countries but has received relatively limited research attention. We need to improve our understanding of why employers hire temporary workers and how far they set out to treat them differently from permanent workers. Secondly, as the proposed European directive implies, it is seen as a form of employment that potentially holds significant disadvantages for some employees. As marginal workers, they may sometimes fall outside the protection offered by collective agreements and the support of trade unions. We therefore need to explore how far the experience of temporary working affects well-being. Thirdly, we have only a very limited understanding of why workers accept temporary employment and the extent to which this choice is made from a position of weakness or strength in the labour market. We need to develop a better understanding of the extent to which workers feel forced into temporary employment or choose it as their preferred option and why. Finally, there are questions about how far other factors, such as being in job of choice or experiencing challenging work compensate for the possible costs of temporary employment. In this context, research by Aronsson and Goransson (1999) has suggested that workers' satisfaction and well-being may be as much affected by being in the occupation and job of choice as being on the employment contract of choice.

Before we turn to the specific focus of the research reported in this book, it is important to note that although there is a general assumption that flexible employment is on the increase, we should be careful not to overstate its adoption. This applies in particular to temporary employment. There are some problems in defining temporary work, a point we return to later in this chapter, but, allowing for this, it appears that across Europe about 14 per cent of the workforce are employed on temporary contracts and this figure is not rising. The average hides considerable variation. In 2005, when we were undertaking the research reported in this book, the figure among the countries in the study ranged between 5.5 per cent in the United Kingdom and 33.3 per cent in Spain (OECD, 2006), suggesting that any analysis needs to take into account national differences in economic, political, and social factors. Although 14 per cent may not seem large, it nevertheless includes many millions of workers who are often considered to be in precarious employment and therefore potentially vulnerable and this justifies a particular focus on their experiences and well-being. With this in mind, we turn to the analytic framework that informed our research.

THE ANALYTIC FRAMEWORK FOR THE STUDY

The analytic model that informs our research is set out in Figure 1.1. This has four core sets of variables. Firstly, there are a range of background or control variables that are included because we believe they may have an influence on employment contracts, the psychological contract, and employee well-being. Secondly, there is the key independent variable that forms the central focus of our study, namely, the nature of the formal employment contract, with a major broad distinction between permanent and temporary contracts. Thirdly, there are a set of intervening variables that might affect the relationship between the independent and control variables and possible outcomes. At the heart of these is the psychological contract but we have also included a range of additional variables that have been identified in previous research as having a significant role to play in shaping worker well-being. Finally, there are a variety of outcomes that centre on aspects of employee well-being but extend to a broader range of attitudes and behaviour.

The background or control variables

There are four levels at which background factors can be considered. The first is the national level. Institutional and cultural factors are likely to affect the presence of temporary employment in each country, how temporary employment is experienced, and how it is regarded. In their analysis of the varied pattern of growth of temporary employment agency work across European countries, Koene, Paauwe, and Groenewegen (2004: 69) conclude that 'the growing use of agency work over the past two decades is not just an economic and numerical fact, but also reflects a normative change in the societal attitude towards temporary work'. We need to take into account

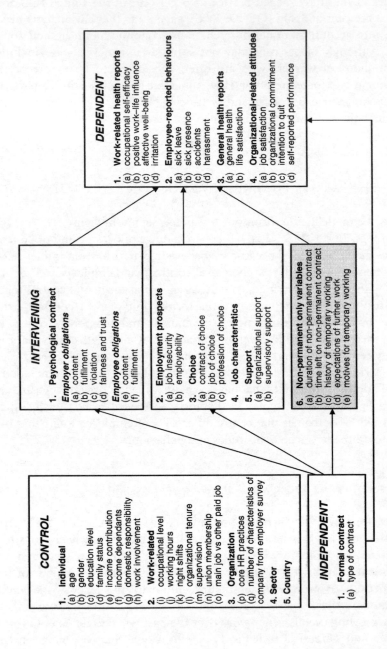

Figure 1.1 The Psycones analytic framework

possible differences in these societal attitudes across countries by including a number of countries in the research.

The second level is the employment sector. The nature of the work in different sectors and the labour market associated with each sector are likely to affect the requirement for temporary employment and how it is experienced. For example, the requirements of a relatively stable manufacturing environment and a more volatile retail sector might lead to differing use of temporary workers. Sectors such as agriculture and hotels and catering are more susceptible to seasonal fluctuations in demand for labour and may therefore be more predisposed to employ some workers on a temporary basis. To address these issues the research therefore needs to cover a number of distinctively different sectors.

The third level that needs to be addressed is the organization. We need to understand why organizations employ temporary workers, the kinds of roles in which they are deployed, how they are regarded by employers, and how this affects the ways in which temporary workers are treated. Features of the organizational context are also likely to affect the experience of being a temporary worker. The presence of a trade union might ensure better treatment; the same may be the case in organizations where more advanced human resource practices are widely applied so that practices that are adopted for permanent workers, such as access to training and development and feedback on their performance, are extended to temporary workers as well.

The final level of analysis is the individual worker. Temporary work may suit some people but not others. It will therefore be important to consider a range of background factors such as qualifications, family income obligations, and dependent relationships that may have a bearing on this. We will also need to link these to motives for undertaking temporary employment. Indeed, the issue of motives is likely to be sufficiently important to merit specific analysis in its own right. This is reflected in the location of motives for temporary employment within the analytic model. Other factors at the individual level that might affect reactions to temporary employment and also have a bearing on well-being, and therefore need to be considered in the analysis, include work-related experiences such as working hours, any shift-working, level in the organization, any supervisory responsibilities, and tenure with the organization.

While all these background factors at the country, sector, organizational, and individual level serve as control variables to enable us to assess the independent impact of the employment contract, they also inform the extent and form of temporary working. They are therefore of interest in their own right, not least because some have potentially important policy implications. As Peel and Boxall (2005) have argued, it is particularly important to understand the basis for management decisions about employing temporary workers and to consider how far they seek arrangements that are mutually beneficial to both workers and organizations. This highlights the need to collect information on the features of background and context from both employers and employees. In the chapters that follow, we will take into account how the various background factors affect the employment contract, the psychological contract, and aspects of well-being.

Employment contracts

The key independent variable in our study is the employment contract and in particular the distinction between temporary and permanent contracts. As noted earlier, the concept of standard employment, defined in terms of full-time, permanent employment with a single employer, is growing less tenable with the growth of flexible forms of employment. Any deviation from this towards part-time working or multiple job holding is still defined as atypical. When the contract is temporary, the employment attracts other labels such as 'contingent', 'precarious', or 'casual'. The role of the self-employed complicates the picture still further. In the United States, they may be regarded as temporary workers (Connelly and Gallagher, 2004), but in Europe, their position is less clear-cut.

For practical purposes, the Eurostat/OECD definition of temporary employment appears to provide a useful point of departure. It states that:

A job may be regarded as temporary if it is understood by both employer and employee that the termination of the job is determined by objective conditions such as reaching a certain date, completion of an assignment or return of another employee who has been temporarily replaced. (Eurostat, 1996, p. 45)

This definition emphasizes the nature of the relationship rather than the employment status of those holding the temporary job. Some problems remain since, for example, it includes consultancy activities that may be carried out by permanent employees of a major consultancy, or by a self-employed consultant, or by an individual who is hired as a temporary employee of the organization. If we adapt this definition to treat 'job' as a synonym for 'employment', then we come close to an acceptable definition of temporary employment, at least from the perspective of the individual worker. In doing so, we exclude the self-employed since they maintain that employment status even when they are not undertaking a specific job or assignment. We will therefore accept the Eurostat/OECD definition of temporary employment with the proviso that 'employment' is substituted for 'a job' at the start of the definition. While this definition provides a basis for comparisons across countries and organizations and is a useful starting point, we should recognize that national differences in legislation, including legislation about the rights of permanent, temporary, and self-employed workers, make highly specific and finely grained consistent comparisons almost impossible.

While the OECD definition offers a broad understanding of the distinction between temporary and permanent contracts, it does not provide any clues to the range of possible forms of temporary employment. For example, it is possible to be employed directly by an employer or through an agency and to be employed on an open-ended contract or on one of fixed duration. There are also a range of temporary contracts that arise as a result of probationary periods, training arrangements, or national job creation schemes. Arriving at a systematic classification of these presents a daunting task. The problem may be further exacerbated by national differences in some of the definitions such as the distinction between a probationary contract and a fixed-term contract. Any employment through an agency is commonly regarded as temporary employment and fits the OECD definition; but it breaks down when the worker has a permanent contract with the agency. Those employed by consultants and by subcontractors may appear from the perspective of an organization to be temporary, and the relationship is maintained only until the end of an assignment. But the worker may have a permanent contract with their employer.

For the purposes of this study, we draw three main distinctions. Firstly, we distinguish whether the employment is through an agency or directly with an organization. Secondly, we distinguish whether the contract is open-ended or of a fixed term. Thirdly, we distinguish the basis for the employment. This third category is the most problematic. However, it is possible to differentiate

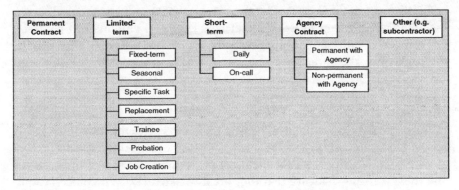

Figure 1.2 Types of employment contract

temporary contracts introduced to fill a short-term requirement, including seasonal jobs and provision of cover for absent workers, from contracts created to develop and assess competence such as trainee, probationary, and job creation scheme positions. It is also possible to differentiate temporary employment that is one-off in nature, such as providing cover for a specific maternity leave or assisting in a specific project, from more indeterminate but very short-term arrangements, such as providing on-call or daily cover to deal with unpredictable variations in demand. Yet in services such as teaching or home care, very short-term temporary contracts of this nature may be on the increase. These distinctions are set out in Figure 1.2.

An important implication of the preceding analysis is that we should recognize temporary employment as potentially heterogeneous. The reasons for undertaking it and therefore the characteristics of those engaging in it may be very different depending on the type of temporary employment arrangement. The choices are also likely to be determined by national employment institutions and the requirements of employers. Therefore, in our analysis, we distinguish between the different types of temporary contracts as well as take account of national, sectoral, organizational, and individual circumstances that might play a part in determining their prevalence and their impact on worker well-being.

Intervening variables

The model in Figure 1.1 suggests that a range of factors above and beyond the type of employment contract is likely to determine worker well-being and other worker attitudes and behaviours. Furthermore, reviews of the literature on temporary work (see e.g. Connelly and Gallagher, 2004; De Cuyper et al., 2008; Guest, 2004a) identify a number of potentially important variables that are likely to affect the impact of temporary employment on worker well-being including employment prospects, preferred choice of employment contract, job content, organizational support, and, as a central feature of the analysis, the psychological contract.

Employment prospects

In our analysis, employment prospects are concerned with two interrelated issues. One is perceived job insecurity and the other is perceived employability. Job insecurity is widely cited as a problem of temporary employment and there is strong evidence that they are associated (De Witte and Naswall, 2003; Parker et al., 2002; Sverke, Gallagher, and Hellgren, 2000). Not all the evidence supports this association; for example, Pearce and Randel (1998) found no differences in levels of job security between permanent and temporary US aerospace industry workers. Nevertheless, the evidence overwhelmingly supports an association and it is widely acknowledged that job insecurity reduces employee well-being (see e.g. De Witte, 1999; Sverke, Hellgren, and Naswall, 2002). Therefore, in so far as job insecurity is associated with temporary employment, it could explain any negative consequences of temporary contracts. Employability has also been identified as an important factor in shaping the experience of temporary work (Guest and Conway, 1998). Those who are confident that they could find another job of the same or better quality are likely to be more relaxed about being in temporary employment than those who believe that they would struggle to find another job.

Contract choice

This has been identified in previous research as a key factor in shaping the experience of temporary employment (Krausz, Brandwein, and Fox, 1995; Marler, Barringer, and Milkovich, 2002). Those who, for whatever reasons, actively seek temporary work might be expected to be more positive when they are in temporary positions than those who would prefer permanent employment. The research of Aronsson and Goransson (1999) suggests that this is likely to extend to choice of job and occupation. Motives for engaging in temporary employment are perhaps best considered as part of the wider issue of choice and volition.

Job content

This has been less consistently studied in previous research on temporary employment. However, the economic arguments in favour of temporary employment (Williamson, 1985; Boxall and Purcell, 2008) suggest that routine and easily replaceable jobs are particularly suited to temporary work. At the same time, infrequently needed professional jobs might also be suitable for temporary contracts. We therefore need to consider whether workers at these potential extremes of job content respond differently to the experience of temporary work. We also need to gain a better understanding of whether temporary jobs are more constrained with respect to skill use, autonomy, and work load than permanent jobs (Parker et al. 2002). For example, we might hypothesize that temporary workers are given the more marginal, routine tasks that require less insider knowledge of networks and informal procedures. This, in turn, may influence their attitudes and behaviour.

Organizational support

Organizational support has been widely recognized as an important variable affecting satisfaction, commitment, and well-being at work. Organizational support can be defined as a feeling of being valued by an organization (Eisenberger et al., 1986). It can be complemented by the more local concept of supervisor support which addresses the extent to which an individual believes their supervisor values their contribution and cares about their well-being (Kottke and Sharafinski, 1988). These concepts are grounded in exchange theory and therefore fit well with the broad analytic model that informs our study. We include both levels of support in our model on the grounds that the extent to which newcomers to an organization and those who are only with the organization for a short period feel supported while they are in the organization seems likely to have an important bearing on their satisfaction and well-being during their employment (Eisenberger et al., 1997).

Characteristics of temporary work

For those engaged in temporary work, their experience of such work, and reactions to it are likely to be shaped in part by the specific characteristics of their employment. We therefore need to take into account the duration of the contract, the time left on the contract, previous experience of temporary employment, expectations of a contract extension, and, as noted above, the motives for engaging in temporary work. In doing so, we recognize that temporary workers are potentially a heterogeneous group with a wide range of experiences and preferences that are likely to affect their reactions to their employment status.

THE ROLE OF THE PSYCHOLOGICAL CONTRACT

The final and, for this analysis, the key intervening variable is the psychological contract, which lies at the heart of our model. The concept of the psychological contract has attracted growing attention in recent years as a useful analytic framework within which to explore the consequences for workers of changes in organization and employment. Its origins can be traced back to the 1960s and to the recognition that employment contracts, like all contracts, are only partial and that informal understandings develop that can have a major bearing on attitudes and behaviour at work (Argyris, 1960; Levinson et al.,

1962; Schein, 1965). Its reintroduction as a focus of contemporary research owes much to the work of Rousseau (1989, 1995).

Informal understandings may take the form of perceived obligations, with strong normative implications about appropriate behaviour. For example, an employee is likely to believe, as a minimum, that an employer is obliged to provide safe working conditions and an environment free from any discrimination and harassment. The employer, in turn, is entitled to expect that the employee will arrive at work at agreed times and behave honestly. Beyond these and other basic obligations, both parties may make promises, perhaps in the context of a performance appraisal or possibly in the context of asking, as a favour, to have some time off work, that create expectations and commitments. Sometimes these will be explicit, sometimes more implicit; and at other times one party will believe a promise has been made while the other party does not. There is invariably some scope for miscommunication; and a turbulent environment can often mean changes in personnel so that when a boss moves on, the implicit and informal promises will often move on with him or her. There is therefore plenty of scope for breach of the understandings that form the core of the exchange in the psychological contract.

The influential work of Rousseau (1995) has dominated much of the research on the psychological contract. She has defined the psychological contract as 'individual beliefs, shaped by the organization, regarding terms of an exchange agreement between the individual and their organization' (Rousseau, 1995: 9). This approach deliberately adopts a one-sided view, emphasizing workers' perceptions of the contract, partly on the grounds that it is inappropriate to anthropomorphize the organization. However, others have argued that if the psychological contract is to be viewed as an exchange, then it is important to consider both parties to that exchange. By the same token, the metaphor of a contract inevitably entails two parties or at least their agents, and in this context, managers can act as agents of the organization (Arnold, 1996; Guest, 1998; Coyle-Shapiro and Kessler, 2002*b*). Partly acknowledging this, some of Rousseau's more recent work has emphasized the importance of mutuality (Rousseau, 2005). Indeed, in one of Rousseau's more recent definitions, she suggests that '[p]sychological contracts are the individual belief systems held by workers and employers regarding their mutual obligations. Every employment relationship is subjectively understood and experienced by each participant—the employee, contractor, manager-employer' (Rousseau, 2005, 81). Taking these issues into account, for this study, we defined the psychological contract as '*the perceptions of both parties to the employment relationship—organization and individual—of the reciprocal promises and obligations implied in that relationship*' (Guest and Conway, 2002*b*).

Rousseau (2005) has argued that the growth of employment flexibility and the pace of change affecting organizations have meant that psychological contracts have tended to become less collective and more idiosyncratic or individual. The need to manage a range of slightly different 'deals' presents new challenges for management and also creates more scope for breaches of the psychological contract and for invidious comparisons with the deals that others may have managed to negotiate. It also means that issues of fairness and trust become more salient (Guest, 2004*b*).

McLean Parks, Kidder, and Gallagher (1998) have presented an analysis of the possible dimensions along which the psychological contracts of temporary workers might be considered. They propose seven dimensions. Two are concerned with time and address whether the contract is of short or long duration and of precise or imprecise duration. Stability is concerned with the extent to which the psychological contract is fixed or evolving. Scope is concerned with the breadth of the psychological contract. Tangibility addresses the extent to which the contract is explicitly defined and observable. This overlaps a little with the next dimension, focus, which is concerned with whether the psychological contract is more about socio-emotional, relational factors or economic, transactional factors. Finally, particularism is concerned with the extent to which what is exchanged in the psychological contract is unique and non-substitutable. Although this is a conceptual framework, it provides some useful dimensions to take into account in developing an empirical study of the psychological contracts of temporary workers. In a comparison of two case study organizations, Koene and van Riemsdijk (2005) have shown how these dimensions can be utilized to explore different approaches to human resource management and the employment of temporary workers. The dimensions also highlight the potential variability of the psychological contracts of temporary workers and provide a warning against treating temporary workers as a homogeneous group.

There are several reasons why we have chosen the psychological contract as a major analytic framework for our study of the impact of temporary employment on worker well-being. The first is that it expands the metaphor of the contract from the employment contract to the range of other issues that inform the employment relationship. This is important in a context where there is anecdotal evidence as well as a range of popular assumptions that employers may be more ready to treat temporary workers less favourably in a range of respects than their permanent employees. It therefore permits us to explore and compare the implicit and informal aspects of the employment relationship of both permanent and temporary workers.

A second reason is that the psychological contract effectively captures the exchange at the heart of the employment relationship, focusing on the substantive issues in that exchange from the perspective of both parties. Thirdly, in focusing on the exchange at the individual level, the psychological contract is able to capture elements of the idiosyncrasy that appears to be a key feature of contemporary flexible employment in a way that is less feasible when adopting a more traditional collective perspective. At the same time, and this is a fourth argument in favour of the use of the psychological contract, it provides a framework within which to explore the contemporary employment relationship in those work settings where collective arrangements are either absent or largely dormant. If the analytic framework is extended to incorporate issues of fairness and trust, then it comes close to addressing most of the core issues in more traditional employment relations (Guest, 2004*b*).

A fifth reason for utilizing the psychological contract in this context is that its focus on the exchange between the employer and workers places the worker at the heart of this exchange. Since worker well-being is a central concern of the study, this is particularly appropriate. Finally, the way in which the psychological contract has been analysed by researchers such as Guest and Conway (1998, 2002*a*; Guest, 2004*b*), Coyle-Shapiro and Kessler (2002*a*), and others offers an analytic framework that, by setting out causal links and addressing antecedents and consequences, points to a range of policy implications and possible interventions to improve the psychological contract.

In the reviews of the evidence about the impact of temporary employment on workers' attitudes and behaviour (see e.g. Connelly and Gallagher, 2004; De Cuyper et al., 2008; Guest, 2004*a*), it emerges that there is no consistent evidence that temporary workers feel disadvantaged. Instead, much depends on the set of moderating or mediating variables that we have incorporated into our model such as contract preference and concerns about job security and employability. However none of the research to date incorporates the range of potential influences or takes account of sectoral and national factors that may help to shape the extent to which temporary work is adopted and how society views such employment. They therefore confirm that there is a need for a fuller exploration of the consequences of temporary employment, and in particular of the factors that help to determine its impact on employee outcomes. The common perception among many of those who seek to shape EU policy and legislation is that temporary employment is predominantly harmful. This may be the case; but first we need to gain a better understanding of the circumstances under which its effect on workers is likely to be negative or positive. As a final step in the analytic framework, we need to consider the nature of relevant worker outcomes. With this in mind, we turn to a discussion of worker well-being.

WORKER WELL-BEING

We have alluded several times to the concept of worker well-being. There has been a growing interest in well-being and related concepts such as happiness among social scientists. For example, in the United States and the United Kingdom, economists like Easterlin (2001) and Layard (2005) have noted the failure of job satisfaction to follow the predictions of classic economic theory and rise in line with increasing national affluence in advanced industrial societies. At a policy level, several European countries have become concerned at the rise in the proportion of workers who are absent from work or have quit work as a result of long-term mental health and stress-related problems (Jones et al., 2003; Lidwall, Marklund, and Skogman Thoursie, 2005). One of the explanations that has been offered is that the growing demands at work, allied to increasing insecurity brought about by rapid and unpredictable change, are causing many workers to feel distressed. Helliwell (2003) in a forty-country comparison of values and life satisfaction found that three of the factors likely to reduce the level of happiness in a country are being unemployed, a sense of job insecurity, and the national level of unemployment. It seems likely that workers on temporary contracts will be among the more vulnerable in such contexts. This has been the major driver behind moves within the European Union to provide greater protection for temporary workers and it is also a central focus of our study.

Danna and Griffin (1999) define well-being as 'comprising the various life/ non-work satisfactions enjoyed by individuals, work-related satisfactions and general health' (p. 368). Warr (1987, 2002, 2007) suggests that well-being may be considered as general or context-specific. While our interest is primarily in work-related well-being, we are also interested in its broader implications, and Roxburgh (1996) among others has shown that there is a spillover from work-related well-being to well-being in life more generally. In his thorough review of work-related well-being and how to measure it, Warr (1987, 1990) identifies three core dimensions. These are pleasure–displeasure, which in practice means satisfaction–dissatisfaction; enthusiasm–depression; and contentment–anxiety. Responses associated with dissatisfaction, depression, and anxiety, and more particularly some combination of these, may be associated with mental health problems which are an increasingly dominant factor in long-term absence from work. Although these are different from physical health, there is some possibility of overlap between physical and mental health. Indeed, the World Health Organization definition of health is 'a state of complete physical, mental and social well-being and not merely the absence of disease or infirmity' (WHO, 1998).

This brief analysis suggests that both work-related well-being and well-being in life are multifaceted. We need measures of psychological health such as those identified by Warr; measures of life satisfaction and general health; and measures of the interface between work and life outside work, including work–life balance, that address possible spillover. Although the definitions of well-being and health cited above tend to highlight positive features and experiences, well-being at work can also be defined as freedom from mental and physical harm which suggests that well-being will be manifested in an absence of negative experiences such as accidents, bullying, and harassment and undue pressure to attend work, even when feeling unwell. Accepting this broad perspective on well-being, we will include these variables in the study. This will provide an opportunity to determine which aspects of well-being are likely to be affected by, or associated with, flexible working and more particularly temporary employment contracts. Through this we can begin to provide a more comprehensive answer to the question of whether flexible working is associated with positive or negative outcomes for those who experience it.

Although our main interest is the link between new patterns of flexible working and worker well-being, we should recognize that there is a long tradition of research in work and organizational psychology that is interested in the link between satisfaction and performance (Schneider et al., 2003; Staw, 1986). This raises the question of whether flexible working including temporary employment affects both well-being and performance. To determine this, we will need information on organizationally relevant outcomes. Some of these can be obtained from managers. Others might be measures of performance, commitment, and intention to stay as long as possible with the organization. We will therefore incorporate these into our analysis to provide a rounded picture of the impact of flexible working.

In summary, the aim of the study reported in this book is to evaluate the impact of a particular form of employment flexibility—temporary employment contracts—on worker well-being and work-related attitudes and behaviour. A closely related aim is to assess the role of the psychological contract in helping to understand the relationship between employment contracts and worker well-being. The study, which we have labelled PSYCONES (PSYchological CONtracts across Employment Situations), was funded by the European Union under its Fifth Framework Agreement. It builds on an earlier extensive pilot study supported by SALTSA (Samarbetsprogram mellan Arbetslivsinstitutet), the Swedish trade union organization.

THE STRUCTURE OF THE BOOK

Following this introductory chapter, Chapter 2 describes how we explored these issues and in particular the characteristics of the sample of workers and organizations that we studied. Since our focus is on developments within Europe and our concern is with whether country factors, including different national institutions and policies, have an impact on flexible working, we need to compare experiences in a number of different countries. We therefore included seven countries in the study. To further minimize the risk of bias, we additionally focused on three rather different sectors in each country. The result is a large study comprising over 200 organizations and over 5,000 workers of whom about one-third are employed on various kinds of temporary contract. In each organization, data were collected at both the individual and organizational levels through separate interview/questionnaire schedules. The methods of data collection are described and details of the sample are presented. Fuller information about the detailed construction and analysis of the questionnaires and measures is included in Appendix 2.

Chapter 3 explores the employers' perspective, reporting their reasons for employing temporary workers and considering the ways in which they treat temporary workers compared with permanent workers. Here, and in subsequent chapters, we set the findings in the context of the relevant literature. The findings confirm that employers use temporary workers primarily to provide flexibility, with organizational characteristics determining the type of flexible workers required. Managers report a different, more transactional relationship with temporary workers. Overall, they also report higher levels of satisfaction with the performance of temporary workers compared with permanent workers.

Chapter 4 presents the core findings comparing workers employed on temporary and permanent contracts. It covers the range of variables explored in the study including the intermediate items such as job insecurity and job content, and outcome variables such as job satisfaction, absence, the various measures of health, and subjective indictors of performance. The chapter also explores the motives for undertaking temporary employment and reports the differences between the responses of those engaged in the various types of temporary employment. On the basis of this initial comparison, and contrary to our initial assumptions, temporary workers report generally more positive attitudes and well-being.

Chapter 5 focuses specifically on the psychological contract. After developing further some of the conceptual and research issues raised in this introductory chapter, it explores the content of the psychological contracts of temporary and permanent employees. It covers the various elements within our conceptualization of the state of the psychological contract including the extent to which promises and obligations have been met, the levels of trust and fairness, and the extent to which the psychological contract is perceived to have been breached and violated. Because the study collected perceptions of the promises and obligations of both the organization and workers as judged by both the employer and workers, there is a rich basis for comparison of breadth of promises and levels of fulfilment. This analysis reveals some imbalance in the psychological contracts of temporary workers in particular, since they generally seem to promise more to the employer than the employer offers in return and employers admit that they do not always fulfil their promises and obligations.

Chapter 6 builds on the previous chapter by analysing the causes and consequences of the psychological contract. The analysis of the determinants takes account of factors at the individual, organization, sectoral, and national levels as well as paying particular attention to the nature of the employment contract. The key finding is that even after controlling for the range of background factors, temporary workers report a more positive psychological contract. Taking the analysis a step further, the results suggest that the psychological contract partly mediates the link between employment contract and outcomes but those on temporary contracts still report a number of more positive outcomes.

Chapter 7 compares the reports of employers and workers on various aspects of the psychological contract. To date, only a very limited number of studies have collected data from both employers and workers within the same organizations. A key question is whether a higher level of agreement on the various dimensions of the psychological contract is associated with more or less positive outcomes from the perspectives of both organization and workers. This is explored in relation to both permanent and temporary workers and the results indicate that a higher level of agreement between parties is not consistently associated with more positive outcomes.

Chapter 8 provides a full test of the model that informs the study. In Chapter 6 we established that the psychological contract partially mediates the relationship between type of employment contract and outcomes. In this chapter, we incorporate the full range of potential mediating variables so that we can take account of being on contract of choice, job insecurity, employability, organizational support, and job content as well as the psychological contract. The results suggest that these further mediate the association between type of employment contract and outcomes. Nevertheless, those on temporary contracts still report some significantly more positive outcomes.

The incorporation of the full set of potential mediators also provides an opportunity to determine which are most strongly associated with the various outcomes. Therefore, in addition to providing a stern test of the influence of employment contracts, there is also a unique opportunity to consider the relative importance of the psychological contract alongside a number of other well-established variables.

Chapter 9 focuses on national and sectoral differences. As we have noted, there are considerable national differences in the proportions of workers on temporary contracts and we speculated that a range of national factors might help to shape the experience of temporary employment. To explore this possibility, we developed a range of measures of institutional and cultural factors that have emerged in previous research and in this chapter present some findings based on these. However, a comparison on the basis of these factors reveals only limited differences between the countries included in the study and analysis of our data reveals that both country and sector have a relatively minor impact on attitudes and outcomes. It appears that experiences in the workplace have the greatest impact on well-being in general and work-related well-being in particular.

Chapter 10 draws together the findings. The results are contrary to expectations and we consider why this should be so. Since they are consistent across the seven countries, we are reasonably confident that they are robust. On the other hand, we need to be able to justify them in the light of some competing evidence and the widespread assumption that temporary workers are significantly disadvantaged. We consider factors including changing expectations, the growing interest in work–life balance, and the increasing demands that appear to be placed on those in permanent positions. We finish by briefly reviewing the empirical and theoretical advances resulting from this study and outlining some policy implications at both the national and organizational levels.

2

Investigating the Experience
of Temporary Workers

Thomas Rigotti, David E. Guest, Michael Clinton, and Gisela Mohr

INTRODUCTION

Our study set out to evaluate the impact of temporary employment on the well-being, attitudes, and behaviour of temporary workers. As outlined in the previous chapter, we developed a clear conceptual framework within which to explore the role of temporary contracts that also allowed us to consider a range of other influences on workers' outcomes. A central feature of this framework is an emphasis on the psychological contract. This chapter describes how we conducted the study. It therefore outlines the methods adopted and how we validated the measures, the process of conducting comparative research, the data analysis and how we resolved the various issues that arose. It also provides information about the sample and how we selected it. Details of the measures we used are included in Appendix 1, and the sources of data and the statistical properties of the measures are presented as a Technical Report in Appendix 2.

THE GENERAL APPROACH TO DATA COLLECTION
AND ANALYSIS

The core aim of the research was to explore the experience and consequences of temporary working across a number of European countries from the perspective of workers and employers. Given the desire to gain systematic information across a range of contexts in each country, an early decision was taken to use a survey instrument as the major means of data collection with workers. While a similar decision was agreed with respect to representatives of employers, the data included some qualitative information that could be more easily collected in the context of a face-to-face interview. Therefore, an interview, based on a structured schedule, was recommended as the preferred method of collecting data from employers.

There are established and well-validated measures for some of the topics we wanted to cover in our surveys; for others, we had to create new measures. Developing new survey instruments that can be used in a number of countries requires extensive preparatory work. The research team was therefore fortunate in gaining sponsorship from SALTSA, the Swedish trade union organization, to conduct a sizeable pilot study to develop and test the measures. This funding also provided an opportunity for extensive discussions among members of the team about the analytic framework, for reviews of the relevant literature, and for an analysis of the current policies and practices in each of the participating countries. The results of this extensive pilot work, involving 1,685 workers, were presented in a report to SALTSA (Isaksson et al., 2003a) and can be found in De Cuyper, Isaksson, and De Witte (2005). The pilot study confirmed that the survey instruments, with some modifications, would be suitable for collecting the kind of data that would meet the aims of the study.

Data collection

We needed to develop instruments to collect information from three sources. The first was the sample of temporary and permanent workers; the second was the employers of these workers; and the third was the group of experts who could provide information about national institutional and cultural arrangements that might affect the experience of temporary working. We will consider each in turn.

The survey of workers

The central aim of the study was to collect information about the backgrounds, experiences, attitudes, and well-being of temporary and permanent workers covering the issues set out in the analytic framework described in Chapter 1. Most of the variables we were interested in had been explored in previous studies, and in many cases, there were standard and well-validated measures available. However, they had typically been used in some but not all of the countries in our study and only some of them had previously been applied to the potentially distinctive case of temporary workers. As noted above, we decided at an early stage to use a structured questionnaire survey approach based on an extensive pilot study, and to undertake careful cross-

and back-translation in line with the established best practice for comparative research (Werner and Campbell, 1970; Behling and Law, 2000). We also needed to establish that even the previously validated measures retained acceptable levels of reliability in each country.

The extensive pilot study allowed us to determine the reliability and validity of the scales. In most cases, the measures worked well and in a few cases some mainly minor modifications were required. Some of the more challenging decisions related less to the scales than to certain background/control variables such as a basis for comparing education levels across countries. However, with this thorough pilot testing, we were confident that we had a sound means of data collection.

The choice of variables to measure was determined largely by the conceptual framework that informed the study. However, this still left plenty of scope concerning choice of scale. Following extensive debate, we settled upon a mix of measures developed initially in a number of different countries, reflecting the international and comparative nature of the study. The full set of variables used in the survey of workers is set out in Table 2.1, while the source of the actual instruments and the number of items in each scale are set out in Appendix 2. It should be noted that the questionnaire for temporary workers contained a number of additional items that were not included for permanent workers. These consisted of items on motives for temporary working, on expectations of further work with their current employer, and some information on the length of their existing contract and history as a temporary worker.

The survey of employers

A core assumption in our study was that the experience of temporary workers would be shaped not only by individual characteristics, previous experiences, and motives but also by the specific organizations in which they were working. For those temporary workers who move rapidly from one work setting to another, often staying in each for a matter of days rather than weeks or months, the policies and practices of the organization in which they are located at the time of our survey may not be of much significance. However, as our information on the temporary sample indicates, the average tenure of our temporary workers is 32 months. This suggests that they typically stay in an organization for sufficient time to be affected by the policies and practices in operation. In anticipation of this, we decided to collect information from managers about any distinctive ways in which they managed temporary workers and, in particular, any differences in the application of a number of key human resource practices to temporary and permanent

Table 2.1 The variables included in the worker survey

Independent	Control	Intervening	Dependent
1. Formal contract	1. Individual characteristics	1. Psychological contract	1. Work-related well-being
(a) type of contract	(a) age	*Employer obligations*	(a) job satisfaction
	(b) gender	(a) content	(b) influence of work on life
	(c) education level	(b) fulfilment	(c) work-related anxiety
	(d) family status	(c) violation	(d) work-related depression
	(e) income contribution	(d) fairness and trust	(e) irritation
	(f) income dependants	*Employee obligations*	(f) occupational self-efficacy
	(g) domestic responsibility	(e) content	
	(h) work involvement	(f) fulfilment	2. Organizational-related attitudes
	(i) occupational self-efficacy		(a) organizational commitment
		2. Employee prospects	(b) intention to quit
	2. Work-related	(a) job insecurity	
	(i) occupational level	(b) employability	3. General well-being
	(j) working hours		(a) general health
	(k) night shifts	3. Choice	(b) life satisfaction
	(l) organizational tenure	(a) contract of choice	
	(m) supervision	(b) kind of work of choice	4. Employee-reported behaviours
	(n) union membership	(c) motives for temporary work	(a) sick leave
	(o) main job vs. other paid job		(b) sick presence
		4. Job characteristics	(c) accidents
	3. Organization	(a) role clarity	(d) harassment
	(p) core HR practices	(b) autonomy	(e) self-reported performance
		(c) skill utilization	
		(d) workload	
		5. Support	
		(a) organizational support	
		(b) supervisory support	

workers. We also sought information about the reasons for employing temporary workers and about employers' perceptions of the performance of temporary compared with permanent workers.

Since a core focus of our study was the role of the psychological contract, which, within our definition, we viewed as a two-way process, a distinctive feature of our approach was to collect parallel information from both employer and workers about the psychological contract. We therefore asked the management representative to report the obligations and promises made to both permanent and temporary workers on the part of the organization and how far they had been met, their views about the obligations to the organization of permanent and temporary workers, and also how far these had been met.

The information we sought from the managers consisted of predominantly quantitative data but also included some qualitative elements and was therefore best collected using a structured interview. The data were collected from the most senior person at the workplace responsible for human resource and employment policies and practices. The specific types of data we collected through this process are summarized in Table 2.2.

Table 2.2 Data collected from employer representatives in each organization

Number of employees within organization
Number of permanent and temporary employees within organization
Ownership of organization
Local HR policy and practice responsibility
Types of temporary contracts present in organization
Union density/influence
Recent changes to workforce size/make-up
Anticipated future changes to workforce size/make-up
HR practices in place for permanent and temporary employees
Motives for use of temporary contracts
Ease of recruitment
Performance ratings for permanent and temporary employees
Psychological contract for permanent and temporary employees

The survey of experts

As noted earlier, we sought to develop a more extensive set of information about societal factors and related institutional arrangements in each country that might affect the experience of temporary working. We identified the potentially relevant dimensions through a review of the literature and consultations with academic experts. Some of these dimensions, such as the level of unemployment, could be collected from national statistics. We were also able to obtain data from Schwartz, an acknowledged expert on national cultures (see Schwartz, 1999), on the seven dimensions of national cultures that he has identified. Other information that the existing literature had identified as potentially important was less easy to obtain from existing sources. This included information on four topics: the zone of negotiability, sanctions for violations, strength of family ties, and societal attitudes towards working mothers. We gained information on these four dimensions through Web-based surveys of experts identified in each country. This resulted in a set of scores for each country on the key dimensions we had identified.

The data collection process

Having set the parameters for data collection including the number of organizations from each sector and the number of temporary workers in each organization, the research teams in each country were left to arrange access in whatever ways they considered appropriate. It was anticipated that access would be obtained through an initial approach to organizations, followed by an interview, based on the agreed structured interview schedule, with the human resource manager or the person responsible for human resource and employment policies and practices. This would then be followed by the distribution of questionnaires to a random sample of permanent and temporary workers at each site. The size of the sample and the proportion of workers covered seemed likely to depend on the size of the organization or the specific establishment. The bulk of the data were collected between 2003 and 2005.

In practice there were a number of variations on this approach. In some countries, the researchers found it easier to gain access than in others. It seems that researchers in Germany, the United Kingdom, and Sweden faced most difficulties in gaining access. In a number of cases, the organization was willing simply to provide research access; in others, they expected a report or other types of feedback in return. Some organizations understood the importance of a randomly selected cross-section of the relevant categories of workers. In other cases, this was far more difficult to achieve, and in a minority of extreme cases, the sample was largely controlled by the management of the organization. Usually, data from workers were collected through self-completion and return of the questionnaire. In some organizations, this was facilitated by provision of time for groups of workers to complete the survey in the workplace, sometimes in groups with the researchers present to deal with any queries or possible misunderstandings. This process proved to be useful in providing further confirmation that the questionnaire could be understood and completed by different types and levels of workers. Nevertheless, one consequence of the varying degrees of control over the survey completion process was that a number of the returns contained missing items or indications that the response categories had been misunderstood or treated inappropriately. As a result, if the analysis used list-wise deletion, whereby a questionnaire was excluded from the analysis if any item had been omitted or completed in a blatantly incorrect way, the sample size could fall quite considerably and this is reflected in the variation in sample sizes in some of the later chapters.

Data analysis

The large sample and the complex set of data covering temporary and permanent workers as well as employer data across three sectors and seven countries provide a major challenge for data analysis. We proceeded in five main steps.

The first step was to establish the continuing validity of the measures. This was largely achieved through a series of factor analyses and reliability analyses across the total sample and each country sub-sample. The relevant results are summarized in Appendix 2. The second step was to provide descriptive statistics for temporary and permanent workers and for each country together with some bivariate statistics to test for any significant differences. The third step was to test the core model focusing on the comparison of the experiences of temporary and permanent workers, through a series of regressions. Linked to this, we also explored the extent and consequences of matching the responses of employers and employees, particularly on the psychological contract. The fourth step was to test for mediating effects of the various intervening variables, including the psychological contract, on the link between the type of employment contract and employee well-being. (We acknowledged the potential value of testing for moderator effects but decided at this stage against adding further potential complexity to what was already a full and detailed body of data.) The final step was to undertake a form of multilevel analysis, derived mainly from the regressions, to determine the size effects of national and sectoral differences. A further step would have been to undertake a more detailed analysis of the societal and institutional factors on outcomes. However, we did not follow this up through detailed statistical analysis since, as we shall see, the main analysis indicated that national factors explained only a very small proportion of the variation in results.

The results of these various analyses are presented in the following chapters. There is the potential to provide a large amount of technical detail and quite complex statistical analysis. We have tried to keep this to a minimum and although there are a number of tables containing detailed results, we have attempted to ensure that these are clearly explained in the text.

THE SAMPLE

National comparisons

Temporary working is an international phenomenon that, as we have noted, is likely to be shaped by national institutional factors. It is therefore essential that to accommodate such factors we conducted our study in a number of countries. Our research was funded by the European Union, reflecting the policy interest in the subject, and this meant that we largely restricted our sample to countries in Europe. The study was initiated before the most recent influx of new members in the European community. The aim in selecting countries was therefore to select from across Europe, from the north and south, from the east and west, and from those with a high and low incidence of temporary working. On the basis of these criteria, we selected Sweden, Spain, the United Kingdom, and Germany, but with some emphasis on East Germany, Belgium, and the Netherlands as central in the 'old' Europe. We also included Israel as a comparator country.

Institutional comparisons

While 'country' serves as an important proxy for national policies, it does not tell us which of the policies is exerting an influence. Following a review of the literature, we therefore additionally explored a range of national societal or institutional factors within each country building in particular on what had been learnt in the earlier EU-funded New Understanding of European Work Organization (NUEWO) project that explored the institutional and economic factors affecting the changing use of temporary agency workers in four European countries (Stjernberg and Bergstrom, 2003). The factors we identified as potentially relevant in shaping both the extent of temporary working and reactions to being a temporary worker were laws and regulations, the industrial relations system, the labour market, the education system, family structure, and cultural values. These were further divided into a number of more specific issues. For several of them we were able to obtain statistical information. Where this was not available, for example, with respect to the strength of family ties and societal attitudes towards working mothers, both of which form part of the family structure construct, we identified a panel of expert informants and sought their views. In almost all cases, we were able to arrive at a consensus view. On this basis, we could rate each country as high, medium, or low on each dimension, providing an additional institutional level input to the comparative analysis.

Sector comparisons

A core assumption in the literature on temporary working and in the development of national and EU policy initiatives is that some temporary workers are likely to constitute a disadvantaged and potentially exploited minority, operating on the margins of employment in insecure jobs. These are likely to be very different from the portfolio workers identified by Handy (1989) and others who may choose temporary working as an expression of their freedom. It was therefore essential that we obtained a cross-section of temporary workers. We sought to achieve this by careful selection of the sectors in which we conducted our study.

Our initial thoughts were that we should focus on a declining, an expanding, and a stable sector. However, our pilot study and early investigations indicated that it would prove very difficult to gain access to a declining sector that was common across the seven countries. We therefore altered the focus and established a further set of criteria. These were that the sector should be well represented in all countries, that it should cover a reasonably broad class of organizations, that it employed a reasonable number of temporary workers, and that it was likely to be important in future employment. If possible, we aimed to cover both the public and private sectors. We also wanted to compare routine work, intermediate work, and professional work since this appeared to map the academic debates about the less and more advantaged types of temporary workers. As a result, the sectors we focused on were food production, retail services, and education. Food production is a low-skill sector that often has seasonal peaks and troughs in demand and therefore a requirement for a numerically flexible workforce. We agreed to focus on blue-collar workers in this sector. Retail services covers a potentially wide range of organizations from shops to insurance sales and is generally seen as a stable or expanding sector in which there are plentiful job opportunities and a range of skill requirements. Education is viewed as a sector that employs a large number of professional teachers as well as semi-professional support staff, and we agreed to focus on these categories of workers in this sector.

Organizational comparisons

Since policies and practices are likely to vary quite considerably across different organizations, it was essential that we explored the experience of temporary working in a number of different organizations. We set a target of seven organizations in each sector in each country to facilitate multilevel comparisons. Furthermore, we set parameters whereby no more than a third of the workers in our study should come from any one organization within each country. We also set a target of 100 temporary workers from each sector in each country to ensure sufficient numbers for full statistical analysis. In the event, although not all countries achieved this target, and some flexibility had to be permitted in a few cases to incorporate a wider range of types of manufacturing and service organizations, the number of organizations in the sample across the seven countries was 206. Details of the sample of organizations are set out in Table 2.3.

The information in Table 2.3 confirms that we obtained a good cross-section of organizations in each sector and each country. There are quite marked national differences in the average size of the organizations that largely reflect national industry structural characteristics. There was also diversity in the proportion of the workforce of these organizations that were temporary workers. While for some companies, only a small percentage of the workforce was temporary, for others, up to 95 per cent of the workforce were temporary workers. For just over a quarter of the organizations, temporary workers made up at least half of the workforce.

The majority of organizations (51%) in the sample employed between 50 and 250 workers and can be classified as medium-sized enterprises (according to the European Commission classification); 16 per cent of the organizations employed less than 50 people and can be classified as small enterprises; and 32 per cent employed more than 250 staff and can thus be regarded as large enterprises. In general, manufacturing organizations were larger than retail services organizations, which in turn were larger than organizations in the educational sector. Almost one-third (31%) of all organizations were from the public sector.

		Sweden		Germany		The Netherlands		Belgium		United Kingdom		Spain		Israel		Total	
		Mean	SD	Mean	SD	Mean	SD	Mean	SD	Mean	SD	Mean	SD	Mean	SD	Mean	SD
Organizational characteristics	Mean size (no. employees)	194	185	203	217	1005	1420	223	506	1927	2150	467	1091	196	311	538	1124
	Percentage of temporary workers	38 (n)	29 (%)	35 (n)	26 (%)	28 (n)	21 (%)	32 (n)	22 (%)	29 (n)	28 (%)	26 (n)	29 (%)	36 (n)	24 (%)	31 (n)	26 (%)
Sector	Manufacturing	7	29	9	28	9	26	7	30	5	26	17	37	7	26	61	30
	Retail services	8	33	9	28	14	40	8	35	6	32	10	22	9	33	64	31
	Education	9	38	14	44	12	34	8	35	8	42	19	41	11	41	81	39
Organizational ownership	Public ownership	7	29	5	19	10	32	5	23	11	65	7	16	16	67	61	32
	Private ownership	17	71	22	81	21	68	17	77	6	35	36	84	8	33	127	68
	Single, independent establishment not belonging to another body	0	0	14	52	15	48	10	45	8	53	19	46	11	48	77	42
	Head office of different establishments	0	0	4	15	3	10	2	9	3	20	5	12	3	13	20	11
	One of a number of establishments within a larger nationally owned organization	22	92	9	33	6	19	5	23	4	27	15	37	7	30	68	37
	Sole establishment of a foreign-owned organization	0	0	0	0	3	10	0	0	0	0	0	0	0	0	3	2
	One of a number of organizations within a larger foreign-owned organization	2	8	0	0	4	13	5	23	0	0	2	5	2	9	15	8

Note: In some cases, information on ownership and type of establishment was unclear (e.g. partly publicly owned). The numbers for the full sample therefore vary between 206 and 183.

Temporary and permanent worker comparisons

Temporary workers are typically viewed as being at a disadvantage compared with permanent employees. It was therefore decided that both should be included in the sample. To ensure that the use of temporary workers by organizations was likely to be a deliberate policy decision, we set as a target a minimum number of five temporary workers in each of the organizations in the sample. There was no minimum set on the number of permanent workers, but we assumed that in most cases, it would be easier to gain access to permanent workers. This proved to be the case, and the eventual total sample consisted of 1,981 temporary workers and 3,307 permanent workers, providing an overall sample of 5,288. The details are set out in Table 2.4.

The results show that the overall sample size varied between 628 in Germany and 960 in Israel. Approximately 55 per cent of the sample was female. However, this hides quite large variations between country and sector. For example, only 41 per cent in the food manufacturing sector were female, a figure which rises to 63 per cent in retail services and 65 per cent in education. The average age across the sample was 37 years with fairly small national variations, although the Israeli sample, with an average age of 40, is significantly older and the Spanish sample, with an average age of 34, is significantly younger than the other country samples. There was some tendency for those in retail services to be younger and those in education to be a little older than average. Average working hours across the whole sample was 35 hours a week although the standard deviation of 12 suggests quite a lot of variation within each sector and country. Those in food manufacturing work an average of 40 hours a week compared with 33 in retail services and 31 in education; however these overall figures hide some quite marked variations between the country patterns within the sample. For example, the teachers in the Israeli sample work an average of only 25 hours a week compared with the UK teachers who work 36 hours a week. Although it is not shown in the table, as we might expect, 67 per cent of the employees in the manufacturing sector were unskilled or skilled blue-collar workers, 62 per cent of the employees in the retail services sector were lower-level and intermediate white-collar workers, and 85 per cent of the participants from the educational sector were intermediate and upper white-collar workers. These comparisons are based on Goldthorpe's classification (Evans, 1992).

Table 2.4 Characteristics of the sample across country and sector

		Temporary	Permanent	Total	Number of organizations	Percentage of females	Age Mean (SD)	Hours per week Mean (SD)
Sweden	M	62	197	259	7	36	33(11)	37(6)
	R	40	139	179	8	56	30(11)	31(12)
	E	97	195	292	9	69	45(11)	32(13)
	Total	**199**	**531**	**730**	**24**	**54**	**37(13)**	**34(11)**
Germany	M	91	124	215	9	38	37(11)	38(9)
	R	79	108	187	9	61	33(11)	34(9)
	E	116	110	226	14	55	41(12)	32(12)
	Total	**286**	**342**	**628**	**32**	**51**	**37(12)**	**35(10)**
The Netherlands	M	96	125	221	9	30	37(10)	37(6)
	R	89	163	252	14	56	31(10)	30(11)
	E	113	171	284	12	52	42(10)	31(11)
	Total	**298**	**459**	**757**	**35**	**47**	**37(11)**	**32(10)**
Belgium	M	88	123	211	7	57	35(10)	38(6)
	R	106	111	217	8	69	35(11)	26(11)
	E	100	111	211	8	70	38(11)	33(12)
	Total	**294**	**345**	**639**	**23**	**65**	**36(11)**	**32(11)**
United Kingdom	M	64	324	388	5	54	37(12)	39(7)
	R	31	109	140	6	72	37(10)	34(11)
	E	62	52	114	8	75	41(11)	36(13)
	Total	**157**	**485**	**642**	**19**	**61**	**38(12)**	**37(9)**
Spain	M	156	224	380	17	45	34(9)	42(8)
	R	115	154	269	10	50	30(9)	41(8)
	E	104	179	283	19	59	39(10)	31(9)
	Total	**375**	**557**	**932**	**46**	**52**	**34(10)**	**38(9)**
Israel	M	130	252	382	7	24	41(11)	44(13)
	R	97	132	229	9	82	37(12)	36(12)
	E	145	204	349	11	79	41(11)	25(12)
	Total	**372**	**588**	**960**	**27**	**58**	**40(11)**	**35(15)**
Total	M	687	1369	2056	61	41	36(11)	40(9)
	R	557	916	1473	64	63	33(11)	33(11)
	E	737	1022	1759	82	65	41(11)	31(12)
	Total	**1,981**	**3,307**	**5,288**	**206**	**55**	**37(11)**	**35(12)**

Note: M = Food manufacturing, R = retail services, E = education.

Comparisons of type of temporary workers

We were very conscious that there are many forms of temporary employment. The analysis presented in the introductory chapter sets out the various forms that temporary working might take. Given the challenges of obtaining a satisfactory sample of temporary workers in the first place, we did not set any explicit targets for the type of temporary employment contract. In the event, our sample consisted of a considerable variety of forms of temporary employment but at the same time was dominated by fixed-term contracts. Indeed, the vast majority of temporary workers in our study can be classified as fixed-term contract workers (62%), followed by temporary agency workers (8%) and seasonal employees (7%), who can be found mainly in the manufacturing sector. A relatively large group of temporary workers are on training (5%) or probationary (5%) contracts. A further 5 per cent are daily or on-call workers. The remaining categories, including workers involved in job creation and subcontracting, each make up only 2 per cent or less of our sample. The pattern of distribution is illustrated in Figure 2.1.

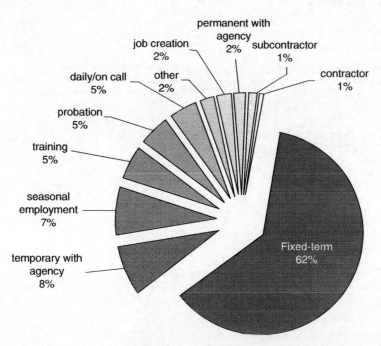

Figure 2.1 Share of different employment contracts within the group of 1,981 temporary workers

The composition of our temporary workers sample may partly reflect national factors; for example, Spain, which has the highest proportion of workers in Europe on temporary employment contracts, typically makes extensive use of fixed-term contracts. When we compare our sample with the available national statistics (OECD, 2008) the actual distribution of types of temporary work in each country reflects the make-up of our sample. For example, national statistics show that the proportion of temporary workers employed on fixed-term contracts ranges from 76.5 per cent in Spain to 50.4 per cent in Germany. Temporary agency workers range from 22.1 per cent in Belgium to 3.5 per cent of the temporary workforce in Sweden. Apprentices make up 17.2 per cent of temporary workers in Germany but only 1.1 per cent in Spain.

We can compare the background characteristics of temporary workers in the dominant group in our sample—those on fixed-term contracts—with the other main categories. This reveals that as we might expect, those on training contracts are significantly younger, with an average age of 24, while those on seasonal contracts, with an average age of just over 35, are significantly older than workers on fixed-term contracts whose average age is 32. There are no marked differences in gender across the main categories of temporary workers. Those on fixed-term contracts have significantly higher educational qualifications and more senior positions in organizations than temporary agency workers, and more particularly temporary seasonal workers. The average organizational tenure, as well as contract duration, is hard to compare as the variance even within the different employment types is very large. As one may expect, temporary agency workers have the shortest contracts, while training offers the longest contracts.

Other sample characteristics

As noted earlier, we collected quite a considerable amount of additional information about all the participants on the grounds that their personal circumstances might affect their experience of temporary working. At the same time, we collected information on aspects of their current employment such as the level of their current job, their union affiliation, and whether they worked shifts. These variables are primarily included as background control variables although they are sometimes of interest in their own right. The descriptive results for the sample from each country are presented in Table 2.5.

The results show that there are some national variations in the domestic circumstances of the sample. For example, the proportion living with a partner ranges from 73 per cent in Germany to 36 per cent in Israel while in Sweden 28 per cent live alone. Despite these variations, the role in terms of

Table 2.5 Background and work-related characteristics of the national samples

		Sweden (%)	Germany (%)	The Netherlands (%)	Belgium (%)	United Kingdom (%)	Spain (%)	Israel (%)
Sex?	Female	54	51	46	65	62	52	58
	Male	46	49	54	35	38	48	42
Do you live with a partner?	Yes	59	73	72	69	67	43	36
	No with family/ parents/friends	13	17	14	18	18	49	57
	No, alone	28	10	14	13	15	8	6
What is your financial contribution to the household income?	Sole earner	34	30	28	22	24	20	23
	Main earner	16	20	26	17	22	16	22
	Joint earner	35	29	20	24	27	30	27
	Contributory earner	16	21	26	37	27	35	28
Are you in your household the person mainly responsible for ordinary shopping and looking after the home?	Yes	47	39	32	47	48	24	40
	Equally responsible	44	39	43	37	37	48	45
	No, someone else	9	22	25	16	15	28	15
Job level?	Unskilled blue collar	30	26	13	24	37	15	24
	Skilled blue collar	10	16	14	10	5	9	13
	Lower-level white collar	15	18	23	22	16	17	15

Intermediate white collar	38	30	19	38	18	23	35
Upper white collar	5	9	29	5	15	34	12
Management or director	2	1	2	2	9	3	2
Night shifts?							
No	86	87	97	88	82	94	73
Yes	14	13	3	12	18	6	27
Supervisory role?							
No	84	82	78	86	65	74	72
Yes	16	18	22	14	35	26	28
Union member?							
No	25	80	79	47	79	81	37
Additional job(s)?							
No	79	89	91	92	94	94	84
Yes	21	11	9	8	6	6	16
Education levels?							
ISCED Level 0	0	0	1	2	0	4	0
ISCED Level 1	6	0	2	3	20	9	3
ISCED Level 2	14	13	18	14	28	5	4
ISCED Level 3	27	35	35	24	13	17	29
ISCED Level 4	22	5	2	10	9	0	18
ISCED Level 5	27	44	41	46	29	53	40
ISCED Level 6	4	3	1	0	1	11	7

financial contribution does not vary greatly across countries. Close to 50 per cent of the sample from each country except Belgium and Spain are the sole or main earners in the family. In Belgium this figure falls to 39 per cent and in Spain to 36 per cent. In Spain, the respondents are also less likely to be mainly responsible for household activities.

There are quite marked variations in the reported skill levels in the samples of the various countries. In Sweden, Germany, and the United Kingdom, approximately 40 per cent of the sample are in blue-collar jobs compared with less than 25 per cent in Spain and the Netherlands. At the other end of the spectrum, 37 per cent of the Spanish sample are in upper-level white-collar jobs or in management compared with 7 per cent in Sweden and Belgium. These differences are also reflected in the educational levels of the national samples. Using the standard International Standard Classification of Education (ISCED) definitions, 64 per cent of the Spanish sample fall into the top two categories compared with about 30 per cent for Sweden and the United Kingdom. The United Kingdom has a disproportionately large number, 48 per cent, in the lower three levels compared with only 7 per cent in Israel and 13 per cent in Germany. With respect to other work-related characteristics, 75 per cent of the Swedish sample belong to a trade union compared with closer to 20 per cent in Germany, the Netherlands, the United Kingdom, and Spain. A sizeable minority have more than one job. This ranges from a high of 21 per cent in Sweden to a low of 6 per cent in Spain and the United Kingdom. There are also sizeable variations in shift-working with 27 per cent in Israel reporting that they work shifts compared with 3 per cent in the Netherlands and 6 per cent in Spain. Finally, 35 per cent of the UK sample say that they have a supervisory role, implying responsibility for other people, compared with 14 per cent in Belgium and 16 per cent in Sweden.

Overall, therefore, there are quite marked variations in the backgrounds, domestic responsibilities, and work requirements of the people in our sample. We will take these factors into account in considering the impact of temporary employment on attitudes and behaviour. Although these background characteristics are not a central focus of our study, they are nevertheless interesting in their own right and we will highlight any circumstances in which they have a strong bearing on the outcomes.

SUMMARY

In this chapter, we have set out, in non-technical language, the process whereby we collected and analysed the data and have presented a description of the sample on which our study is based. Details of the measures and the statistical analyses demonstrating the validity of the measures are provided in Appendix 2.

We were able to obtain a large sample of workers, including temporary workers, from three sectors in seven countries. These provide a range of types of temporary workers and, for both permanent and temporary workers, a wide range of occupations and skill levels. They include those who might be expected to fall into the categories of disadvantaged temporary workers and also knowledge workers who may value the freedom of temporary employment. We have also obtained proportions of types of temporary workers, including fixed-term, agency, and seasonal contract workers, that are broadly representative of the actual proportions in each country.

The next chapter presents the first set of results, focusing initially on the management responses that cover organizational policies and practices in the employment of temporary workers.

3

Flexible Employment and Temporary Contracts: The Employer's Perspective

Kerstin Isaksson, José Maria Peiró, Claudia Bernhard-Oettel, Amparo Caballer, Francisco J. Gracia, and José Ramos

INTRODUCTION

Research into the effects and consequences of employment contracts has predominately been carried out from the employees' perspective. To date, little research has considered the employers' perspective. Consequently, there is very little literature examining the challenges and opportunities for human resource (HR) policies and practices presented by temporary work (Burgess and Connell, 2006). In order to address this deficiency, the Psycones study collected information from management representatives in over 200 organizations across seven countries. This chapter explores a range of management issues surrounding the use of temporary contracts.

The aims of this chapter are threefold. First, we attempt to identify the reasons for hiring temporary workers and, more generally, the factors affecting the number of temporary workers hired by the organizations. In doing so, we distinguish external, contextual factors, and internal factors. Second, this chapter explores the HR practices reported to be in use by the organizational representatives and assesses whether they indicate equal treatment of temporary and permanent workers. Finally, the chapter analyses whether the reported HR decisions and employment strategies are related to some relevant organizational outcomes. More specifically, we investigate whether the reasons for hiring temporary workers and the HR practices applied to permanent and temporary workers appear to have an effect on their turnover rates, dismissal rates, and on managers' satisfaction with their performance.

Wherever possible, the information was collected from the most senior manager in the workplace responsible for HR and employment policies and practices. The manager was therefore the most likely to be well-informed about relevant policies and practices. The same managers provided information on the content and fulfilment of the psychological contract as a representative of the organization. In large workplaces, a senior manager might not always be in the best position to know about practices on the ground. In smaller workplaces, this is likely to be less of a problem. Nevertheless, it is important to bear this issue in mind, and in Chapter 7, we compare these management responses with those of permanent and temporary workers. One question we consider is whether a closer agreement between them affects the nature of the outcomes. However, in this chapter, we restrict our focus to the responses provided by the managerial representatives of the organizations.

The first section presents descriptive information about the relevant policies, practices, and outcomes in the organizations. We then address the three aims listed above. In each case, we provide a brief conceptual background and then report the relevant results of our analysis. In the final section of the chapter, we discuss the main findings and their implications.

COMPANY EMPLOYMENT POLICY AND PRACTICE WITH RESPECT TO TEMPORARY WORKERS

Table 3.1 gives an overview of various indicators of employment and staffing based on information provided by the managers in each organization. The table shows variations between country and sector on trends in employment of temporary workers, problems experienced in filling vacancies, the degree of equal treatment of permanent and temporary workers, the influence of trade unions, rates of voluntary quitting and dismissal, and employers' satisfaction with the performance of temporary and permanent workers.

The results show that the average proportion of temporary workers in the organizations in our sample varies between 25 per cent in the Netherlands and 38 per cent in Sweden with an overall average of 30 per cent. Furthermore, the table shows that 41 per cent reported an increase in the use of temporary workers over the past three years. However, these overall figures mask quite wide national variations, with organizations in Germany and the United Kingdom most likely to have reported an increase over the past three years and those in Sweden and Spain the least likely to do so. Just over a third expect their workforce as a whole to increase in the future, though we are not in a

Table 3.1 Description of staffing policies, practices, and outcomes, and differences between countries and sectors

		Country										Sector				
	N^a	Total	Swe	Ger	NL	Bel	UK	Sp	Is	χ^2	F	Food	Retail	Educ	χ^2	F
Staffing (per cent of organizations)																
Temporary workers (%)	194	30.9	38.4	35.1	25.1	31.8	28.8	25.2	36.5		1.38	27.6	38.8	27.3		4.1*
Report increase in temporary workers (%)	193	40.9	22.2	59.3	36.1	45.5	56.3	33.3	47.8	11.2		39.0	45.0	39.2	0.6	
Expect general increase in staff (%)	193	33.7	33.3	11.1	19.4	38.1	56.3	46.5	39.1	16.7**		39.7	39.0	25.0	4.2	
Problems filling vacancies (range 1–5)	193	2.73	2.48	2.70	2.73	3.35	2.91	2.62	2.67		2.33*	2.6	2.8	2.7		1.0
Equal treatment of perms and temps (%)	194	53.0	40.7	66.7	30.6	50.0	63.8	74.4	39.1	27.4**		50.8	56.7	52.0	2.5	
Union influence (% high/very high) over:																
Employment contract	191	14.7	25.9	14.8	19.4	5.0	6.7	11.4	13.6	6.1		28.1	10.0	8.1	11.8**	
HR policy	191	17.8	55.6	7.4	22.2	5.0	6.7	6.8	18.2	35.9***		26.3	13.3	14.9	4.1	

(continued)

Table 3.1 Continued

	N^a	Country										Sector				
		Total	Swe	Ger	NL	Bel	UK	Sp	Is	χ^2	F	Food	Retail	Educ	χ^2	F
Working conditions	191	29.8	63.0	23.3	27.8	15.0	13.3	22.7	27.3	19.6**		43.9	21.7	25.7	7.9*	
Turnover (% in most recent year)																
Permanent workers	158	6.4	9.9	2.1	7.9	1.1	22.8	2.8	6.3		6.05***	6.6	10.8	2.9		5.7**
Temporary workers	154	9.0	9.8	5.3	5.2	7.5	46.7	2.9	11.7		6.07***	11.2	13.2	3.9		2.4
Dismissal (% in most recent year)																
Permanent workers	158	2.1	0.6	1.6	3.4	1.1	3.0	1.0	4.8		6.07***	3.0	3.1	0.6		5.7**
Temporary workers	193	47.5	50.1	48.1	53.0	54.6	28.7	42.3	46.2		0.05	47.4	47.3	47.6		0.1
Satisfaction with performance (range 1–7)																
Permanent workers	188	5.30	5.44	5.30	5.45	5.00	5.40	5.35	5.00		1.07	5.17	5.19	5.49		2.47
Temporary workers	188	5.35	5.15	5.78	5.27	5.38	4.93	5.36	5.41		1.89	5.08	5.33	5.58		5.20**

$*p \leq .05, **p \leq .01, ***p \leq .001$
^{a} The number of companies this table is based on varies, because some organizations had no records specifying the required information. This is particularly the case for voluntary turnover and dismissal.

position to speculate about any increase in the proportion of temporary workers and it is, of course, possible that changing economic circumstances have considerably altered these expectations. There are marked differences in expectations about an expansion in the use of temporary workers. Just over a third expect some growth in the future, but this figure is significantly higher in the United Kingdom and significantly lower in Germany compared with most other countries. Problems with filling vacancies are generally moderate, although they are significantly higher in Belgium followed by the United Kingdom than in other countries.

Just over half claim that they give the same treatment and opportunities to permanent and temporary workers. Interestingly, there are significant differences between the countries, with equal treatment apparently less likely in those countries where trade union influence is the greatest, namely, Sweden, the Netherlands, and Israel. More generally, the influence of trade unions is only rated as high in a small minority of organizations concentrated in these three countries and most notably in Sweden. Union influence is also consistently higher in food manufacturing than in the other two sectors.

Labour turnover is just under 50 per cent higher among temporary than among permanent staff. The table shows significant country differences with very low labour turnover rates in both groups in Spain, while in the United Kingdom they are very much higher than elsewhere. This may reflect differences in employment law or in the interpretation of voluntary turnover compared with dismissal. The results in Table 3.1 indicate that almost half of all temporary workers were dismissed in the previous year compared with just over 2 per cent of permanent workers. These figures are fairly consistent across countries except the United Kingdom where there is much less dismissal of temporary workers, reinforcing the possibility of some substitution between voluntary turnover and dismissal.

Satisfaction with the performance of both permanent and temporary workers is high and although the differences are not large, it is higher, on average, for temporary workers. This is the case in four of the seven countries, although we should stress that these differences are not statistically significant. Satisfaction with the performance of temporary workers is higher in the retail services and education sectors compared with food manufacturing and here the differences are significant. The generally high levels of satisfaction with temporary workers suggest that the high reported rates of dismissals reflect the termination of the requirement for temporary labour rather than dissatisfaction with their performance.

ANTECEDENTS OF TEMPORARY EMPLOYMENT:
FLEXIBILITY AS A RESPONSE TO PRESSURES AND DEMANDS

Changes in the environment are forcing companies to change their employment policies. In this context, flexibility has emerged as a key concept for many organizations. Within the general trend of cutting costs by means of downsizing, mergers, re-structuring, and other changes in work systems, flexible employment strategies and the externalization of the work force have become more prevalent (Pfeffer and Baron, 1988).

Flexible employment is often discussed with a reference to Atkinson's model (1984) of 'The Flexible Firm' that configures within the same firm a primary and a secondary labour market. While the core group of full-time permanent employees in the primary labour market performs crucial functions for the company and enjoys a high level of job security, adaptation to environmental changes is achieved with the secondary labour market. Employees who are easy to substitute are often employed on the periphery. Employers may use time-limited contracts, employment agencies, subcontracting, and outsourcing as strategies to adapt the size of the workforce to variations in work requirements. Following this logic, in the context of economic downturn, temporary workers will be among the first to have their employment terminated.

According to this conceptualization, temporary employment is used primarily to cope with fluctuations in demand or to replace permanent employees during shorter periods of absence. However, the nature of temporary employment is changing partly due to contextual factors and partly due to profound changes in employers' use of labour (Stanworth and Druker, 2006). Many organizations regard temporary employees as a critical part of their HR strategies regardless of whether these strategies aim at reducing cost or gaining additional non-organizational-specific expertise and knowledge (Lepak and Snell, 1999; Marler, Barringer, and Milkovich, 2002; Silla, Gracia, and Peiró, 2005). Stanworth and Druker (2006) describe four distinct reasons for using agency labour depending on whether organizations are acting strategically or reactively and whether the aim is to supplement permanent employees or substitute for them. Their conclusion is that boundaries between 'core' and 'periphery' are sometimes redrawn, usually shrinking the former and increasing the latter. Temporary employment is therefore used not only to replace permanent workers or to cope with the fluctuations in demand, as the human capital theory states, but also for jobs in the primary market, extending job flexibility to new and more diverse forms and situations. The use of temporary workers is therefore no longer limited to blue-collar or service jobs with low qualifications. Professionals, consultants, and other skilled knowledge workers have become a growing part of the temporary work force, although they do still form a minority (Guest, 2004*a*). Hence, changes in company policy and in the labour market have given rise to a more diversified body of flexible workers, employed for many different reasons. To clarify what functions organizations aim to fulfil with temporary employment, we asked managers why they currently employed temporary workers.

Reasons for using temporary workers

Table 3.2 shows a list of twelve possible reasons for employing temporary workers that had been identified through the pilot study and presents the average responses to a question about the importance of each reason. Responses were provided on a scale from 1, not at all important, to 5, extremely important, and are listed in order of priority.

Our results show that the most commonly cited reasons for hiring temporary workers among employers participating in the Psycones study were to fill vacancies during maternity leave and other long-term absence of permanent workers and to meet peaks in immediate demand. Another common reason was to employ newly recruited personnel for a trial period before offering a permanent contract. Reduction of costs through savings on training, salary, or fringe benefits, on the other hand, was found to be among the least prevalent reasons.

The middle section of the table summarizes any significant differences between countries. It shows that managers in Sweden and Belgium in particular were more likely to cite use of temporary workers to cover maternity leave or other longer periods of absence in contrast to Germany and Israel. Sweden and Israel were more likely to offer temporary trial periods in contrast, in particular, to Belgium and the United Kingdom where managers were significantly less likely to cite this as a reason. Spanish managers were more likely to say they hired temporary staff because otherwise they could not fill vacancies in contrast to Sweden, Germany, and Israel where this was significantly less likely to be a factor. Managers in the Netherlands were more likely to hire to temporary workers because of a freeze on permanent numbers in contrast to Sweden and Germany. Finally, Israeli organizations were more likely than those in Sweden in particular to use temporary staff to cut fringe benefit costs. Generally the pattern of most frequently reported reasons for hiring temporary workers is fairly similar across countries.

Table 3.2 Reasons for employing temporary workers across countries and sectors

Reasons	Mean (1–5)	Swe	Ger	NL	Bel	UK	Sp	Is	Country difference	Sector difference[b]
It covers maternity leave or longer periods of staff absence	3.25	3.85	2.73	3.39	3.86	3.20	3.21	2.21	B, Sw >I[a]	
It helps to match staff to peaks in demand	3.19	2.85	3.62	3.22	2.86	3.20	3.18	3.47		F, R > E
We offer trial periods before employing a permanent employee	3.12	4.22	2.54	3.11	2.41	2.29	3.10	3.84	Sw > G, B, UK, I > G, B, UK	F, R > E
It covers staff short-term absence	2.80	2.96	2.56	2.72	3.32	3.20	2.69	2.42		
We are otherwise unable to fill vacancies	2.12	1.74	1.35	2.09	2.14	2.47	2.92	1.71	Sp > G, I, Sw	E > F
We can bring in specialist skills	2.00	1.81	1.54	2.39	1.55	2.40	2.12	2.06		E > R
We need to freeze on permanent staff numbers	1.97	1.33	1.60	2.69	1.95	1.57	1.95	2.39	N > Sw	
It can improve our performance	1.78	1.73	1.81	1.89	1.73	2.14	1.52	1.94		
It saves wage costs	1.71	1.44	1.92	1.94	1.36	1.43	1.65	2.11		
We would like to have personnel for unusual working hours (e.g. night-time, evening, weekend)	1.69	2.30	1.42	1.53	1.73	1.71	1.54	1.74		F, R > E
It saves fringe benefit costs	1.48	1.07	1.58	1.53	1.14	1.36	1.52	2.26	I > B, Sw	
It saves training costs	1.19	1.07	1.04	1.22	1.09	1.29	1.17	1.63	I > G, Sw, B	

[a] Sw = Sweden, G = Germany, B = Belgium, N = Netherlands, UK = United Kingdom, Sp = Spain, I = Israel

[b] F = Food manufacturing industry, R = Retail sector, E = Education sector

A general tendency is that some countries (Sweden, the Netherlands, and Belgium) have substitution-related items at the top of the list, whereas the other countries (Germany, United Kingdom, Spain, and Israel) describe peaks in demand as the most common reason.

Whether these reasons, together with other critical organizational factors, explain variations in the rate of temporary workers in a company is investigated in the next section and helps to address the first aim in this chapter, namely, to analyse the organizational antecedents of the use of temporary workers.

Factors predicting the proportion of temporary workers

In order to predict the proportion of temporary workers employed by an organization, we conducted a hierarchical regression analysis including a range of factors that we considered might have an impact. We therefore included country and sector differences together with a range of structural factors such as size, ownership, whether the organization is independent or

Table 3.3 Antecedents of the percentage of temporary workers in the organization ($N = 173$)

Percentage of temporary workers	
Sweden	−.01
Germany	.08
Netherlands	−.17*
Belgium	.01
United Kingdom	.14
Spain	−.17*
Manufacturing sector	−.23**
Education sector	−.10
Size of organization	−.17*
Private ownership	.08
Independent unit	.04
Union influence	.10
HR practices to all employees	−.03
Reasons for employing temps:	
-short-term substitutes	−.20**
-specialist skills	.04
-unusual hours	.31***
-lower wage costs	−.05
Adjusted R^2	.16***

$^*p \le .05, \,^{**}p \le .01, \,^{***}p \le .001$

part of a larger group, reasons for using temporary workers, and equal application of HR practices to permanent and temporary workers ('HR practices to all employees'). This last item is based on the number of HR practices, from a list of five common practices, about which managers explicitly reported that the practice was applied to both permanent and temporary workers.

The final set of items in the regression analysis concerns motives for hiring temporary workers. Factor analysis of the twelve possible reasons for using temporary workers listed in Table 3.2 resulted in four factors, representing different reasons for employing temporary workers. However the internal consistency of these factors was low and scales could not be constructed. For this reason, we chose to include the four single items with the highest factor loadings to represent the four factors in the regression analyses. The first item was 'replacement of permanent workers during absence', as an important reason for hiring temporary workers. The second item was 'need for specialist skills', third was 'lowering of costs', and the final item concerned the 'need for personnel during unusual hours', as a reason to employ temporary workers. Table 3.3 shows the results of the analysis aiming to identify factors related to the proportion of temporary workers in the organization.

After controlling for country and sector, the structural factors are mostly insignificant. It should be noted that there are some significant differences between countries and sectors but we must be cautious in interpreting them since our organizations are not nationally representative. This is a point we address more fully in Chapter 9. Hiring temporary workers to work unusual hours appears to be the factor most strongly associated with a large proportion of temporary workers. This is an issue that is likely to be particularly important in the retail sector and there is some support for this in the negative beta weights indicating somewhat lower proportions of temporary workers in manufacturing and education. Interestingly, in firms that reported the reason 'to cover short-term absence' as less prevalent, the percentage of temporary workers in the organization appears to be higher. A possible explanation for this is that firms with a large percentage of temporary workers already have the built-in flexibility to cover short-term absences of permanent staff.

In summary, therefore, it is the distinctive reasons for hiring temporary workers and more particularly the need to cover unusual hours, rather than structural features of the organizations, that offer the strongest explanations for variations in the proportion of temporary workers in the workforces of the organizations in the Psycones study.

EMPLOYMENT RELATIONS, HR POLICIES AND PRACTICES, AND EQUAL TREATMENT

As we have noted, changes in labour markets and in competitive pressures have led to more flexible employment arrangements. Von Hippel et al. (1997) summarize the benefits of these changes for employers. They highlight cost reduction, effectiveness, and efficiency as potential outcomes. However, other scholars have suggested that for some of the workers affected by this, and in particular temporary workers, there is a downside to this trend which could induce a high level of job insecurity, losses, and stigmatization for employees (Boyce et al., 2007). Furthermore, temporary employment and externalized work arrangements have been found to restrict opportunities for training and development, supervisor support, and/or representation and influence (for a summary, see Bergström, 2003). As Isaksson, De Cuyper, and De Witte (2005) stated:

The benefits for core employees would be secured at the expense of employees at the periphery, with the latter group running the risk of being trapped in poorly qualified jobs with few or no prospects. (p. 5)

The regulation of non-permanent types of employment has been the subject of debates within the European Union during the past decade. One of the challenges for European governments, policy makers, and social agents is to find a balance between employment flexibility and job security for the employees (Reilly, 1998; Hesselink and Van Vuuren, 1999). As an attempt to secure acceptable employment conditions for all workers, the Council of the European Union approved a Council Directive in 1999 stating in clause 4 that:

fixed-term workers shall not be treated in a less favourable manner than comparable permanent workers solely because they have a fixed-term contract or relation unless different treatment is justified on objective grounds. (Vigneau et al., 1999, p. 26)

More recently, the Temporary Agency Workers Directive has been introduced to ensure equal treatment on basic employment terms and conditions for those employed by temporary agencies and the European commission has developed principles to guide a common strategy for 'flexicurity'.

Against this background, a relevant question motivating our second aim in this chapter is to investigate whether there is equal treatment or whether a different employment status implies differences in HR practices. HR practices are an important way for organizations to articulate relationships with their employees and to communicate the terms and conditions of their employment policies (Rousseau and Wade-Benzoni, 1994). Whether or not managers and employees agree about the HR practices is discussed in Chapter 7.

Following the EU regulation, unfair treatment should only occur for justifiable objective reasons. However, according to the Atkinson model we might expect these practices to differ for temporary and permanent workers. Furthermore, as Bergström (2003) discusses, in practice equality principles are hard to ensure because they require the identification of criteria to which the rules apply and an identical core worker to whom the temporary worker is compared. We should also bear in mind that the legislation on Temporary Agencies was agreed after the data for this study had been collected. The following sections summarize the results concerning management reports about equal treatment obtained in our study. It may be useful to bear in mind that a majority of the temporary workers in our sample were employed on fixed-term contracts.

Application of HR practices to temporary and permanent employees

We collected information from organizations about HR policies and practices in two ways. For five practices, we asked whether each practice was in place and if so whether it applied equally to permanent and temporary workers. For a further three items, it was more appropriate to ask about the proportion of permanent and temporary workers to which the practices applied. The first five practices concerned the following issues: an opportunity to express views concerning the job; an attempt to design interesting and varying jobs; provision of support for non-work responsibilities (e.g. childcare facilities, flexible hours, financial planning); active equal opportunity practices; and active prevention of harassment and bullying. Figure 3.1 shows the proportion of

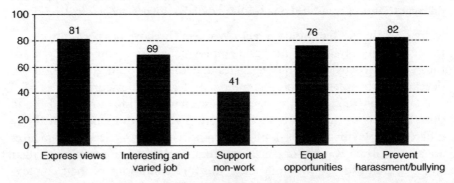

Figure 3.1 Percentage of employers reporting equal treatment of permanent and temporary workers on specific HR practices

workplaces where managers reported that these practices were in place for both permanent and temporary workers.

As can be seen, HR managers in a large majority of organizations claim that four out of the five practices are applied equally to both permanent and temporary workers. The exception is support for non-work responsibilities, which, if it is applied at all, is often only provided for permanent employees. In addition, nearly one-third of managers report unequal treatment when designing interesting and varying jobs. There is therefore some indication that in a number of organizations, temporary workers receive less favourable treatment on these five practices. It is important to bear in mind that equal treatment may indicate that the practice applies equally to both categories of workers or to neither.

The three topics on which managers were asked to identify the proportion of workers to which they applied covered training and development, performance appraisal, and performance-related pay. Inspecting the results summarized in Figure 3.2, two general trends are apparent. First, HR practices on training and feedback are more widespread than the application of performance-related pay. Second, all three practices are more often implemented for the permanent workforce; hence, temporary workers receive less training ($t = 5.58$, $p < .001$), less feedback ($t = 3.75$, $p < .001$), and are less likely to have access to performance-related pay ($t = 4.09$, $p < .001$). Although these differences are statistically significant, the percentage differences are not always very large. However they confirm the general tendency for managers,

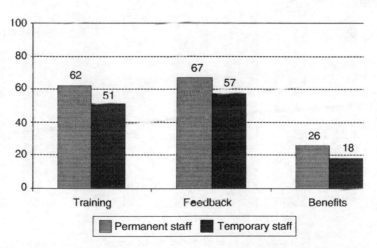

Figure 3.2 Percentage of employers reporting equal treatment of permanent and temporary employees on training and development, feedback, and performance-related pay

on average, across the organizations included in the Psycones study to report somewhat less favourable treatment of temporary workers compared with those on permanent employment contracts.

Equal treatment for temporary and permanent employees—overall judgement

Apart from these specific HR practices, we asked all managers to judge the overall treatment of temporary compared with permanent workers. Figure 3.3 reveals that just over half, 53 per cent, of all managers reported that they apply a policy of equal treatment. However, 35 per cent of managers report small differences while 11 per cent report large differences in the way permanent and temporary staff are treated.

Figure 3.3 also shows the country comparisons. Managers in Spain, followed by Germany and the United Kingdom, were the most likely to say they applied equal treatment and opportunities. In contrast, in the Netherlands, Israel, and to a lesser extent Sweden a majority of managers reported that there were differences in the treatment of permanent and temporary workers. When asked to give examples of unequal treatment, managers predominantly

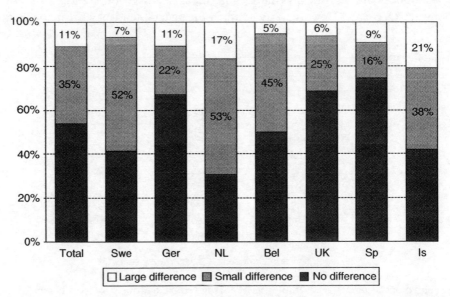

Figure 3.3 Percentage of employers reporting equal treatment of permanent and temporary workers

referred to better opportunities for permanent employees in terms of internal career, personal advancement, and/or participation in training.

In summary, this section has provided evidence indicating that managers in a sizeable minority of organizations apply a number of HR practices less favourably to temporary workers. Taking this a step further, and exploring the issues more broadly, almost half the organizations agree that permanent and temporary workers do not receive equal treatment and opportunities, a view that is supported more strongly by managers of organizations in some countries, notably those with a stronger trade union presence, than others.

ORGANIZATIONAL CONSEQUENCES: PERFORMANCE, LABOUR TURNOVER, AND DISMISSALS

An apparent challenge for management today is to create organizational flexibility while maintaining or increasing individual and organizational performance (Tsui et al., 1997). Whether or not this is possible may to some extent depend on the context; for example, in high-performance work systems the effectiveness of employing temporary workers has been questioned (Ford and Slater, 2006). However, the choice of management strategy and HR approach applied may be relevant, since some appear to be more critical than others for improving business performance. Differences between organizations in the use of HR practices may, for example, relate to the core competences required (Cappelli, 1999), the nature of the customer market (Sherer and Leblebici, 2001), and the relative contributions of human and other types of capital (Lepak et al., 2002). Furthermore, they may differ depending on the strategic value and uniqueness of contributions that different employee groups make to the firm (Lepak and Snell, 1999). Some scholars suggest that one way to improve effectiveness when employing temporary workers is to ensure equal treatment as a basis for higher motivation (Nollen and Axel, 1998). Empirical investigations reveal that better employee performance may also be achieved when employers engage in a mutual relationship with their employees or over-invest in their employees (Tsui et al., 1997). To summarize, the application of (equal) HR practices, organizational context, and strategic decisions (such as the reasons for employing temporary workers) may be decisive factors in ensuring favourable organizational outcomes in companies with a diversified workforce.

Wherever possible, we gained information from managers on a limited number of outcomes including voluntary quits, dismissals, and subjective

Table 3.4 Antecedents of employer's satisfaction with performance and of levels of turnover and dismissal of permanent and temporary workers

	Satisfaction with performance		Voluntary quitting		Dismissal	
	Perm N = 168	Temp N = 168	Perm N = 146	Temp N = 141	Perm N = 146	Temp N = 167
Sweden	.23**	.05	.03	−.07	−.17#	.09
Germany	−.09	.23**	−.25**	−.18*	.08	−.01
Netherlands	.08	.01	.04	−.33***	.09	.06
Belgium	−.16#	.07	−.24**	−.06	−.08	.04
Spain	.03	.01	−.19*	−.32***	−.16#	−.03
United Kingdom	.07	−.33***	.49***	.67***	.12	−.06
Manufacturing	−.04	−.08	−.10	−.16#	.04	−.03
Education	.17#	.13	−.18	−.10	−.14	.03
Size of organization	−.03	.11	.09	.24***	−.03	.35***
Private ownership	.27***	.09	.06	.11	.13	.01
Independent unit	.13#	.13#	−.04	.14	.11	.08
Percentage 'temps'	−.07	.00	.29***	.21**	.19*	−.14#
Union influence	.01	−.05	−.04	.21**	−.00	.01
HRM practices apply to all employees	.09	.05	.06	−.06	−.07	−.06
Reasons for employing temps:						
Short-term substitutes	.05	−.07	.02	−.11	.05	−.16*
Specialist skills	.03	.01	−.02	−.01	−.16*	−.06
Unusual hours	−.31***	−.10	.02	.17*	−.04	.16*
Lower wage costs	.08	.02	−.05	.03	.13	−.14#
Adjusted R^2	0.12	0.08	0.26	0.36	0.16	0.08

Israel serves as the reference category for country and retail services for sector
#$p \leq .10$, *$p \leq .05$, **$p \leq .01$, ***$p \leq .001$

ratings of their satisfaction with the performance of permanent and temporary workers. The results are summarized in Table 3.4. The aim here is to determine whether features of the organizations, the application of HR practices, and the reasons for hiring temporary workers relate to these outcomes.

Table 3.4 shows the results of the regression analyses of organizational factors such as size, ownership, independence, and HR practices applied to all workers and reasons for employing temporary workers on employers' satisfaction with performance, voluntary quitting rates, and dismissals of workers during 2003, the year prior to the start of our data collection.

Separate analyses were performed for permanent and temporary workers controlling for country and sector. The table shows standardized beta values in the last step of the analyses.

Satisfaction with performance

The table shows that managers of private organizations tended to be more satisfied with the performance of their permanent employees than managers of public organizations but there are no significant differences in satisfaction with temporary workers. No other features of organizational structure or HR practices are significantly associated with satisfaction with the performance of either permanent or temporary workers. It is, however, worth noting that UK employers are notably less satisfied with the performance of temporary workers than managers in all the other countries while German managers tend to be more satisfied. Among the reasons for employing temporary workers, the table shows that organizations that need to employ temporary workers to work unusual hours were less satisfied with the performance of their permanent employees. However, none of the listed reasons for employing temporary workers is related to employers' satisfaction with their performance.

Labour turnover

The results in Table 3.4 indicate that organizations with a higher proportion of temporary workers appear to have higher levels of labour turnover both among permanent and temporary employees. Quitting among temporary workers was also reported more frequently in larger organizations and in organizations with a high level of union influence. There are also marked differences between countries, with particularly high levels of voluntary labour turnover among both permanent and temporary workers in the United Kingdom. Reasons for employing temporary workers had no significant effect on labour turnover among permanent workers but organizations that reported hiring temporary workers to provide cover for unusual hours reported higher levels of quits among temporary workers. An interesting but slightly unexpected finding was that variables in our analysis were able to explain a much higher proportion of the variance in labour turnover than in either dismissals or satisfaction with performance (36% of variance in quitting of temporaries compared to levels around 10% for the other dependent variables). Possible explanations could be differences in labour market legislation and general functioning of the labour market across countries.

Dismissals

Background and structural factors have a very limited influence on dismissals of either permanent or temporary staff. Organizations with a higher proportion of temporary workers report more dismissals of permanent staff and larger organizations report more dismissals among temporary staff. Since larger organizations also report more labour turnover among temporary workers, this may help to explain why they are likely to report a lower proportion of temporary staff in their workforces.

Hiring temporary workers with specialist skills was related to lower levels of dismissal of permanent employees. Temporary workers seem to be at a higher risk of dismissal in organizations that employed temporary workers to cover unusual hours. Conversely, in organizations that often hired workers as short-term substitutes or to lower costs, dismissals of temporary workers were significantly lower.

SUMMARY AND DISCUSSION

Despite its rather exploratory nature, this is one of the few studies of temporary employment that takes the employers' perspective into account. We started this chapter by providing an organizational context for the results, particularly with respect to the use of temporary staff and the influence of trade unions. Our first main aim was to explore the reasons reported by organizations for hiring temporary workers and the factors affecting the size of the temporary workforce. Our second aim was to explore the extent to which there was equal treatment of temporary and permanent workers, particularly with respect to the application of HR practices. The third aim was to explore any association between reasons for hiring temporary workers, features of the organizational context, and the application of HR practices for three outcomes, namely satisfaction with the performance of permanent and temporary workers, levels of voluntary turnover, and dismissals of permanent and temporary staff.

With respect to our first major aim, seeking to understand the reasons for hiring temporary workers, we found that three main reasons emerged. These concerned the need to cover long-term and short-term absences, the need to meet peaks in demand, and the desire to hire people for a trial period before possibly offering them permanent employment. When we looked at how these and other factors affected the proportion of temporary workers in an organization's workforce, motives for hiring tended to be more important than structural factors. More specifically, hiring to provide cover for unusual working hours was associated with higher proportions of temporary workers while hiring to cover short-term absences was associated with lower proportions.

The second aim was to determine how far managers believed that they treated permanent and temporary workers equally, particularly with respect to the application of HR practices. Our results revealed that many managers admitted that they did not treat the two groups of workers equally and that temporary workers were disadvantaged. This applied with respect to specific HR practices and also when a more general question about equality of treatment and opportunities was asked. Somewhat contrary to expectations, those countries with a stronger trade union presence were more likely to report a lack of equal treatment. This raises the question of whether unions use their influence to promote the interests of permanent workers at the expense of temporary workers. It is possible that since the time when we collected this data, the picture has changed somewhat with the advent of European legislation to promote the rights of temporary agency as well as fixed-term contract workers. It may also have altered as a result of the influence of the international financial upheavals on the way firms operate.

The third aim was to determine how far the size of the temporary workforce, the reasons for hiring temporary workers, and the more or less equal application of HR practices affected three outcomes, namely, satisfaction with performance, levels of labour turnover, and levels of dismissals. An initial important finding was that most managers were quite highly satisfied with the performance of both permanent and temporary staff and, if anything, were marginally more satisfied with the performance of their temporary staff. Despite this, levels of voluntary turnover and more particularly dismissals of temporary staff were high. Given the high levels of satisfaction with performance, we must assume that the dismissals mainly relate to removing temporary workers when they are no longer required.

Very little in our model predicted variations in performance among temporary workers. With respect to the performance of permanent workers, this was rated more highly in private-sector organizations and received a lower rating in those organizations that gave some emphasis to the need to cover unusual hours as a major reason for hiring temporary workers. We can speculate that this may be linked to the reluctance of permanent workers to work during unusual hours. Voluntary quitting was higher among both permanent and temporary workers in those organizations with a higher proportion of temporary workers and, with respect to temporary workers, in larger organizations and where union influence was higher. Dismissals of temporary staff were higher in larger organizations, confirming the important role of organizational size, while both quits and dismissals of temporary staff were higher in organizations that hired temporary workers to cover unusual hours. Finally, there are some interesting national differences, with the UK organizations reporting much higher dissatisfaction with temporary workers than elsewhere and much higher voluntary quitting among both permanent and temporary staff. Organizations in Spain and the Netherlands, by way of contrast, report much lower levels of voluntary quits among temporary staff. Sweden is distinctive in a rather different way because, as reported in the New Understanding of European Work Organization (NUEWO) project (Storrie, 2003), the unions have a strong influence over aspects of relevant policy. In spite of this, or maybe because of it, temporary workers appear to be particularly disadvantaged with respect to equal application of HR practices.

In conclusion, it appears that a range of influences at a variety of levels operate to affect these outcomes. The results confirm that, at least in the organizations in our sample, which, given the size of their temporary workforce are mostly not representative of their national organizations, numerical flexibility is in operation to provide cover where necessary but, contrary to assumptions in sections of the literature, not primarily to reduce costs.

4

Individual and Organizational Outcomes of Employment Contracts

Nele De Cuyper, Hans De Witte, Moshe Krausz, Gisela Mohr, and Thomas Rigotti

This chapter presents the core findings of comparing the attitudes and behaviour of workers on permanent and temporary contracts, and identifying any differences between them. Firstly, we investigate the impact of contract type on various psychological variables, including both work-related and general well-being, attitudes towards the job and the organization, and behavioural indicators. Secondly, there is a detailed examination of the processes underlying possible differences between temporary and permanent workers. More specifically, we highlight the importance of job characteristics, psychosocial working conditions, job insecurity, and human capital issues. Thirdly, in the context of the debate on the heterogeneity of temporary workers, we identify a number of dimensions along which temporary workers may differ, and we explore their impact on psychological outcomes.

TEMPORARY EMPLOYMENT AND PSYCHOLOGICAL OUTCOMES

A review of the existing evidence

Conventional thinking suggests that the effects of temporary employment are likely to be negative for employees. For example, European and national legislations (e.g. De Jong and Schalk, 2005*b*) have implemented actions to further the social protection of temporary workers on fixed-term contracts, and to establish equal treatment of fixed-term and permanent employees.

This was based on evidence that temporary employment may increase the risk of inequality in the distribution of rewards such as compensation or training (Beard and Edwards, 1995; Davis-Blake and Uzzi, 1993; OECD, 2002). These actions also recognize the weaker labour market position of temporary workers in terms of characteristics of race, age, education, and gender (Saloniemi, Virtanen, and Vahtera, 2004). Furthermore, the disadvantaged position of temporary workers has been highlighted in socio-economic theories such as the Flexible Firm Model (Atkinson, 1984) and Human Capital Theory (Becker, 1993). Basically, these theories suggest that temporary workers occupy positions on the organization's periphery, which are characterized by poor job quality, lack of job security, and limited possibilities for development and advancement.

Accordingly, most psychological studies hypothesize poor well-being, unfavourable attitudes, and unsatisfactory performance among temporary workers as compared to permanent workers. However, the balance of research evidence shows that this cannot be offered as a general conclusion. Reviews of European (De Cuyper, Isaksson, and De Witte, 2005; De Cuyper et al., 2008) and US (Connelly and Gallagher, 2004) research conclude that results on the impact of temporary employment are inconclusive. This goes for job-related and general well-being, as well as for attitudes towards the organization and behavioural indicators. For example, while Dutch (De Jong and Schalk, 2005b), Spanish (Caballer et al., 2005), and German (Rigotti and Mohr, 2005) research has established that temporary workers report lower job satisfaction than permanent workers, Belgian studies (De Cuyper and De Witte, 2005a) do not find contract-based differences. Similarly, inconsistent results have been reported in the review by Virtanen et al. (2005) on various indicators of health and well-being. Inconsistent results are also found on organizational variables: for example, temporary workers as compared to permanent workers report either lower (e.g. Van Dyne and Ang, 1998; Sverke, Gallagher, and Hellgren, 2000), or higher (e.g. McDonald and Makin, 2000), or equal (e.g. De Witte and Naswall, 2003) levels of organizational commitment. Consistent results have only been reported for turnover intention: temporary workers are more likely to quit the organization than permanent workers. However, as pointed out by Guest and Clinton (2005), they may not intend to quit before their contract expires. Finally, studies on behavioural indicators are scarce: initial evidence points to non-significant differences on sick leave (Goudswaard, Kraan, and Dhondt, 2000) or more frequent sick leave among permanent workers (Virtanen et al., 2001).

One obvious explanation for the inconsistent findings across studies may be the huge variation in research designs (Connelly and Gallagher, 2004). Comparison across studies has been hampered by factors such as sample selection, specific national contexts including labour market indicators and legislation, choice of measures, and selection of controls. Moreover, this questions the possibility of generalizing findings. The heterogeneity of the Psycones study's sample, its sample size, the rigorous selection of sectors and organizations, the participation of six European countries plus Israel, and the use of reliable measures may address these concerns.

We investigated differences between temporary and permanent workers on various psychological outcomes using analysis of covariance (ANCOVA), and controlling for individual,[1] work-related,[2] as well as context[3] variables in all analyses. Detailed information about the relevant measures and their reliability, as well as information on the procedure of data collection and on sample characteristics, is reported in Chapter 2 and in Appendix 2.

Employment contracts and psychological outcomes in the Psycones study

Well-being among permanent and temporary workers

Table 4.1 presents the results of ANCOVA with regard to well-being. In general, results show poorer work-related well-being among permanent workers as compared to temporary workers: specifically, temporary workers report significantly lower scores on irritation, anxiety, and depression, and

Table 4.1 Temporary versus permanent employment: well-being (ANCOVA)

Well-being[a]	Means[b]		F	R^2_{adj}
	Temporary	Permanent		
Pos. influence of work	3.23	3.15	5.02	.20
Irritation	2.46	2.76	42.46**	.13
Job satisfaction	4.13	3.91	56.04**	.13
Anxiety	1.85	2.01	33.15**	.13
Depression	1.33	1.50	45.99**	.20
Self-efficacy	3.56	3.51	3.70	.15
Life satisfaction	5.69	5.61	4.27	.11
Health	4.27	4.18	5.63*	.05

[a] Responses on all scales ranged from 1 to 5, except for irritation and life satisfaction (1 to 7)
[b] Means including controls
*$p < 0.01$, **$p < 0.001$

higher scores on job satisfaction. Similar results are found for general well-being: permanent workers report poorer health than temporary workers. Temporary and permanent workers do not differ significantly with respect to the positive influence of work on life outside work, self-efficacy, and life satisfaction, although in each case there is a tendency for temporary workers to report slightly more positive outcomes. The explained variance (R^2_{adj}) ranges from 20 per cent for work-related depression and the influence of work on life outside work to only 5 per cent for general health. This suggests that there are likely to be other factors influencing general health besides those included in the model.

Attitudes and behavioural outcomes among permanent and temporary workers

The results of organizational attitudes and behavioural indicators are shown in Table 4.2. In most cases, there are no significant differences between permanent and temporary workers. Specifically, there are no differences between temporary and permanent workers on organizational commitment, performance, sick leave, accidents, and incidents of harassment and violence. However, temporary workers as compared to permanent workers report lower turnover intentions and lower sickness presence. The distinctive circumstances of temporary workers imply that we need to treat any comparisons

Table 4.2 Temporary versus permanent employment: attitudes towards the organization and behavioural indicators (ANCOVA)

Attitudes and behaviour[a]	Means[b]		df	F	R^2_{adj}
	Temporary	Permanent			
Organizational commitment	3.92	3.91	3,922	.22	.30
Turnover intention	.64	.82	3,921	30.50**	.23
Performance	4.13	4.14	3,896	.02	.11
Sick leave[c]	1.50	1.60	3,240	4.05	.10
Sickness presence[c]	1.91	2.06	3,239	7.05*	.10
Accidents[c]	.98	.99	3,245	0.00	.07
Incidents of harassment/violence[c]	.74	.79	3,238	1.68	.04

[a] Responses on all scales ranged from 1 to 5
[b] Means including controls
[c] In order to have sufficient variation in responses, we established a one-year time period for reports on sick leave, sickness presence, accidents, and incidents. This implies that organizational tenure was conditional for employees' responses. Accordingly, analyses are performed only with temporary workers whose contract tenure was at least one year.
*$p < 0.01$, **$p < 0.001$

of turnover intentions with considerable caution. The explained variance is low for accidents and incidents of harassment and violence: these may be related to factors not included in the model, such as interpersonal conflicts or organizational culture. The explained variance (R^2_{adj}) exceeds 10 per cent for all other outcomes, and is particularly high for organizational commitment.

Summary

In sum, the initial analyses of the results from this study do not support hypotheses about the unfavourable impact of temporary employment. On the contrary, we find either no differences between permanent and temporary workers, or poorer results for permanent workers on various measures of work-related and general well-being, organizational attitudes, and behavioural indicators. It is notable that there are no well-being, attitudinal, or behavioural outcomes on which permanent workers report significantly more positive results than temporary workers. In the following sections, we will explore the possible explanations for these results, by first looking at variables that are central to most theories of work-related well-being and satisfaction, and then by exploring the heterogeneity of temporary workers to determine whether certain types of temporary work have a major bearing on these results.

THE INFLUENCE OF TEMPORARY EMPLOYMENT ON THE EXPERIENCE OF WORK

A review of existing evidence

Most previous studies have focused on the negative rather than the potentially positive features of temporary employment. For example, several studies show that job insecurity is exacerbated in temporary employment arrangements (e.g. De Witte and Naswall, 2003; Kinnunen and Nätti, 1994). Furthermore, results from the Third European Survey on Working and Living Conditions show that temporary workers experience lower job control and fewer possibilities for skill utilization than permanent workers (Goudswaard and Andries, 2002). While these studies underline potential risks associated with temporary employment, they may not capture the complex dynamics that together account for employees' responses.

Some studies have highlighted the possibility that unfavourable job characteristics may be compensated by others that are more favourable. For example, Parker et al. (2002) replicate previous research confirming the negative consequences of temporary employment, through job insecurity and low participative decision making, and for job strain. However, they also establish that temporary employment is associated with reduced role overload. In turn, lower role overload is associated with reduced job strain. Similarly, in the study by Saloniemi, Virtanen, and Vahtera (2004), fixed-term employees report fewer problems than permanent employees with psychosocial working conditions, most notably with regard to workload demands. It is also possible that temporary workers may perceive higher social support than permanent workers partly because they are newcomers to the organization and not yet familiar with organizational procedures and practices, and they receive extra attention and help.

Many temporary workers may have learned to cope with the possible negative effects of job insecurity. In this respect, recent studies have demonstrated that permanent and temporary workers may differ in their reactions to job insecurity. In particular, job insecurity was found to lower job satisfaction and organizational commitment among permanent workers, but not among temporary workers (De Cuyper and De Witte, 2006, 2007; De Witte and Naswall, 2003; Mauno et al., 2005). These effects were replicated for positive influence of work on life outside work, turnover intention (De Cuyper and De Witte, 2005b), and psychological distress and health (Bernhard-Oettel, Sverke and De Witte, 2005; Sverke, Gallagher, and Hellgren, 2000; Virtanen et al., 2002). While job security is of crucial importance for permanent workers, temporary workers may rely on employability to safeguard their labour market position (Forrier and Sels, 2003; Galunic and Anderson, 2000). Hence, these potentially compensating aspects should be given due consideration in all analyses of temporary employment.

A significant proportion of temporary workers are hired to replace permanent workers (see Chapter 3), and many temporary workers are employed on contracts of relatively long duration. This suggests that temporary and permanent workers often perform exactly the same job, and hence their job characteristics and working conditions may be quite similar (Beard and Edwards, 1995). In some countries (e.g. Sweden), long contract duration gives access to various benefits, implying that some temporary workers may be similar to permanent workers also with regard to legal rights. European legislation now extends this to all workers on fixed-term contracts. This possibly explains why some studies do not find differences between temporary and permanent workers. For example, Krausz, Brandwein, and Fox (1995) do not find differences on role-related issues, and Scandinavian studies show no association between contract type and social support (Bernhard-Oettel and Isaksson, 2005).

Relying on temporary workers may have hidden implications, in that it may affect permanent workers' perceptions. On the one hand, temporary workers may safeguard the position of permanent workers in times of restructuring, which may enhance feelings of security among permanent workers. On the other hand, temporary workers are often hired when the workload is too high for permanent workers, and when working overtime no longer offers a solution. This implies that permanent workers may perceive demands that are too high to cope with when temporary workers enter the organization. In addition, temporary employment may create feelings of increased responsibility and supervision demands among permanent workers, for they may be assigned the task of monitoring temporary workers. Furthermore, permanent workers in organizations with many temporary workers may perceive fewer developmental and internal mobility opportunities and less job security (Davis-Blake, Broschak, and George, 2003; Kraimer et al., 2005; De Cuyper et al., 2009). These perceptions, in turn, may negatively affect permanent workers' trust, organizational commitment, and turnover intentions (Davis-Blake, Broschak, and George, 2003; George, 2003).

In sum, different perspectives on the employment of temporary workers have been outlined. Most researchers have highlighted the association between temporary employment and negative job characteristics, most notably job insecurity, limited possibilities for skill utilization, and lack of control and autonomy. However, others have argued that temporary employment may be beneficial in other respects. Specifically, the lower scores on various indicators of autonomy among temporary workers may be balanced with lower workload demands. Similarly, the negative effects of job insecurity may be buffered by the positive effects of employability. A further possibility is that there may be few differences in reported work experiences between temporary and permanent workers, because they may perform similar jobs and also because permanent workers may experience less visible but equally harmful stressors. One of the aims of our research was to address these issues and to resolve some of the apparently conflicting perspectives through carefully designed comparative research.

Temporary employment and work experiences: the Psycones findings

In the following section, we present a detailed analysis of the data that address the possible advantages and disadvantages of temporary and permanent

Table 4.3 Temporary versus permanent employment: job characteristics, psychosocial working conditions, job insecurity, and employability (ANCOVA)

Work aspects[a]	Means[b]		df	F	R^2_{adj}
	Temporary	Permanent			
Autonomy	3.56	3.69	3,892	17.70**	.35
Workload	3.01	3.23	3,907	48.37**	.24
Role clarity	4.35	4.38	3,904	1.15	.11
Skill utilization	4.60	4.58	3,900	.82	.42
Perceived organizational support	3.65	3.50	3,920	24.58**	.34
Support from supervisor	3.70	3.51	3,922	37.46**	.25
Job insecurity	2.24	1.56	3,921	400.62**	.23
Employability	2.14	2.28	3,917	4.01	.20

[a] Responses on all scales ranged from 1 to 5
[b] Means including controls
* $p < 0.01$, ** $p < 0.001$

employment. Table 4.3 summarizes the results of ANCOVA. The same controls are used that were used previously. The results show that on the negative side, temporary employment is associated with significantly lower autonomy and much higher job insecurity. However, on the positive side temporary workers report a significantly lower workload and higher levels of organizational support and support from the supervisor. Finally, temporary and permanent workers do not differ on role clarity, skill utilization, and employability. With the exception of role clarity, the total explained variance (R^2_{adj}) is fairly high, ranging from 20 per cent for employability up to 42 per cent for skill utilization.

Do work experiences mediate the relationship between employment contracts and outcomes?

The mix of positive and negative experiences associated with temporary employment raises the question of how far the results we reported earlier in the chapter indicating that temporary workers reported higher well-being and more positive work attitudes are a result of their work experiences. To explore this possibility, we conducted a series of regression analyses to establish the extent to which these work experiences may explain the relationship between contract type and the psychological outcomes through a process of mediation. In order to limit the number of analyses presented here, we focus on and discuss the results for job satisfaction. Job satisfaction was selected for two reasons. First, job satisfaction reflects a topical theme in the realm of research on temporary employment, and it is considered an important indicator of well-being at work. Second, earlier analyses showed that contract type was related to job satisfaction, which is a condition for mediation. More extensive tests of mediation, based on fuller versions of the Psycones model, are presented in Chapters 6 and 8.

Table 4.4 summarizes the results. There are three steps in the regression. Step 1 introduces the control variables; Step 2, shown in the first column of Table 4.4, shows the influence of contract type; and Step 3 shows the influence of the various work experiences. The results for Step 2 show that there is a significant negative association between being on a permanent contract and job satisfaction. If work experiences mediate this association, then in Step 3, where they are introduced, any association between a permanent contract and job satisfaction should disappear. However the results in Table 4.4 show that contract type remains significant after introducing the various work experiences. This suggests that work experiences cannot account for the differences in job satisfaction between permanent and temporary workers. Set against this, it should be noted that all the work experiences, except for workload and employability, help to explain variations in job satisfaction above and beyond contract type. Skill utilization, organizational support, and support from the supervisor exert the strongest influence.

Table 4.4 Summary of hierarchical regression analyses: work experiences as predictors of job satisfaction

	Job satisfaction[b]	
Predictors[a]	Step 2	Step 3
Permanent contract	−.11**	−.10**
Autonomy		.08**
Workload		−.01
Role clarity		.09**
Skill utilization		.23**
Organizational support		.26**
Support from supervisor		.15**
Job insecurity		−.08**
Employability		−.02
R^2_{adj}	.30	.50
ΔR^2_{adj}		.20**

[a] Responses on all scales ranged from 1 to 5
[b] Only Steps 2 and 3 of the regression are presented.
*$p < 0.01$, **$p < 0.001$.

Summary: differences in work experiences

Overall, our results suggest that explanations in terms of job characteristics and other work experiences may not explain the results on the psychological impact of temporary employment. We find evidence that temporary employment is associated with both positive and negative work experiences compared with permanent employment, and that it is quite similar to permanent employment in other respects. Furthermore, permanent employment is associated with higher workload and lower support, which provides some evidence for hypotheses about possible hidden stressors for permanent workers. However, when tested with respect to outcomes, and in particular to job satisfaction, these elements do not explain the effects of contract type. Even after taking into account differences in work experiences, temporary workers report higher job satisfaction than those with permanent contracts.

THE HETEROGENEITY OF TEMPORARY WORKERS

Theoretical considerations

So far in this chapter, we have treated temporary workers as a homogeneous group. A major thesis in the literature suggests that the inconsistent and often contradictory findings on the psychological impact of temporary employment may result from the heterogeneity of the temporary workforce (Connelly and Gallagher, 2004; McLean Parks, Kidder and Gallagher, 1998). While most studies have focused upon fixed-term contract workers or temporary agency workers, others have included contractors or on-call workers. However, others do not even define the specific contract type. Temporary contracts may differ greatly in employment stability (Virtanen et al., 2005) and in future employment prospects (Chambel and Castanheira, 2005). For example, UK research shows that fixed-term workers report equal or higher levels of job satisfaction as compared to permanent workers, while seasonal, casual, and temporary agency workers are least satisfied with their job (Guest and Clinton, 2005). Similarly, Virtanen et al. (2003) find no differences in subjective health between permanent workers and fixed-term contract workers, while seasonal workers and employees on probation report more health problems. The authors suggest that this pattern of results follows the core–periphery stratification in the labour market: health effects appear to depend upon the stability of the formal contract. These studies clearly show the risks of generalizing results from one type of temporary employment.

A limitation of most research on temporary employment is the country-specific nature of the analysis and the high risks involved in any attempt to generalize the results across countries. For example, fixed-term employment may not offer the same stability everywhere due to differences in national legislation. Also, agency workers are temporarily employed in some European countries, while they have permanent contracts with the agency in others. Furthermore, there is no Belgian, German, Israeli, or Spanish equivalent for on-call workers, while these contracts are legally defined in the Netherlands, Sweden, and the UK.

Measures of contract duration, time left before the contract expires, and personal history of temporary contracts may provide more useful and objectively verifiable indicators of employment (in)stability than the formal type of temporary contract. Contract duration may be particularly important. Longer-duration temporary contracts may reduce differences between temporary and permanent workers, for example with regard to access to HR practices such as training, and to benefits and privileges including legal rights such as a longer period of notice. In fact, Engellandt and Riphahn (2005) found that long-term temporary workers are more likely to put in extra effort as compared to those on short-term contracts. Furthermore, little time left before the contract expires may negatively affect employees' responses because of increased job insecurity. For example, Ichino and Riphahn (2001) found increased absenteeism among employees whose probationary contracts were about to expire. A long history of repeated temporary contracts may signal that the employee is stuck in temporary employment, or that the employee alternates temporary employment with unemployment (Scherer, 2004). Hence, the likely effects are negative for the employee.

The heterogeneity of the temporary workforce is however not limited to objective indicators. It has been argued that research on the psychological impact of temporary employment should include aspects related to perceived future employment prospects, preferences, and motives for accepting such employment. Firstly, perceived future employment prospects may have significant consequences. The prospect of being offered a permanent or renewed temporary contract may increase perceived employment stability (Booth, Francesconi, and Frank, 2002). Also, the employee may think the organization is willing to invest in a long-term employment relationship, and he or she may feel obliged to reciprocate with favourable attitudes and productive behaviour. This hypothesis is supported in the study by Goudswaard, Kraan, and Dhondt (2000): employees perceiving their chance of a permanent or renewed contract as high compared to low, reported higher levels of job satisfaction, and they were less often absent because of sickness.

Isaksson and Bellaagh (2002) and Krausz (2000*a*) suggest that individuals preferring temporary to permanent employment (voluntary temporary workers) might respond in a more favourable way than those not preferring temporary employment (involuntary temporary workers). This issue has been investigated primarily in relation to job satisfaction: voluntary as compared to involuntary temporary workers report higher job satisfaction (Ellingson, Gruys, and Sackett, 1998; Feldman, Doerpinghaus, and Turnley, 1994; Krausz, Brandwein, and Fox, 1995).

A further issue concerns temporary workers' motives for accepting temporary employment. Most authors have grouped possible motives into a voluntary–involuntary dichotomy (e.g. DiNatale, 2001; Tan and Tan, 2002). Voluntary motives include the opportunity to combine work with non-work roles, and the possibility of gaining experience with different tasks and jobs. Involuntary motives refer to the difficulty of finding permanent employment or gaining access to permanent employment. In line with studies on volition, voluntary motives are expected to yield overall beneficial effects. However, the impact of involuntary motives may depend upon the specific motive and the specific outcome under consideration: while the difficulty of finding permanent employment probably reflects dissatisfaction with the current contract, temporary employment as a way to gain permanent employment may have favourable effects, in line with the 'stepping stone' or 'foot in the door' hypothesis (De Cuyper and De Witte, 2008; De Cuyper, Notelaers, and De Witte, 2009; Gagliarducci, 2005; Korpi and Levin, 2001; Tunny and Mangan, 2004). In this case, temporary workers may invest in the current employment relationship to increase their chance of gaining permanent employment. They may perform at high standards, and show constructive attitudes to create the image of a valued employee (Feather and Rauter, 2004).

The heterogeneity of temporary workers: evidence from the Psycones study

The design of the Psycones study provided us with a unique opportunity to explore variations within a disparate sample of temporary workers. Firstly, we have information from workers employed on a wide variety of types of temporary contract. Secondly, we have information from temporary workers employed in seven different countries. Thirdly, as noted in Chapter 2, we asked temporary workers a series of additional questions to establish their temporary employment history, the duration and time left on their current contract, their expectation of contract renewal and future employment prospects, and their motives for accepting temporary employment. Taken together, these provide us with a distinctive opportunity to explore variations within the population of temporary workers and to consider how far these variations might help to explain differences in the previous research findings addressing the experience of temporary employment.

Motives for temporary employment

We asked respondents to rate the importance of each of nine motives for accepting temporary employment on a five-point scale. The motives were drawn from the literature cited above. The results are presented in Table 4.5. We undertook a factor analysis (principal component analysis (PCA), Varimax rotation) to determine the extent to which the items clustered together, and this yielded three factors. The items belonging to each factor are identified on the left-hand side of Table 4.5. Factor 1 (28% of the variance) includes five items. These items are labelled 'voluntary motives' because they describe possible advantages of temporary employment. Factor 2 (17% of the variance) includes two items which are typically considered to describe involuntary motives. However, their intercorrelation is low ($r = .25$, $p < 0.001$). Therefore, we will use the item 'it is difficult for me to find a permanent job' in the analyses, as it is more characteristic of involuntary motives. Factor 3 (12%) includes one item, which points to a more ambivalent or pragmatic motivation towards temporary employment. The final item, 'This way, I hope to gain permanent employment', cross-loads on Factors 2 and 3. Despite this, it is included in the regression analyses described below because it captures the 'stepping stone' or 'foot in the door' motive which is assumed in the literature to be of some importance.

We, therefore, have three sets of motives that largely reflect the existing literature. The first covers voluntary motives, and consists of five items which combine into a scale with an acceptable alpha ($\alpha = 0.74$). The second addresses involuntary motives but is represented by a single item. The third is concerned with the stepping stone motive and is again based on a single item. It is worth noting that the mean scores in Table 4.5 suggest that the stepping stone motive seems to be considered the most important and the voluntary motives the least important in the decision to accept temporary employment.

Our aim in the following section is to evaluate how features of temporary working affect well-being, attitudes, behaviour, and the experience of work among temporary workers. The various indicators of heterogeneity or variability among the temporary workforce form the core predictors in a set of regression analyses using the temporary sample only. In the first step of the analyses, the control variables are introduced. These are not shown in the

Table 4.5 Motives for accepting temporary employment: mean, standard deviation, and frequencies

Factor		M	SD	Not at all important (%)	Not very important (%)	Of some importance (%)	Quite important (%)	Very important (%)
1	It suits my present needs/situation (e.g. family, study, leisure...).	2.44	1.58	46.7	11.1	12.1	12.5	17.7
	It offers me a higher wage than other employment contracts.	1.83	1.19	58.0	17.6	12.5	6.9	5.0
	It gives me more freedom.	2.20	1.34	48.0	13.9	16.9	12.5	8.8
	It offers me a supplementary income.	2.02	1.41	58.4	11.1	10.9	9.4	10.3
	It allows me to gain experience and expertise with different tasks and jobs.	2.96	1.49	27.7	9.8	21.7	20.6	20.2
2	It is difficult for me to find a permanent job.	2.45	1.49	42.1	12.8	17.9	12.8	14.4
2/3	It was the only type of contract I could get.	3.39	1.53	20.0	10.2	16.7	17.7	35.6
	This way, I hope to gain a permanent employment contract.	3.46	1.52	19.4	8.3	15.2	21.2	35.8
3	The contract was offered with the job I wanted.	3.42	1.52	19.4	9.2	16.6	19.6	35.1

tables that follow. In the second step, the heterogeneity measures are included and these are presented in the tables. We include the specific type of contract,[4] objective indicators,[5] and subjective dimensions reflecting preference for temporary employment, described in the tables as 'volition', and motives for accepting temporary employment.

Explanations for variations in well-being among temporary workers

Table 4.6 presents the results exploring factors affecting well-being and related attitudes among the temporary workers in our sample. Unlike earlier studies that identified the specific type of temporary employment arrangement as important in understanding temporary workers' responses, the specific type of contract does not add significantly in explaining well-being. It should be emphasized in this context that we restricted our analysis to a comparison between workers on fixed-term contracts, the dominant form in our sample, and all other types of temporary contract.[6] It might be that country-specific definitions and regulations have affected the results, an issue we consider in more detail in Chapter 9. Time left before the contract expires and personal history of temporary employment also have no significant impact on well-being. Contract duration is positively related to anxiety. This is a rather counter-intuitive finding. However, earlier in the chapter we reported that permanent workers reported higher levels of anxiety than temporary workers and it is possible that temporary workers with long duration contracts begin to assume some of the characteristics of permanent workers.

Among the subjective indicators, it appears that future employment prospects have favourable effects on employees' job satisfaction, depression, and self-efficacy. Similarly, volition is positively related to job and life satisfaction, while it is negatively related to irritation and anxiety. Unsurprisingly, those who deliberately choose temporary employment respond more positively to the experience than those who do not. Even though we might expect a close relationship between volition and both voluntary and involuntary motives, these motives did not predict employees' well-being, except for a positive relationship between voluntary motives and the positive influence of work on life outside work. The stepping stone motive has favourable effects on job satisfaction and depression. Surprisingly, it is negatively related to self-efficacy. Finally, the pragmatic motive, taking the job because it was difficult to find a permanent job, is associated with job satisfaction.

Although these results reveal some significant associations between subjective factors associated with temporary employment and well-being, we should be careful not to overemphasize their importance. The amount of variance explained ranges between 4 per cent for health and 32 per cent for job

Table 4.6 Summary of hierarchical regression analyses: predictors of well-being among temporary workers

Predictors[a]	Pos. influence of work	Irritation	Job satisf.	Anxiety	Depression	Self-efficacy	Life satisf.	Health
Fixed-term contract	−.05	.03	.02	−.03	−.02	−.02	.05	−.01
Contract duration	.04	.03	−.02	.09*	.02	.02	.04	.04
Time left	−.09	.03	−.04	−.00	.04	−.08	−.08	−.03
History	−.01	.02	.06	.01	.04	.02	−.03	−.04
Prospects	.00	−.03	.12**	−.05	−.11**	.11**	.06	.06
Volition	−.01	−.10*	.12**	−.15**	−.09*	−.00	.11*	.04
Voluntary motives	.09*	−.01	−.01	.01	−.04	.06	.01	−.04
Stepping stone motive	.08	.02	.15**	−.04	−.11*	−.10**	.04	.02
Involuntary motive	.02	.01	−.02	.05	.06	.01	−.04	−.01
Pragmatic motive	.07	.02	.10**	.00	−.02	.03	−.04	.02
R^2_{adj}	.23	.18	.34	.14	.21	.19	.16	.07
ΔR^2_{adj}	.03**	.02	.06**	.03**	.04**	.03**	.02	.01

[a] Only Step 2 of the regression is presented.
* $p < 0.01$, ** $p < 0.001$

satisfaction. But although often statistically significant, the amount of added variance explained by the specific measures associated with temporary employment ranges between 0 and 5 per cent. In other words, the indicators of variability within the population of temporary workers do not explain very much of the variation in responses.

Explanations for variations in attitudes and behaviour among temporary workers

Results on the relationship between objective heterogeneity indicators, organizational attitudes, and behavioural indicators are shown in Table 4.7. With one exception, none of the objective contract indicators is significantly associated with any of the attitudinal or behavioural indicators. The exception is an association between longer contracts and a greater likelihood of experiencing an incident of bullying or harassment. Indeed, few of the indicators of variability within the temporary workforce have much impact on these outcomes. The predictors explain most variance in the more attitudinal items of organizational commitment and turnover intention: employment prospects and the stepping stone motive are positively related to organizational commitment, and they are negatively related to turnover intention. Additionally, volition and the pragmatic motive are negatively related to turnover intention. Performance is predicted by employment prospects. Finally, the stepping stone motive is positively related to sickness presence.

Altogether, the results show that objective heterogeneity indicators do not contribute much in explaining the psychological experience of temporary workers. However, the more future-oriented subjective indicators such as future employment prospects, volition, and motives, most notably the stepping stone motive, are stronger predictors for the responses of temporary workers. These variables may characterize different types of temporary workers, and although they explain only a small amount of the variation in the results, it is still possible that differences within the temporary group along these dimensions are larger than those between temporary and permanent workers. This issue will be explored below.

Permanent workers as a reference group

In the previous sets of analyses, we established evidence that subjective factors such as reasons for accepting temporary and future employment prospects may affect the responses of temporary workers. However, these results do not show whether these indicators may contribute in understanding differences between temporary and permanent workers. In fact, few earlier studies

Table 4.7 Summary of hierarchical regression analyses: predictors of attitudes and behavioural indicators among temporary workers

Predictors[a]	Org. comm.	Turnover	Performance	Sick leave[b]	Sickness presence[b]	Accidents[b]	Incidents[b]
Fixed-term contract	−.02	−.03	.02	−.05	−.01	−.05	.06
Contract duration	−.05	.03	.00	.07	.04	.03	.12*
Time left	.03	−.03	−.03	−.00	−.02	.03	−.03
History	−.04	.02	.06	−.01	−.01	.02	.05
Prospects	.14**	−.18**	.11**	−.03	−.02	−.02	−.04
Volition	.04	−.09*	−.06	.01	−.08	−.06	−.06
Voluntary motives	−.01	.03	.09	−.02	−.02	.01	.02
Stepping stone motive	.12**	−.20**	.04	.03	.11*	−.01	.02
Involuntary motive	−.04	−.00	−.08	−.04	−.06	−.05	−.01
Pragmatic motive	.07	−.09*	−.06	−.07	−.05	−.03	−.02
R^2_{adj}	.35	.32	.14	.14	.14	.08	.08
ΔR^2_{adj}	.05**	.09*	.03*	.01	.02*	.01	.02

[a] Only Step 2 of the regression is presented.

[b] In order to have sufficient variation in responses, we established a one-year time period for reports on sick leave, sickness presence, accidents, and incidents. This implies that organizational tenure was conditional for employees' responses. Accordingly, analyses are performed with temps having a tenure of at least one year.

*$p < 0.01$, **$p < 0.001$

included permanent workers as a reference group to evaluate the theoretical significance of differences within the group of temporary workers. In the final set of analyses in this chapter, we address this issue. For each outcome variable, we select one predictor at most, namely the subjective factor that was most predictive of each outcome at a 0.001 level (Tables 4.6 and 4.7).[7] This is done to reduce the number of analyses and not because other predictors may be less relevant. It is possible that the use of single items for various predictors may have affected the results. A median split on each highly significant subjective factor results in two groups of temporary workers: those scoring relatively lower and higher on the specific predictor. These two groups were compared to the permanent group by analysis of variance, including the control variables (ANCOVA).

Future employment prospects were the most important predictor for depression, self-efficacy, organizational commitment, and performance. A median split results in two groups of temporary workers, one perceiving relatively better employment prospects, the other perceiving relatively poorer prospects. These two groups are compared to the permanent group. As we would expect, Table 4.8 shows that temporary workers perceiving better employment prospects as compared to those who perceive relatively poorer prospects, report lower depression, higher self-efficacy, higher organizational commitment, and better performance. However, comparison with permanent workers reveals that permanent workers have the highest levels of depression. They do not differ significantly from temporary workers with poorer prospects regarding self-efficacy. They do not differ from temporary workers with better prospects regarding performance. And they are situated in-between the two temporary groups regarding organizational commitment. Volition was an important predictor of anxiety among temporary workers. The results in Table 4.8 show that permanent workers are more anxious than both more and less voluntary groups of temporary workers. Finally, stepping stone motives were important in predicting job satisfaction and turnover intention among temporary workers. Compared to permanent workers, both groups of temporary workers, those more and less inclined to cite the stepping stone motive, are more satisfied with their job and are less inclined to quit.

These results suggest that differences in motives and employment expectations among temporary workers are of only limited importance in understanding differences between temporary and permanent workers. On three core indicators of well-being, anxiety, depression, and job satisfaction, as well as intention to quit, contract type (temporary versus permanent) seems more important than the differences within the temporary workers group. For self-efficacy, organizational commitment, and performance, the permanent workers fall between the two groups of temporary workers. On each of these

Table 4.8 Differences between temporary workers and permanent workers (ANCOVA)[1]

	Employment prospects				Volition	Stepping stone	
	Depression	Self-efficacy	Org. commitment	Performance	Anxiety	Job satisfaction	Turnover intention
Temp. low	1.37^a	3.47^a	3.84^a	4.07^a	1.91^a	4.02^a	$.80^a$
Temp. high	1.28^b	3.62^b	4.03^b	4.18^b	1.77^b	4.38^b	$.46^b$
Permanent	1.51^c	3.51^a	3.93^c	4.14^b	2.00^c	3.91^c	$.84^c$
df	3,626	3,639	3,651	3,631	3,817	3,722	3,720
F	25.34**	11.46**	13.60**	7.01**	10.29**	39.50**	36.28**

[1] Different letters indicate significant differences

** $p < 0.001$

variables, the temporary workers were differentiated by employment prospects. There is therefore some suggestion that this alone among the quite extensive range of potential indicators of variability within the temporary worker population may be of some significance in explaining a limited set of differences between permanent and temporary workers.

Summary

Some earlier studies found more favourable outcomes among fixed-term contract workers as compared to workers on other temporary employment arrangements (Aronsson, Gustafsson, and Dallner, 2002; Chambel and Castanheira, 2005). Our results do not support these findings, possibly because specific types of temporary arrangement are defined differently across countries, or because our sample includes only a small minority of contracts that are generally considered as extremely precarious such as on-call or daily workers. Furthermore, we found little evidence that objective variations in the contracts of temporary workers including contract duration, time left before the contract expires, and history of temporary employment predicted well-being, attitudes and behavioural indicators among temporary workers. By way of contrast, subjective indicators such as employment prospects, volition, and motives for accepting temporary employment did help to explain some of the variations among temporary workers. However, on most outcomes, permanent workers report more unfavourable results, even after taking into account subjective indicators, suggesting that contract type, in the form of broad comparisons between permanent and temporary contracts, is more important than variations in the experiences and expectations of temporary workers in explaining a range of outcomes. These results challenge a number of assumptions and need further investigation. The following chapters seek to shed further light on why we have found these results and how robust they are.

CONCLUDING REMARKS

The results in this chapter challenge earlier assumptions on the detrimental effects of temporary as compared to permanent employment. In this study, permanent workers as compared to temporary workers report poorer results on several indicators of well-being, organizational outcomes, and behavioural indicators. On other outcomes there are no significant differences and on no outcomes do permanent workers report significantly more positive results than temporary workers. These effects are found after controlling for a large number of individual, work-related, and contextual variables.

We investigated possible explanations for these puzzling findings. The first explanation is based on the assumed impact of job characteristics and psychosocial working conditions. We show that temporary employment may be associated with desirable as well as undesirable job characteristics and psychosocial working conditions, and that the jobs of temporary and permanent workers may be quite similar in other respects. The undesirable job characteristics among permanent workers, most notably lower social support, may reflect hidden social costs of using temporary employment. It might be that temporary workers, at the expense of permanent workers, receive extra attention because they are relatively new on the job, and not yet acquainted with organizational practices (Wikman, Andersson, and Bastin, 1998). This hypothesis on 'hidden costs for permanent workers' may be an important avenue for future research.

Temporary workers report higher levels of job insecurity and lower levels of autonomy than permanent workers. However, our results suggest that work experiences do not explain differences in outcomes between temporary and permanent workers. On the other hand, using job satisfaction as a key example of broad work-related well-being outcomes, job characteristics, support, and job security do make significant contributions to levels of job satisfaction. In other words, even if they do not mediate the link between employment contract type and job satisfaction, they are still important predictors of job satisfaction. Recent studies furthermore show that temporary and permanent workers react differently to job insecurity (Bernhard-Oettel, Sverke, and De Witte, 2005; De Cuyper and De Witte, 2006, 2007; De Witte and Naswall, 2003; Mauno et al., 2005; Virtanen et al., 2002). Future research may want to explore further the effects of interactions between contract type and work experiences on psychological outcomes.

The second possible explanation for our unexpected findings is based on debates about the heterogeneity of the temporary workforce. More specifically, temporary contracts may differ in the employment stability they offer, and this, in turn, is likely to affect temporary workers' well-being, attitudes, and behaviours. In this respect, the type of temporary contract, and more specifically fixed-term versus other types of temporary contracts, does not predict the temporary workers' well-being, attitudes, and behaviour. Objective indicators, such as variations in contract duration, time left before the contract expires, and history of temporary employment, also largely fail to predict differences in outcomes. In contrast, temporary workers' future employment prospects, their contract preference, and motives for accepting temporary employment do help to explain differences in outcomes, although their influence is relatively small. Even these indicators are less important than contract type, reflected in temporary versus permanent employment in explaining workers' well-being.

Overall, the results in this chapter have shown that there are significant differences between workers on permanent and temporary contracts on a number of important outcomes and that generally, if unexpectedly, the outcomes of workers on temporary contracts are more favourable. Explanations in terms of job characteristics, psychosocial working conditions, and differences within the temporary workforce cannot account for more than a small part of this variation. An alternative explanation that was not tested in this chapter is based on social exchange theories. In this respect, the psychological contract is potentially useful and its role will be fully explored in subsequent chapters.

NOTES

1. The individual controls were the following: age, gender, education, family situation, financial contribution to the household, number of persons dependent on the household income, and domestic responsibility.
2. The work-related controls were the following: work involvement, occupational position, weekly working hours, night shifts, tenure, supervision responsibilities, union membership, and core HR practices.
3. The context-related controls were the following: country, sector, organization's size (number of employees), percentage of temporary workers, and type of organization (public versus private; independent versus not independent).
4. Fixed-term contracts versus other temporary arrangements. We did not distinguish between all possible types of temporary arrangements because of the relatively small number of temporary workers on other than fixed-term contracts, and because of the difficulty of finding comparable contracts across countries (see Chapter 2 of this volume).
5. Objective contract characteristics were the following: contract duration, time left before the contract expires, and history of temporary employment.
6. We realize there may be variations in other types of temporary contracts, as well. For example, on-call employment is generally considered more precarious than other forms of temporary employment (for a review, see De Cuyper et al., 2008). However, owing to fairly small numbers of such contracts, we were unable to make further comparisons within the broader group of temporary contracts.
7. Accordingly, we do not perform analyses for positive influence of work on life outside work, irritation, life satisfaction, health, sick leave, sick presence, accidents, and incidents.

5

The Psychological Contracts of Temporary and Permanent Workers

René Schalk, Jeroen de Jong, Thomas Rigotti, Gisela Mohr, José Maria Peiró, and Amparo Caballer

In this chapter, we describe in some detail the concept of the psychological contract that informs the core analytic model for this study. In doing so, we build on and expand the material presented more briefly in Chapter 1. Firstly, we explore the definition and typologies of the psychological contract. Secondly, theories underpinning the psychological contract are discussed, followed by a review of the results of previous studies. Thirdly, we set out the reasons why we expect differences between the psychological contracts of temporary and permanent workers. Fourthly, our approach towards defining and assessing the psychological contract in the Psycones project is outlined and justified. Finally, we present the findings of our study that describe the psychological contracts of temporary and permanent employees. We also report the results for the psychological contract as viewed from the perspective of the employers in our sample.

THE PSYCHOLOGICAL CONTRACT AS A CONCEPTUAL AND ANALYTIC FRAMEWORK

What is the psychological contract?

The later decades of the twentieth century were characterized by a wide range of organizational changes that had serious implications for employees and put the 'traditional' employment relationship to the test. The psychological contract proved to be a very useful concept to describe, analyse, and explain the feelings and reactions of employees to these changes. The rapid growth of interest in the psychological contract as a meaningful concept during this period owes much to the work of Denise Rousseau (e.g. 1989, 1990, 1995). She defined and restricted the psychological contract to an employee's perception of the exchange of mutual promise-based obligations between the employee and the organization. The consequences of the psychological contract were mainly studied in situations in which the so-called violations of the psychological contract occurred (Morrison and Robinson, 1997). These violations resulted in strong attitudinal and behavioural reactions among employees.

Rousseau's definition and approach have been extensively criticized (Arnold, 1996; Guest, 1998; Meckler, Drake, and Levinson, 2003). Before Rousseau, several authors, for example, Argyris (1960), Levinson et al. (1962), Kotter (1973), and Schein (1978) used the concept of the psychological contract in a broader sense, taking both the employee's and employer's perspectives into account. Furthermore, these authors refer to *expectations* that both parties have about their relationship. However, the use of 'expectations' is problematic because it is a very broad category of beliefs covering the subjective perceptions about what you would expect or hope to receive from or to provide to the other party. Rousseau uses the more limited 'promise-based obligations' as the basis of the psychological contract: 'The psychological contract, unlike expectations, entails a belief in what the employer is obliged to provide, based on perceived promises of reciprocal exchange' (Robinson and Rousseau, 1994, p. 246).

There are many different ways to define and measure the psychological contract (Schalk, 2004). However, Conway and Briner (2005), in their critical evaluation of psychological contract theory and research, use Rousseau's definition. They opted for this definition because it captures the subjective interpretation of the essential feature of a contract (exchange), and because promises are a clear and precise construct, which makes the definition conceptually distinct from other constructs. In the Psycones project, we used the same approach and define the psychological contract as the perceptions of all mutual promise-based obligations included in the employment relationship. However, we go beyond Rousseau by also including the employer's view. A major drawback of many studies of the psychological contract is that they are essentially one-sided: only the employee's perspective is included. The employer's perspective, although considered as very important and essential to understand the exchange between employer and employee, is, in most cases, not considered (see, for exceptions, Coyle-Shapiro and Kessler, 2002*b*; Guest and Conway, 2002*b*; Porter et al., 1998). Therefore, we included both perspectives in our study.

Typologies of psychological contracts

The psychological contract in employment situations has as its basis the formal, mostly written, employment contract made between the employer and the employee. The formal contract, as well as the keeping of the contents of this contract, is enforced by institutions, laws, rules, and regulations. These institutions and regulations form the country-specific context in which the employment contract is established. In several European countries, the employment contract between employer and employee falls under the jurisdiction of the so-called central agreements between organizations of employers in a certain sector and representatives of the employees (unions). In these central agreements, general rules and systems determine issues such as salary, minimum wages, secondary benefits, holidays, working conditions, procedures to be followed in case of downsizing and reorganization, and so on.

In the literature on psychological contracts, as in other disciplines such as law (e.g. MacNeil's Relational Contract Theory, 1985) and economics (e.g. Williamson's Transaction Cost Economics, Williamson, 1979), a conceptual distinction is often made between transactional and relational contracts. The basis for this distinction is the idea that some terms of the contract can be conceived of as exchanges of short-term, concrete, economic transactions, for example, an exchange of a specific investment of time and labour for money (MacNeil, 1985; Rousseau, 1989). This kind of contract is considered to be a transactional contract. On the other hand, a relationship that implies a long-term perspective, raises expectations about the future development of the relationship, and extends beyond purely economic transactions is considered to be a relational contract.

The distinction between transactional and relational contracts is not entirely clear. With respect to the specific dimensions underlying the distinction between transactional and relational contracts, only a few empirical studies have been reported (McLean Parks, Kidder, and Gallagher, 1998). Studies often fail to cross-validate which terms can be considered as transactional or relational (Arnold, 1996). There are several other dimensional approaches. Rousseau (1995), for example, distinguishes transactional, balanced, transitional, and relational contracts. Coyle-Shapiro and Kessler (2000) found three dimensions: relational, transactional, and training. Recently, Isaksson et al. (2010) found evidence for a layered model. According to Isaksson et al., transactional terms are included in all psychological contracts. Relational contracts build on this foundation of transactional terms. McLean Parks, Kidder, and Gallagher (1998) attempted a conceptual extension of the distinction by adding dimensions of stability, scope, tangibility, focus, time frame, and volition, which, they hypothesized, would be particularly relevant in exploring the psychological contracts of temporary workers.

Other typologies focus on the psychological contract as an exchange of organizational inducements and employees' investments (e.g. De Jong and Schalk, 2005a; Sels, Janssens, and Van den Brande, 2004; Shore and Barksdale, 1998; Tsui et al., 1997). Research using these typologies focuses mainly on the balance between inducements and investments, or perceived over- or under-investment of one of the parties.

The typologies can apply to either partner in the relationship, and include employee perceptions as well as the views of employers (represented, for example, by supervisors or HR managers). It should be noted that several 'agents' of the organization can be involved in contract-making and contract-keeping (Conway and Briner, 2005; Rousseau, 1995).

In the Psycones project, to measure the psychological contract, we included items that potentially cover a broad range of dimensions and typologies. Our main focus, however, was on the content rather than the dimensions. The content of the psychological contract is transparent, and has been often studied. In contrast, the dimensions of the psychological contract have not been consistently established in empirical research and remain contentious.

PSYCHOLOGICAL CONTRACT THEORY

The psychological contract as a mental schema

If the psychological contract consists of perceptions about mutual promise-based obligations, an important question is how these perceptions are structured. How are the different perceptions weighed, compared, and integrated? What happens when perceptions are incongruent? These questions concern the general psychological processes taking place.

Although theoretical work (cf. Rousseau, 2001; Schalk and Freese, 1997) suggests that there should be internal consistency in the perceptions that together form the psychological contract, which means that the psychological contract should not include inconsistent or contradictory perceptions, there is only limited empirical evidence that this is indeed the case. Only a few studies (e.g. De Vos, Buyens, and Schalk, 2003; Tekleab and Taylor, 2003; Thomas and Anderson, 1998) touch on this issue. Because of the supposed consistency, the psychological contract is often referred to as a (mental) scheme which acts as a kind of a cognitive map that guides actions (Rousseau, 2001). The schema, the general image of the psychological contract, consists of beliefs about the promises made and the mutual obligations in the relationship between employer and employee. In addition, the mental schema acts as a general framework including beliefs about how the relationship should evolve in the future. The mental scheme can easily be conceptualized in theory. Little is known, however, about the actual characteristics of the psychological contract as a mental scheme.

In our study, we consider three aspects that are related to the psychological contract as a schema. Firstly, we assess the breadth of the schema; that is, how many promises are included in the psychological contract. Secondly, we assess the degree of fulfilment and state of the psychological contract. This fulfilment is also part of the schema in that it encompasses a general idea about the results of the exchange. Thirdly, we assess the experience of violation as an emotional reaction that accompanies the evaluation of the psychological contract schema.

SOCIAL EXCHANGE THEORY AND THE PSYCHOLOGICAL CONTRACT

The framework of social exchange theory (Rupp and Cropanzano, 2002) suggests that along with economic expectations, social expectations are relevant for an employee when he or she enters an employment relationship. This means that it is not only the formal employment contract that characterizes the employment relationship. The value of the informal and implicit content of the relationship between employees and their employer should be taken into account too (Shore and Tetrick, 1994).

Social exchange theorists consider the employment relationship as an exchange; for example, loyalty and effort might be offered by employees in return for organizational inducements, such as wages, fringe benefits, and working conditions (Rhoades and Eisenberger, 2002). According to social exchange theory, individuals try to achieve a balance in their exchange relationships (Blau, 1964). The exchange is based on the norm of reciprocity (Gouldner, 1960), which refers to a belief that the commitments or contributions made by one party obligate the other to provide an appropriate return (Dabos and Rousseau, 2004). Reciprocity implies that when an employee perceives that he or she is treated well by the organization, there is an obligation to respond positively and deliver extra effort and/or loyalty. The greater the degree of mutual obligation, the stronger the (social) exchange relationship will be.

According to Blau (1964), a perceived lack of balance in the fulfilment of obligations might lead to negative consequences, as an employee who perceives he or she is not treated well might try to rebalance the exchange by reducing effort. Negative health effects of imbalanced exchange have been demonstrated by Siegrist (1996). Adams's (1965) equity theory is based on the same foundations but adds a dimension of social comparison. It assumes that employees compare their own 'ratio' of how much they contribute to the organization and how much they get back in return to the perceived ratio of relevant others (e.g. co-workers). According to equity theory, employees react and adjust their behaviour according to the extent to which this comparison is favourable, unfavourable, or in balance.

The psychological contract can be regarded as an on-going, implicit, exchange-based contract between the employee and the organization, specifying the reciprocal obligations between the two parties. It specifies what each is expected to give to and receive from the other in the exchange relationship. Perceptions of the exchange are created on both the employee's and the employer's sides. These are likely to include perceptions of the reciprocal conditions under which psychological contracts are formed and how the exchange is evaluated (Coyle-Shapiro and Kessler, 2002*b*; Dabos and Rousseau, 2004; Guest and Conway, 2002*b*). The psychological contract thus operates on both sides of the exchange. In the Psycones project, we accept the importance of recognizing that there are at least two parties to the exchange, and therefore we assess the perspectives of the employer as well as the employee on the exchanges in their relationship.

The distinction between breach and violation of the psychological contract

Both social exchange and psychological contract theories consider expectations and obligations of parties to an exchange. But where social exchange theory emphasizes the reciprocity of the exchange, psychological contract theory includes the evaluation of the fulfilment of obligations. Psychological contract breach is almost always considered from the employees' perspective and occurs when the employee perceives that his/her employer has failed to fulfil one or more promised or implied obligations (Coyle-Shapiro, 2002; Morrison and Robinson, 1997). Breach is essentially the awareness of unmet promise-based obligations and, reflecting a focus on the employees' perspective, can be defined as 'the cognition that one's organization has failed to meet one or more obligations within one's psychological contract' (Morrison and Robinson, 1997, p. 230). The awareness of contract breach may be a relatively short-term phenomenon or it may persist. Alternatively breach could develop into a *violation* of the psychological contract (Pate, Martin, and McGoldrick, 2003).

A violation of the psychological contract is defined by Morrison and Robinson as an 'emotional and affective state that may follow from the belief that one's organization has failed to adequately maintain the psychological contract' (1997, p. 230). This definition suggests a personal and intense response, which goes beyond the failure of the organization to meet expectations (Robinson and Rousseau, 1994). This may flow from and grow out of an initial sense of breach, but it can also reflect an instant response to what is perceived to be a major transgression on the part of the organization or its agents. In the literature, however, breach and violation are often used interchangeably. What is measured in empirical studies is often contract breach, or more specifically non-fulfilment of the psychological contract, even if it is described as contract violation (Bocchino, Hartman, and Foley, 2003; Sutton and Griffin, 2004; Turnley and Feldman, 1999a). A few studies actually assess violation as an 'emotional' construct, which, according to Morrison and Robinson (1997), at the basic level involves disappointment, frustration, and distress or strain, in combination with feelings of anger, resentment, bitterness, indignation, and outrage resulting from the perception that the organization has failed to deliver, resulting in perceptions of betrayal. Morrison and Robinson conceive of contract violation as 'a mental state of readiness for action' (1997, p. 231) that leads to a range of attitudinal and behavioural responses.

In our project, we assess both the cognitive beliefs about the extent to which the organization has fulfilled its obligations, operationalized as the degree of fulfilment or non-fulfilment of promises and obligations, where non-fulfilment can also be described as breach, and the emotional states resulting from this situation, operationalized as positive or negative feelings and described as the degree of violation of the psychological contract. In this way, we accept and utilize the distinction between breach and violation. In addition, we take into account Conway and Briner's finding (2002b) that breach is a commonplace everyday occurrence. Therefore, while breach is important, the main focus should be on violation, capturing the more serious experiences that are particularly likely to affect attitudes and behaviour. In our study we explore both non-fulfilment as an indicator of breach and the specific emotional experience of violation.

The psychological contract, organizational justice, and trust

Many psychological contract theorists have related the psychological contract construct, and more specifically contract breach as well as contract violation, to perceptions of justice or fair treatment. According to Guest (2004b), the status of justice is still uncertain in the context of psychological contract research, as it can be seen as either a determinant, or a dimension, or a consequence of the psychological contract. Therefore, Guest includes justice, together with trust and contract breach, in what he describes as the 'state of the psychological contract'. Guest and Conway (2002b) refer to the state of the psychological contract as addressing whether the promises and obligations have been met, and whether they are fair. In addition they refer to the implications for trust. In their view, the state of the psychological contract influences perceptions of contract violation. Other authors similarly conceptualize violations as an assessment of fairness or organizational justice by the employee (Pate, Martin, and McGoldrick, 2003). Shore and Tetrick (1994), for example, building on existing organizational justice theory, make a distinction between distributive violations (referring to a violation of outcomes of distribution obligations), procedural violations (referring to violations of procedures), and interactional violations (referring to violations regarding expectations of interpersonal treatment).

Reflecting the uncertainty about the relation of justice to the psychological contract, some authors refer to justice perceptions as moderators between psychological contract breach and contract violation. Morrison and Robinson (1997), for example, state that feelings of contract violation are influenced by contract breach, together with the different types of justice. This would imply that justice perceptions trigger feelings of violation. Kickul (2001) and Kickul et al. (2001), however, found a direct effect of the interaction between breach and justice on employee outcomes such as attitudes and performance. The moderating role of justice perceptions on the relation between breach on the one hand, and contract violations or employee outcomes on the other hand, may be similar to an evaluation or comparison to a standard (see also McLean Parks and Kidder, 1994). There is sufficient evidence that assessments of justice and fairness affect outcomes to support the inclusion in this study of a measure of justice perceptions as part of the state of the psychological contract.

In the literature (e.g. Guest and Conway, 2002b), it is assumed that trust is a state that can emerge when promise-based obligations from the other party are fulfilled and the exchange produced between both parties is perceived as fair. Fairness and trust are thus closely related. Trust has been defined by

Rousseau et al. (1998) as a psychological state comprising the intention to accept vulnerability based on positive expectations of the intentions or behaviour of another party. Mayer, Davis, and Schoorman (1995) also emphasize in the notion of trust 'the willingness of a party to be vulnerable to the actions of another party based on the expectation that the other party will perform a particular action important to the trustor, irrespective of the ability to monitor and control that other party' (p. 712). Thus, there are two basic issues in the notion of trust: the voluntary acceptance of vulnerability to another party and the expectation of some return from it. It is the vulnerability that enables the return because it lowers the transaction costs. Costs can be high in the exchange process, and they are usually dramatically reduced when trust is present, increasing the benefits for both parties. Trust is essential when transactions are future-oriented, and deal with open promises that comprise intentions and future, not yet existing, gains. These are the characteristics of relational psychological contracts that make them different from transactional, short-term, and tangible contracts.

Organizations will look for future returns from employees but they have to take into account the risks of not getting them. Employees may be more ready to invest in their future in the company when they perceive that the company has a future-oriented approach and invests in employees for their future benefits. This type of long-term exchange is more likely to take place under conditions of mutual trust. When organizations achieve a high trust relation with their employees, they accumulate a productive social capital that gives them competitive advantage (Lewicki, McAllister, and Bies, 1998).

In summary, the essential component of social capital in organizations is trust because it facilitates the conditions for a relational contract, which is critical to reduce transaction costs, and to create the conditions for future-oriented investment in the organization. Therefore, the conceptual model that underlies the Psycones study (see Chapter 1) considers trust as one of the components of the state of psychological contract.

Expected differences between psychological contracts of permanent and temporary workers

According to McLean Parks, Kidder, and Gallagher (1998) and Rousseau (1995), temporary workers can be expected to have a more short-term, transactional exchange relationship compared to permanent workers. Employment status is thus likely to be an important factor that influences the exchange relationship and therefore the psychological contract (Van Dyne and Ang, 1998).

Three distinctive characteristics of the exchange relationship of temporary workers have been identified. First, it is proposed that temporary workers have narrower psychological contracts (Rousseau, 1995; Rousseau and Tijoriwala, 1998), due to lower reciprocal commitment to developing the relationship (McLean Parks, Kidder, and Gallagher, 1998). Second, the psychological contracts of temporary workers are regarded as less socio-emotional or relation-focused and of a more economic or transactional nature (Coyle-Shapiro and Kessler, 2002*a*; McLean Parks, Kidder, and Gallagher, 1998; Rousseau, 1995), due to the short-term focus of temporary employment contracts. Finally, the psychological contracts of temporary workers are assumed to be less easily violated because narrower, more explicit transactional contracts are less vulnerable to being violated (Guest and Clinton, 2005; Rousseau, 1995). Set against this, we need to consider the possibility that because there is a lower investment in the exchange, both parties to the psychological contract may be more cavalier about reneging on promises and obligations.

The prediction that the psychological contracts of temporary workers will be narrower is generally supported by empirical studies. Several studies have found lower levels of felt employer and employee obligations and inducements among temporary employees compared to permanent workers (Claes et al., 2002; Coyle-Shapiro and Kessler, 2002*a*; Silla, Gracia, and Peiró, 2005; Van Dyne and Ang, 1998).

The assumption that temporary workers will have a more transactional or economic focus in their psychological contract has received only limited support. Consistent with this assumption, Millward and Brewerton (1999) found that contractors with permanent contracts with an organization showed high appreciation for relational exchange characteristics such as equity and development. Temporary contractors, however, scored lower compared to permanent workers on transactional as well as relational dimensions. Other researchers, however, found fewer differences related to employment status (see e.g. Claes et al., 2002; McDonald and Makin, 2000). Both suggest that temporary workers have a considerable relational element in their psychological contract. This result is supported by Chambel and Castanheira (2005), who found that while both direct-hire and temporary agency workers show a predominantly socio-economic focus in their psychological contracts, it is less than that of permanent workers. A possible explanation for the limited differences between permanent and temporary employees might be found in the concern among temporary workers to pursue permanent employment. This implies that temporary workers would view their temporary job merely as a 'stepping stone' to obtaining permanent employment with their current organization (Guest and Conway, 1998; McDonald and Makin, 2000), an issue we explored in Chapter 4.

Guest and Conway (1998) observed a better state of the psychological contract among temporary workers in comparison to permanent workers. However, Claes et al. (2002) and McDonald and Makin (2000) found no significant differences. In summary, based on the findings in previous studies we expect the following with respect to differences between temporary and permanent employees.

Employee perspective:

1. Temporary employees will have narrower psychological contracts: the contract will include fewer promises and obligations from both employees and employers.
2. The content of the psychological contract of temporary employees is expected to have a stronger economic, transactional focus compared to a more relational focus for permanent employees.
3. Because the psychological contract of temporary employees is narrower, it is more easily fulfilled and less easily violated.
4. We expect that permanent workers will report more fairness and trust, because they have a broader and more long-term psychological contract. It should be noted, however, that the results of previous studies are inconclusive in this respect.

Employer perspective:

No previous studies have explored the employer perspective on the employment of temporary and permanent workers. We expect, however, that the employers will mirror the employees' perspective. Therefore, we expect the following:

1. Employers will make fewer promises to temporary employees and receive fewer promises in return.
2. Because the promises and obligations towards temporary employees are fewer in number and more transactional, the degree of fulfilment will be reported as higher.

Bringing this review and these propositions together with the wider literature on temporary employment, there is a general assumption that the psychological contract of temporary workers will be less favourable to employees, if not employers, and therefore that the outcomes of the psychological contract will be less positive among temporary workers compared with their permanent counterparts. The outcomes are considered in Chapter 6. For the remainder of this chapter, we focus on the content, fulfilment and degree of violation of the psychological contract to determine the support for the assumptions outlined above that are based on the available literature.

The measurement of psychological contracts in the Psycones study

We have outlined the conceptual frameworks and relevant literature that have informed the design of our study. To measure the psychological contract, we constructed two closely related survey instruments, one for workers and the other for representatives of the organization. These measures are described in more detail in Chapter 2 and Appendix 2. They were developed through an initial literature review of existing measures followed by an extensive pilot study (Isaksson, et al. (2003a)). The questionnaires for both permanent and temporary workers covered the five core components of the state of the psychological contract outlined in this chapter.

The *content* of the psychological contract asks about the promises and obligations made by the organization to the worker, and about the promises and obligations made by the worker to the organization. A count of the number of items on which promises are made provides the measure of the content or breadth of the psychological contract. *Fulfilment* of the psychological contract measures the extent to which promises and obligations have been kept. This can also be used, in line with many previous studies, as a measure of the degree of breach of the psychological contract. Information about this was collected on a five-point scale ranging from 1 = promise made but not kept at all to 5 = promise made and fully kept.

In addition to the measure of fulfilment, we included in the employee questionnaire a measurement of *violation* of the psychological contract, as well as measures of *trust* and *fairness*. Perceptions of emotional reactions to the psychological contract, including potential violation, were measured using six items. Three were positively worded (happy, pleased, and grateful) and three negatively (angry, violated, and disappointed). Responses were provided on a five-point scale from 'strongly agree' to 'strongly disagree'. The positively worded items were re-coded and the six items then combined to provide the mean score on a measure of violation. Guest and Conway (2002b) relate the state of psychological contracts to the delivery of the promises and obligations, the fairness of the deal, and the degree of trust in whether the promises will continue to be kept in the future. The state of the psychological contract considers the judgements employees make about the equity and fairness of the deal, and the degree of trust in the other party. We measured employee perceptions of the fairness of the deal with four items (e.g. Do you feel fairly treated by managers and supervisors?) on a scale ranging from 1 (not at all) to 5 (totally). We measured trust with four items (e.g. To what extent do you trust senior management to look after your best interests?). The scale of responses ranged from 1 (not at all) to 5 (totally).

The measure of the psychological contract in the survey of employers was somewhat more restricted. The same set of items as those used in the employee questionnaire were included, sometimes reworded slightly to reflect the fact that the respondents were employer representatives. They were asked about their promises and obligations and the extent to which they had been fulfilled; and about the promises and obligations their employees had made and the extent to which they had been fulfilled. These questions were asked separately for permanent and for temporary workers.

The following section presents the results for these core measures of the psychological contract and the state of the psychological contract, first from the perspective of employees, comparing temporary and permanent workers; and then from the perspective of employers, again comparing their views with respect to temporary and permanent workers.

EMPLOYEE REPORTS OF THE PSYCHOLOGICAL CONTRACT

Are broader psychological contracts more difficult to fulfil?

There is some indication in the literature that it may be easier to fulfil narrower, more specific psychological contracts than those that are broader and more embracing. This was explored by examining the association for the whole sample in the first instance, based on Pearson correlations, between the various elements of the psychological contract. The employee responses are shown in Table 5.1.

The number of promises and obligations made by organizations shows a small positive association with contract fulfilment ($r = 0.08$, $p < .01$). However there is no significant association between employee promises to the organization and their fulfilment ($r = 0.01$, $p > .05$). Thus, there is no evidence that broader contracts are significantly harder to fulfil. Perceptions of fulfilled employer promises are strongly correlated with a lower sense of contract violation ($r = -0.58$, $p < .001$), as well as with trust ($r = 0.53$, $p < .001$) and fairness ($r = 0.56$, $p < .001$). Employee claims that they have fulfilled their promises and obligations to the organization are associated with lower employer violation of the psychological contract ($r = -0.19$, $p < .001$), as well as with trust ($r = 0.20$, $p < .001$) and fairness ($r = 0.18$, $p < .001$). The number of employer promises is systematically related to the number of employee promises ($r = 0.49$, $p < .001$). In addition, the two fulfilment measures are interrelated ($r = 0.36$, $p < .001$), supporting the notion within

Table 5.1 Intercorrelations of elements of the psychological contract in the employee questionnaire

		1	2	3	4	5	6
1	Number of employers' promises						
2	Fulfilment of employers' promises	.08**					
3	Number of employees' promises	.49**	.00				
4	Fulfilment of employees' promises	−.04**	.36**	.01			
5	Violation	−.25**	−.58**	−.07**	−.19**		
6	Trust	.30**	.53**	.14**	.20**	−.64**	
7	Fairness	.27**	.56**	.08**	.18**	−.65**	.76**

**p < .01, N = 4874–5227

social exchange theory that individuals tend to strive for balance in a relationship (cf. Blau, 1964; Shore and Barksdale, 1998).

Table 5.2 shows the correlations among the more limited set of psychological contract scales within the employer sample. Employers' representatives were asked to provide separate information about the psychological contracts of permanent and temporary workers and this is reflected in the table. The correlational patterns within the employers' data are quite similar to those in Table 5.1 showing the employees' promises. There are high intercorrelations

Table 5.2 Intercorrelations of elements of the psychological contract in the employer questionnaire

HR managers' perceptions		Permanent employees				Temporary employees			
		1	2	3	4	1	2	3	4
1	Number of employers' promises								
2	Fulfilment of employers' promises	−.14				−.07			
3	Number of employees' promises	.62**	−.07			.54**	−.06		
4	Fulfilment of employees' promises	−.05	.61**	−.15*		.06	.49**	−.06	

*p < .05, **p < .01, N = 173–190 HR managers

for permanent as well as temporary employees, between the number of employer and employee promises and obligations, and between the fulfilment of employer and employee obligations. There is one important respect in which the correlation in the employers' responses differs from those of employees. In the case of temporary and more particularly permanent workers, employers report a negative association between the number of promises and the extent to which they have been kept. Although the negative associations are generally small, this leaves open the issue of whether broader psychological contracts are more difficult to fulfil.

In the following sections, we will present the results comparing the psychological contracts of temporary and permanent workers, using *t*-tests. The results will be discussed in relation to the propositions outlined earlier.

Do temporary employees have narrower psychological contracts?

As Table 5.3 shows, workers report that their employers, on average, have made an average of 8.68 out of 15 potential promises. The standard deviation is quite high, indicating a large degree of variability. As expected, employers appear to have made significantly fewer promises to temporary workers (7.78 on average) than to permanent employees (9.21 on average).

Turning to promises and obligations made by workers to their employer, on average they made 13.39 promises to employers out of a possible 17 and again there is quite a high level of variation in the responses. Temporary employees made significantly fewer promises (12.37 on average) than permanent employees (13.78 on average) and comparison of the standard deviations shows that there was more variability in the responses of temporary workers.

In summary, the findings confirm that temporary workers have narrower psychological contracts than permanent workers.

Do temporary employees experience more fulfilment and less violation of the psychological contract than permanent workers?

On a scale from 1 (promise made but not kept at all) to 5 (promise made and fully kept), the average value of fulfilment of employer obligations perceived by the employees is 3.69, somewhat above the mid-point of the scale. The level of fulfilment among temporary employees, averaging 3.78, is significantly higher than fulfilment among permanent employees which averages 3.64. Permanent employees therefore report that their employers made more promises but that they were less likely to be fulfilled.

Table 5.3 Employee and employer obligations as perceived by the employees

| | Total | | | Type of employment contract | | | | | | | |
| | | | | Temporary | | | Permanent | | | | |
	Mean	SD	N	Mean	SD	N	Mean	SD	N	t	Sig
Psychological contract											
Employer's obligations											
Content	8.68	4.57	5,216	7.78	4.51	1,947	9.21	4.52	3,269	−11.03	.000
Fulfilment	3.69	0.84	4,946	3.78	0.86	1,823	3.64	0.82	3,123	5.88	.000
Violation	2.29	0.86	5,128	2.15	0.84	1,916	2.38	0.86	3,212	−9.03	.000
Fairness	3.18	0.93	5,238	3.31	0.94	1,958	3.10	0.92	3,280	8.11	.000
Trust	3.17	1.00	5,229	3.29	1.01	1,954	3.10	0.99	3,275	6.74	.000
Employee's obligations											
Content	13.39	4.17	5,230	12.73	4.39	1,951	13.78	3.98	3,279	−8.66	.000
Fulfilment	4.31	0.51	5,135	4.36	0.52	1,914	4.29	0.50	3,221	4.80	.000

Analysis of the data in Table 5.3, reporting employee obligations to their employer, reveals a similar pattern, with temporary workers reporting significantly greater fulfilment of their obligations, although the average differences between temporary and permanent workers, while still significant, are quite small (4.36 for temporary and 4.29 for permanent workers).

The average score on the measure of violations is 2.29, where a score of 2 is equivalent to 'somewhat disagree'. This suggests that the general level of violation is quite low, although the standard deviation of 0.84 indicates that there is a fairly wide range of responses. Permanent employees report significantly higher levels of violation (2.38) than temporary employees (2.15).

In summary, in line with initial expectations, temporary employees, who have narrower psychological contracts, report a greater degree of fulfilment of employer obligations, and experience less violation of the psychological contract.

Do permanent employees report higher levels of fairness and trust than temporary employees?

The results in Table 5.3 show that on average the employees scored slightly above the mid-point on both the fairness and trust measures, indicating only moderate levels of fairness in their workplaces and moderate trust in management. The average score among temporary workers was significantly higher than for permanent employees on both the fairness and trust measures. Thus contrary to expectations, the average levels of trust and fairness were higher for temporary than for permanent employees.

Are there differences in the content of the psychological contract between temporary and permanent employees?

Table 5.4 presents the percentages of permanent and temporary employees that report receiving a promise from their employer with respect to each of the fifteen specific items. Most commonly reported by both permanent and temporary employees are promises regarding a safe working environment and a pleasant working atmosphere. The least commonly reported promises are those regarding the provision of a career and help with non-work problems. On each of the items, permanent employees are significantly more likely than temporary workers to report that a promise has been made to them with two exceptions, namely, 'provide a good working atmosphere' and 'provide possibilities to work together in a pleasant way'. The differences are

Table 5.4 Employee perceptions of promises made by the employer and promise fulfilment

		Employee perceptions of promises made by the employer (Yes answers in percentage)			Employee perceptions of promise fulfilment (Mean (SD))		
		Temporary	Permanent	Sig	Temporary	Permanent	Sig
1	Provide you with interesting work?	48.3	52.0	*	3.74 (1.04)	3.56 (1.06)	*
2	Provide you with a reasonably secure job?	52.0	79.4	*	3.57 (1.18)	4.15 (0.94)	*
3	Provide you with good pay for the work you do?	53.0	63.1	*	3.83 (1.08)	3.49 (1.13)	*
4	Provide you with a job that is challenging?	49.4	58.6	*	3.80 (1.03)	3.69 (1.08)	*
5	Allow you to participate in decision-making?	39.6	68.1	*	3.51 (1.08)	3.45 (1.11)	n.s.
6	Provide you with a career?	30.6	47.3	*	3.25 (1.26)	3.36 (1.24)	n.s.
7	Provide a good working atmosphere?	72.7	73.8	n.s.	3.92 (1.04)	3.60 (1.08)	*
8	Ensure fair treatment by managers and supervisors?	65.1	70.9	*	3.95 (1.02)	3.66 (1.10)	*
9	Be flexible in matching demands of non-work roles with work?	53.9	57.7	*	3.84 (1.07)	3.64 (1.06)	*
10	Provide possibilities to work together in a pleasant way?	71.9	72.2	n.s.	4.01 (0.99)	3.69 (1.04)	*

11	Provide you with opportunities to advance and grow?	53.4	66.1	*	3.51 (1.20)	3.38 (1.17)	*
12	Provide you with a safe working environment?	71.0	82.8	*	3.99 (1.00)	3.91 (0.98)	*
13	Improve your future employment prospects?	42.4	50.0	*	3.46 (1.20)	3.46 (1.26)	n.s.
14	Provide an environment free from violence and harassment?	59.9	69.2	*	4.26 (0.94)	4.08 (1.01)	*
15	Help you deal with problems you encounter outside work?	31.0	39.9	*	3.83 (1.08)	3.67 (1.08)	*

*Differences significant at $p < .05$ or stronger

particularly marked with respect to promises concerning job security, participation in decision-making, and career provision supporting the view that permanent workers are more likely to have relational contracts. However, we could find no statistical support for a clear differentiation between relational and transactional psychological contracts and the evidence suggests that permanent workers are likely to report more and temporary workers to report fewer of the items that might fall into each of these categories.

When we look at the extent to which each of the promises was reported to have been fulfilled (see Table 5.4), it seems that promises that are reported as being received more frequently are also reported as being fulfilled to a higher degree. The promises that were most fulfilled for both groups were therefore concerned with providing a safe and violence- or harassment-free working environment. There may be a logic to this as organizations may be more likely to make a promise that is easier to fulfil and *vice versa*. However, there are exceptions to this general rule, such as the item on participation in decision-making. The promises reported by both permanent and temporary workers as least likely to be kept were providing a career, providing opportunities to advance and grow, and improving future employment prospects. All three are relational items concerned with employment and career advancement. The differences between permanent and temporary workers with respect to fulfilment of promises by the employer were statistically significant on all but three of the fifteen items. However, the permanent workers generally reported that more promises were made to them, whereas the temporary workers were more likely to report that promises had been kept. Indeed, this applied to all the items on which there were significant differences with the predictable exception of 'provide you with a reasonably secure job'.

What promises are made by workers to the organization?

Details of the specific promises made by workers to their employer are shown in Table 5.5. As noted earlier, workers tended to report that they made more promises to the organization than vice versa. A number of promises, including 'respect for the norms and regulations of the company', 'meet the performance expectations of your job', 'be punctual', and 'be a good team player', were

Table 5.5 Employee perceptions of promises made by themselves and promise fulfilment

		Employee perceptions of promises made by themselves (Yes answers in percentage)			Employee perceptions of promise fulfilment (Mean (SD))		
		Temporary	Permanent	*Sig*	Temporary	Permanent	*Sig*
1	Go to work even if you don't feel particularly well?	49.7	58.3	*	4.28 (0.88)	4.31 (0.83)	n.s.
2	Protect your company's image?	72.3	80.5	*	4.39 (0.78)	4.35 (0.76)	n.s.
3	Show loyalty to the organization?	74.9	84.5	*	4.44 (0.74)	4.41 (0.73)	n.s.
4	Work overtime or extra hours when required?	77.7	85.6	*	4.46 (0.80)	4.45 (0.78)	n.s.
5	Be polite to customers or the public even when they are being rude and unpleasant?	76.6	83. 7	*	4.45 (0.71)	4.35 (0.73)	*

6	Be a good team player?	90.0	92.6	*	4.52 (0.64)	4.45 (0.64)	*
7	Be punctual (prompt)?	91.6	93.4	*	4.61 (0.65)	4.59 (0.65)	n.s.
8	Assist others with their work?	85.9	91.7	*	4.52 (0.66)	4.47 (0.62)	*
9	Volunteer to do tasks outside your job description?	76.4	83.2	*	4.28 (0.84)	4.24 (0.80)	n.s.
10	Work enthusiastically on jobs you would prefer not doing?	82.3	88.8	*	4.34 (0.75)	4.25 (0.74)	*
11	Meet the performance expectations for your job?	92.5	93.6	n.s.	4.46 (0.64)	4.39 (0.64)	*
12	Accept an internal transfer if necessary?	53.3	53.5	n.s.	4.25 (1.05)	4.10 (1.06)	*
13	Provide the organization with innovative suggestions for improvement?	55.3	71.1	*	3.72 (1.06)	3.81 (0.97)	*
14	Develop new skills and improve your current skills?	71.6	81.5	*	4.01 (0.92)	3.99 (0.86)	n.s.
15	Respect the norms and regulations of the company?	93.3	95.1	*	4.59 (0.64)	4.49 (0.67)	*
16	Develop competencies to be able to perform efficiently in your job?	74.5	82.9	*	4.04 (0.88)	3.89 (0.87)	*
17	Be responsible for your career?	70.4	78.9	*	4.24 (0.86)	4.11 (0.89)	*

*Differences significant at $p < .05$ or stronger

reported by almost all of the employees. In contrast, 'going to work even if you don't feel particularly well' and 'accepting an internal transfer if necessary' were promised by only about, or slightly over, half of the respondents. Permanent employees were significantly more likely to make promises on all but two of the items. The exceptions are 'meet the performance expectations of the job' and 'accept an internal transfer if necessary'. The differences between temporary and permanent workers are largest on relational items concerned with 'providing the organization with innovative suggestions for improvement' and 'developing new skills and improving your current skills'.

Workers generally believe that they largely fulfil their promises and obligations to their organization. They report that they are most likely to fulfil those promises and obligations concerning 'being punctual', 'respecting the norms and regulations of the company', and 'assisting others with their work'. Once again, the promises that are most likely to be made are also the most likely to be fulfilled. Temporary workers are generally more likely than permanent workers to report that they fulfil their promises. In most cases the differences are quite small, although they reach statistical significance on ten of the seventeen items, and on nine of the ten the temporary workers are more likely to report that they fulfil their promises and obligations than the permanent workers. Differences are largest on the items concerning 'accept an internal transfer if necessary' and 'develop competencies to be able to perform efficiently in your job'. In both cases, temporary workers are more likely to claim that they have fulfilled their promises and obligations.

In summary, there do appear to be differences between the psychological contracts of temporary and permanent workers, based on accounts provided by workers. Firstly, permanent workers say they both receive more promises and make more in return. Secondly, the temporary workers are more likely to say that both the promises made by the organization and those that they themselves make have been fulfilled. Thirdly, although we can find no convincing statistical distinction between transactional and relational psychological contracts, permanent workers are more likely than temporary workers to report promises on items that could be classified as relational. Fourthly, it is the relational items in psychological contracts that are most likely to be reported as unfulfilled. Fifthly, permanent workers report lower fairness and trust and greater violation of the psychological contract than temporary workers. Finally, the apparent absence of an association between the number of promises and their fulfilment, reported for the full sample in Table 5.1, alters when the permanent and temporary workers are considered separately. More specifically, permanent workers report more promises and less fulfilment while temporary workers report fewer promises and more fulfilment.

THE EMPLOYER PERSPECTIVE

Do employers make fewer promises to, and receive fewer promises from, their temporary employees?

The average number of promises made by the employers, according to their own report, is 11.1 out of a possible 15 (see Table 5.6). The employers also report that on average they make significantly more promises to the permanent (11.6) than to temporary employees (10.5).

According to reports from employers, the average number of promises made by employees is 14.4 out of a possible 17. Employers report that on average permanent employees make 14.4 promises, a figure slightly, but not significantly, higher than the average of 14.2 promises made by temporary workers. On this basis, we can see that employers do indeed make fewer promises to temporary workers but do not receive significantly fewer in return.

Is the degree of fulfilment of the psychological contract by employers higher for temporary than for permanent employees?

As the results in Table 5.6 show, the degree to which employers believe they fulfil their promises to temporary workers (average 2.8) is slightly but significantly lower than the level of fulfilment of promises to permanent workers (average 2.9). It is interesting to recall that among the employees the perception was reversed: temporary employees perceive that the employers keep more of the promises made to them than the permanent workers do.

Turning to employers' perception of fulfilment of the promises made by employees, average levels of fulfilment (3.1) are the same for both permanent and temporary employees. It is also important to note that employers share with employees the perception that they, the employers, are less likely to keep their promises and commitments to employees than the employees are to keep their promises to the organization. In summary, employers report a significantly higher degree of fulfilment of their promises and obligations towards permanent employees compared with their temporary workers but perceive no differences in the extent to which permanent and temporary workers keep their promises to the organization.

Table 5.6 Employee and employer obligations as perceived by the employers

| | Total | | | Type of employment contract | | | | | | | |
| | | | | Temporary | | | Permanent | | | | |
	Mean	SD	N	Mean	SD	N	Mean	SD	N	t	Sig
Psychological contract											
Employer's obligations											
Content	11.10	3.60	340	10.5	3.7	171	11.6	3.4	169	2.9	.004
Fulfilment	2.90	1.00	374	2.8	1	171	3.1	.9	185	3	.003
Employee's obligations											
Content	14.4	3.5	337	14.2	3.6	153	14.6	3.4	168	1	.31
Fulfilment	3.1	.9	365	3.1	.86	166	3.1	.81	181	.54	.6

Do employers report differences in the content of their psychological contracts with temporary and permanent employees?

The results in Table 5.7 show that more promises are made to permanent workers on twelve out of the fifteen items, with significant differences on seven of these. On two of the remaining items (provides interesting work and provides opportunities to work together in a pleasant way) the scores are identical while on one item (provides an environment free from violence and harassment) more promises are made to temporary workers. On all fifteen items, over half the employers said their organization had made a promise to permanent workers; this fell to twelve out of fifteen for temporary workers. Promises are most likely to be made (based on over 80 per cent saying a promise has been made to both permanent and temporary workers) with respect to providing fair treatment, a good working atmosphere, a safe working environment, and an opportunity to work together in a pleasant way. Employers are significantly more likely to make promises to permanent workers about providing job security, an opportunity to participate in decision-making, a career, opportunities to advance and grow, future employment prospects, help with problems outside work, and flexibility to match work and non-work roles. These items on which there are significant differences are all relational and reflect a long-term association.

The results in Table 5.6 indicated that, overall, employers are more likely to keep their promises to permanent than to temporary employees. However, when we look at specific items in Table 5.7, there are seven on which they say they are more likely to keep their promises to temporary rather than permanent workers. On another seven, they are more likely to keep their promises to permanent workers. The differences are generally small and there are only four items on which there are significant differences between permanent and temporary employees. In the case of three items, covering job security, opportunities to advance and grow, and participation in decision-making, fulfilment for permanent employees is higher than for temporary employees. For the item, 'provide employees with a good working atmosphere', fulfilment is higher for temporary than for permanent employees.

Table 5.8 provides information on employers' perceptions of the specific promises made by employees. Employers believe that permanent workers are more likely than temporary workers to make promises on twelve out the seventeen items. The differences are significant on five of them covering showing loyalty to the organization, assisting others with work, providing suggestions for improvements, developing new skills, and taking responsibility for their career. Employers believe temporary workers are more likely to

Table 5.7 Employer perceptions of promises made by themselves and promise fulfilment

		Employer perceptions of promises made by themselves (Yes answers in percentage)			Employer perceptions of promise fulfilment (Mean (SD))		
		Temporary	Permanent	*Sig*	Temporary	Permanent	*Sig*
1	Provide employees with interesting work?	59.4	59.4	n.s.	3.80 (0.72)	3.81 (0.70)	n.s.
2	Provide employees with a reasonably secure job?	62.9	80.7	*	4.00 (0.86)	4.31 (0.73)	*
3	Provide employees with good pay for the work they do?	65.4	67.3	n.s.	4.22 (0.79)	4.16 (0.84)	n.s.
4	Provide employees with a job that is challenging?	59.9	63.9	n.s.	3.83 (0.82)	3.83 (0.71)	n.s.
5	Allow employees to participate in decision-making?	55.9	73.3	*	3.43 (0.97)	3.64 (0.91)	*
6	Provide employees with a career?	43.6	61.9	*	3.50 (0.93)	3.47 (0.92)	n.s.
7	Provide a good working atmosphere?	83.2	85.2	n.s.	4.10 (0.71)	4.02 (0.72)	*
8	Ensure fair treatment by managers and supervisors?	83.2	85.6	n.s.	4.21 (0.75)	4.17 (0.77)	n.s.
9	Be flexible in matching demands of non-work roles with work?	57.4	66.3	*	3.83 (0.75)	3.85 (0.77)	n.s.
10	Provide possibilities of working together in a pleasant way?	80.2	80.2	n.s.	4.11 (0.73)	4.07 (0.76)	n.s.
11	Provide employees with opportunities to advance and grow?	61.4	79.7	*	3.67 (0.88)	3.75 (0.82)	*

12	Provide employees with a safe working environment?	83.7	84.7	n.s.	4.26 (0.69)	4.24 (0.68)	n.s.
13	Improve future employment prospects of employees?	45.5	52.0	*	3.59 (0.87)	3.61 (0.92)	n.s.
14	Provide an environment free from violence and harassment?	78.2	77.7	n.s.	4.36 (0.72)	4.34 (0.79)	n.s.
15	Help in dealing with problems employees encounter outside work?	45.1	53.5	*	3.72 (0.85)	3.77 (0.88)	n.s.

*Differences significant at $p < .05$ or stronger

make promises on four of the items including one, developing competencies, where they rate temporary workers significantly higher. Scores on the remaining item, about going to work when you do not feel well, are identical. In general, managers believe that both permanent and temporary workers are more likely than not to make promises on all the items.

The pattern of the managers' perception of employee fulfilment of their promises and obligations to the organization is presented in Table 5.8. Managers believe that in general employees are highly likely to fulfil their promises and obligations to the organization and are more likely than the organization to keep their promises and commitments. The responses do not differ greatly with respect to permanent and temporary workers. Interestingly, however, managers report that temporary workers are more likely to keep their promises on eleven of the items while permanent workers are higher on only six. There are significant differences on only three items. Permanent workers are rated more likely to keep promises about protecting the company image and showing loyalty to the organization while temporary workers are rated more likely to accept an internal transfer.

In summary, the results in this section provide further confirmation that managers believe that there are differences between the psychological contracts they have with temporary and permanent workers. These differences are greatest with respect to the promises and obligations they offer permanent and temporary employees rather than those they believe they

Table 5.8 Employer perceptions of promises made by employees and promise fulfilment

		Employer perceptions of promises made by the employees (Yes answers in percentage)			Employer perceptions of promise fulfilment (Mean (SD))		
		Temporary	Permanent	Sig	Temporary	Permanent	Sig
1	Go to work even if they don't feel particularly well?	54.0	54.0	n.s.	3.43 (0.90)	3.40 (0.92)	n.s.
2	Protect their company's image?	77.2	78.7	n.s.	3.64 (0.92)	3.83 (0.80)	*
3	Show loyalty to the organization?	76.7	81.7	*	3.60 (0.93)	3.84 (0.81)	*
4	Work overtime or extra hours when required?	77.7	82.2	n.s.	3.79 (0.88)	3.86 (0.84)	n.s.
5	Be polite to customers or the public even when they are being rude and unpleasant?	79.7	80.2	n.s.	3.83 (0.72)	3.91 (0.69)	n.s.
6	Be a good team player?	83.2	85.6	n.s.	3.82 (0.72)	3.85 (0.67)	n.s.
7	Be punctual (prompt)?	86.6	86.1	n.s.	3.89 (0.78)	3.79 (0.81)	n.s.
8	Assist others with their work?	78.7	84.7	*	3.75 (0.74)	3.70 (0.76)	n.s.
9	Volunteer to do tasks outside their job description?	75.7	79.2	n.s.	3.49 (0.93)	3.39 (0.91)	n.s.
10	Work enthusiastically on jobs they would prefer not doing?	73.7	74.8	n.s.	3.35 (0.93)	3.34 (0.90)	n.s.
11	Meet the performance expectations for their job?	86.1	85.6	n.s.	3.77 (0.63)	3.76 (0.60)	n.s.
12	Accept an internal transfer if necessary?	63.9	62.9	n.s.	3.75 (0.89)	3.44 (0.93)	*

13	Provide the organization with innovative suggestions for improvement?	58.9	68.3	*	3.24 (0.98)	3.28 (0.89)	n.s.
14	Develop new skills and improve their current skills?	73.8	80.7	*	3.50 (0.78)	3.47 (0.75)	n.s.
15	Respect the norms and regulations of the company?	88.1	88.6	n.s.	3.97 (0.70)	3.93 (0.70)	n.s.
16	Develop competencies to be able to perform efficiently in their job?	92.6	78.7	*	3.45 (0.90)	3.37 (0.89)	n.s.
17	Be responsible for their career?	60.9	70.8	*	3.37 (0.93)	3.27 (0.93)	n.s.

*Differences significant at $p < .05$ or stronger

receive in return. A feature of these differences is that the exchange appears to be more uneven for, and to work to the disadvantage of, temporary workers. Managers report that they make fewer promises to temporary workers and are less likely to fulfil those that they do make; at the same time, they acknowledge that temporary workers are more likely than the organization to keep their promises. This would appear to provide a basis for some dissatisfaction among temporary workers.

DISCUSSION AND CONCLUSIONS

The general picture that emerges from the results is that there are differences between the psychological contracts of permanent and temporary employees. The psychological contracts of temporary employees include on average fewer promises and obligations on both the employer and employee side. Whereas psychological contracts of temporary employees tend to focus on transactional issues, psychological contracts of permanent employees focus more on both transactional and relational items. The level of fulfilment of obligations, and levels of trust and fairness are higher among temporary employees, who also experience less violation of their psychological contract. The narrower, more transactional psychological contracts of temporary employees are therefore associated with a more positive evaluation of these contracts.

A simple explanation for this phenomenon could be that when more promises are made, the chance of breaching one of them is greater. At first sight, looking at the evidence reported in Table 5.1, there appears to be no support for the proposition that broader contracts are less fulfilled or might be harder to fulfil. However, when we look just at permanent workers, there is evidence both of more promises and less fulfilment while among temporary workers there are fewer promises but greater fulfilment. Closer inspection reveals that it is the relational items, more often cited by permanent workers, that are the least likely to be fulfilled. This suggests that we need to consider both breadth and the specific content of psychological contracts when seeking to understand levels of fulfilment. It also confirms that permanent and temporary workers tend to have different frames of reference when considering their psychological contracts. Finally, we should not lose sight of the possibility that being employed longer with the same organization might increase the chances of experiencing events leading to perceived violations. These experiences would then influence the overall evaluation of the psychological contract.

With respect to the fundamentals of the exchange process between employer and employee, employees perceive they make more promises and fulfil them to a significantly higher degree than they believe their employers do. Employers broadly agree with this. The imbalance appears to work to the disadvantage of temporary workers in particular and provides a basis for perceptions of imbalance in the exchange. Despite this, as the previous chapter indicated, temporary workers report higher levels of satisfaction and well-being, raising questions we need to explore in the subsequent chapters.

Although the level of fulfilment of the promises, from the employer as well as the employee perspective, is perceived, on average as only 'half kept', this apparent breach does not invariably lead to the experience of violation of the psychological contract. Indeed, there are only modest average levels of perceived violation. On the other hand, the correlation of −0.58 between fulfilment and violation reported by the whole employee sample suggests that the two are strongly associated and that, in line with the proposals of Morrison and Robinson (1997), at a certain level of non-fulfilment or breach of the psychological contract, feelings of violation come into play.

Taken together, the findings provide a rich picture of the specific promises and obligations both from the employee and the employer perspective in the countries that were included in our study. It is important to know that employers feel particularly responsible for providing a physically and socially acceptable work environment to employees. It is also notable that, in general, they are more likely to consider that career issues and matching work and family life are the responsibility of the employees. Employers do treat temporary and permanent employees differently. However it is permanent employees who appear to be at a disadvantage when it comes to evaluating the psychological contact. This may be partly a consequence of their longer tenure and partly due to greater emphasis on relational items in their psychological contracts.

To move beyond speculation about the causes of differences in the psychological contracts and their consequences, we need to take account of a much wider range of background factors. This is the focus of Chapter 6, which explores both the antecedents and the consequences of the psychological contract and begins to enable us to set the importance of the different types of employment contract in context.

6

Causes and Consequences of the Psychological Contract

David E. Guest and Michael Clinton

INTRODUCTION

The previous chapter described the nature and content of the psychological contract in some detail. In this chapter, we set out to answer two core questions; what determines the nature and content of the psychological contract, and what are the consequences of different types of, and different states of the psychological contract? We will also consider whether the psychological contract mediates the relationship between employment contracts and outcomes. In other words, can the somewhat surprising finding that temporary workers report a higher level of well-being and other more positive attitudes and behaviour be explained by their psychological contract? To answer these questions, we have to consider a large body of data since we have information from workers about their own promises and obligations as well as those of their employer together with other indicators of the state of the psychological contract.

In addition, we have information from employers about their perceptions of the promises and commitments they have made to both permanent and temporary workers and the extent to which these have been fulfilled, and information about employers' perceptions of the promises and obligations of permanent and temporary workers to their organization and the extent to which these have been fulfilled. Some of the core results of the data collected from employers were presented in Chapter 3. In this chapter, we build on this to explore how the role of the psychological contract, as judged by the employer, affects a number of key organizational outcomes. In doing so, we provide a much fuller picture of the role of the psychological contract from both the employee and employer perspective than is normally provided in the available literature.

ANTECEDENTS AND CONSEQUENCES OF PSYCHOLOGICAL CONTRACTS: A BRIEF REVIEW

Antecedents of and influences on the process of psychological contract formation

Rousseau (2001) distinguishes four phases in psychological contract formation and evolution. Firstly, in the pre-employment phase, professional norms and societal beliefs play a general role. Secondly, more specific components of psychological contracts are formed in the recruitment process. During recruitment, psychological contracts develop through an interactive process in which promises are exchanged, and the actions and messages of both the employer and the workers are evaluated (Rousseau, 1990; De Vos, 2002; Millward-Purvis and Cropley, 2003). Sutton and Griffin (2004) found that the expectations that new employees have before starting to work about an organization (their pre-entry expectations) significantly affect their post-entry expectations and experiences. Thirdly, psychological contracts are adapted and refined through post-entry expectations and experiences and especially through socialization, which includes the acceptance and assimilation of assumptions, values, and expectations of the organization's culture. In a fourth and later stage, experiences in the ongoing process of exchanges of promises, for example, in situations that involve organizational changes, are incorporated into the psychological contract.

From this analysis of stages in psychological contract formation, it is clear that societal (macro-level), organizational (meso-level), and individual (micro-level) factors are involved (De Vos, 2002; Conway and Briner, 2005). At the societal level, economic, political, legal, cultural, and even sub-cultural factors, such as perceptions about employer–employee obligations, and perceptions of what constitutes violation (Thomas, Au, and Ravlin, 2003), can play a part. At the organizational level, the signals provided by human resource (HR) policies and practices can play a crucial role in contract formation. More specifically, HR practices such as performance reviews, compensation, and benefits and training are likely to influence psychological contracts (Guzzo and Noonan 1994; Rousseau and Greller 1994).

At the level of the individual employee, important factors to take into account include, for example, work values, career strategy, and personality factors, such as locus of control, and exchange orientation (De Vos, 2002). In addition, information retrieved from the interaction with organizational representatives, employees' perceptions of organizational culture (Turnley and Feldman, 1999*b*), experiences from previous employment relations, and availability of alternative employment (Guest, 2004*a*) have been shown to have an impact. The information that shapes pre- and post-entry expectations is acquired in several ways. Information-seeking processes such as inquiry, monitoring, and negotiations are influenced by messages that employees receive from the organization, recruiters, and managers, and from co-workers (Shore and Tetrick, 1994). Building on this literature, there is a wide array of factors that we need to consider when exploring issues that help to shape psychological contracts.

Antecedents of breach and violation of the psychological contract

So far we have discussed factors influencing the development of the psychological contract. Once it is established, how do perceptions of contract breach and violation develop? Morrison and Robinson (1997; see also Robinson and Morrison, 2000), in their model of the development of violation of the psychological contract, suggest that reneging and incongruence are two important causes of the perception of contract breach. Reneging occurs when the organization knowingly fails to follow through its obligations, due to inability or unwillingness on the part of the organization and its agents within management. In a situation of incongruence, however, the agents of the organization believe they have fulfilled the promises made to the employees but employees perceive that they have failed to do so, leading to perceptions of unmet expectations. According to Morrison and Robinson (1997), incongruence is caused by factors such as divergent schemata (i.e. people make sense of events and situations in different ways), and the complexity and ambiguity of obligations. Different schemata evolve because of differences in sociocultural influences such as institutional and organizational contexts (Dick, 2006). Therefore, whether the employee perceives a breach of the contract as a violation depends on how he or she interprets the breach. In this process, issues such as trust and fairness are likely to play an important role.

Consequences of the psychological contract

The psychological contract and its various constituent elements, such as content, breach, and violation, have frequently been cited as influencing employee attitudes and behaviour. There are many studies of the consequences of contract breach and violation. The consequences of different types of content of the psychological contract, however, have been a relatively neglected research area. An exception is a study by Hui, Lee, and Rousseau (2004), who examined the relationship between transactional, relational, and balanced contract forms on the one hand, and organizational citizenship behaviour (OCB) on the other hand. They found a direct effect of transactional contracts on OCB. The effects of relational and balanced contracts on OCB, however, were mediated by a form of instrumentality reflected in perceptions of how valuable and worthwhile OCB was perceived to be.

Most studies have found that employee perceptions of contract violation and/ or breach lead to various forms of unfavourable reactions among employees. Robinson (1993; in Shore and Tetrick, 1994), for example, distinguishes five potential employee responses to violation: voice, silence, retreat, destruction, and exit. Turnley and Feldman (1999a) added 'neglect' to these responses. Several studies (for an extensive review, see Conway and Briner, 2005) found an association between psychological contract breach and/or violation, and employee attitudes and behaviour such as organizational citizenship behaviours (Coyle-Shapiro, 2002), job satisfaction (Sutton and Griffin, 2004), intention to leave (Tekleab and Taylor, 2003), trust (Robinson, 1996), organizational commitment (Coyle-Shapiro and Kessler, 2002b) and in- and extra-role performance (Robinson, 1996). The associations are invariably negative. The effects of violations of the psychological contract are not limited to organization-related outcomes, however. Several studies report effects of psychological contract violations and breach on occupational health and stress symptoms, such as emotional exhaustion (Bocchino, Hartman, and Foley, 2003; Gakovic and Tetrick, 2003), leading to health-related behaviour such as absenteeism (Pate et al., 2003).

In addition, several studies identified moderator variables of the relationship between contract violation and employee responses. Turnley and Feldman (1999a, b) found evidence for several moderating effects, including the availability of attractive employment alternatives, justifications for the violation, procedural justice perceptions, and personality factors such as affectivity, conscientiousness, and equity sensitivity (see also Kickul and Lester, 2001). Ho, Weingart, and Rousseau (2004) found two other personality traits, neuroticism and agreeableness, that influenced responses to contract violation. Job dissatisfaction has been shown to moderate the relation between contract violation and outcomes (Turnley and Feldman, 2000). Finally, Ho (2005) found that employees' evaluations of psychological contract fulfilment are influenced by social information from referents.

Building on these various research findings, and reflecting the distinctive focus on worker well-being of the Psycones study, we included a large number of outcome measures. These included established indicators of work-related well-being; some widely used work-related attitudes such as job satisfaction, organizational commitment, and intention to quit; several indicators of work-related health; some general measures of life satisfaction and work–life balance; and some organizationally relevant performance indicators. These were outlined in Chapter 2 and were used in the analyses presented in Chapter 4 comparing the well-being and other outcomes of workers on permanent and temporary contracts.

The results reported in Chapter 5 indicated that permanent workers had broader psychological contracts than temporary staff but that they were less likely to report fulfilment of their psychological contracts. They also tended to report significantly poorer outcomes, more particularly on the measures of well-being; indeed, there were no outcomes on which permanent workers reported significantly more positive results than temporary workers. It is possible that the psychological contract and related factors such as fairness and trust provide a useful explanatory framework that can help us to understand why permanent workers report poorer outcomes. Therefore, in this chapter, we present the results describing the causes and consequences of the psychological contract, and we also address the underlying question of whether the differences between permanent and temporary workers' outcomes can be explained in terms of the psychological contract or whether we need to look further to understand these differences.

A review of the analytic framework

The model set out in Chapter 1 is worth recalling at this point since it provides an organizing framework within which to consider the results presented in this chapter. It shows that there are five broad groups of factors that might help to explain variations in the psychological contract. These are individual, work-related, organizational, sectoral, and national characteristics. In addition, we need to take account of the central focus of our study: the nature of the employment contract. The framework highlights the various aspects of the psychological contract that we will be focusing on. It also identifies the range of additional potential mediating variables that might affect the outcomes. These will not be considered here but are explored in Chapter 8. Finally, the model identifies the range of outcome variables that have been included in the study and which we will be considering in the analyses. See Figure 1.1, page 10.

The following sections of the chapter focus on the factors that explain the psychological contracts of workers and then on the role of the psychological contract and the background factors in explaining workers' well-being, attitudes, and performance. In so doing, we will examine how far the psychological contract serves as a mediator of the relationship between the type of employment contract and employee outcomes.

WHAT DETERMINES THE PSYCHOLOGICAL
CONTRACTS OF EMPLOYEES?

We used seven core measures in this study to examine the psychological contract from the perspective of employees. Firstly, there are a set of measures of the promises and obligations of the employer to the employee, the extent to which these are fulfilled, perceptions of any violation of the psychological contract, and perceptions of fairness of treatment and trust. This combination of elements is sometimes referred to as the state of the psychological contract (Guest, 2004*b*). Secondly, there are the promises and obligations made by employees to the organization and the extent to which employees believe that they have fulfilled these. The descriptive results on each of measures were presented in Chapter 5.

There are five broad sets of background factors, at five different levels, that might influence the psychological contract. More specifically, these factors can be classified as operating at the individual, workplace, organization, sector, and national levels. Descriptive information about these background factors is presented in Appendix A2.1 along with a table of intercorrelations between the measures reported in this section of the chapter. A key purpose in exploring this range of background factors is to determine whether, once they are taken into account, the employment contract continues to show any association with the psychological contract.

To identify the impact of the background factors, we need to explore each one in turn while controlling for the effect of all the others. This can be achieved through the use of hierarchical linear regressions. These also allow us to control for the effects of a large number of background variables of our choosing. In addition, we can enter independent variables into the regression over a series of steps to examine the effect they have on the dependent variable and any changes that result in the importance of variables previously entered in the regression equation. In practice, the data we report in this chapter show the findings after all the background variables have been entered into the analysis.

Workers' perceptions of the state
of their psychological contracts

The key results from the regression analyses are presented in Table 6.1. The table presents the beta weights and the asterisks indicate those that are statistically significant. Given the large sample size, and in line with practice in previous chapters, we will focus on results that are significant at the $p < .01$ level or better. When all the background factors are taken into account, they explain between 26 and 28 per cent of the variation in the responses to four of the five measures of the psychological contract. This is a moderately high level of explanation and suggests that the measures we have used capture some but not all of the important influences. The exception is the fulfilment of the psychological contract. The background factors that we have included are able to explain only 19 per cent of the variation in responses, which is a little lower than we might hope for and suggests that there are other factors exerting influence that we have not been able to take into account. We will review the influence of factors at each level in turn.

At the individual level there are no very strong and consistent findings. There is some indication that those with heavier domestic responsibilities report less fulfilment and more violation of their psychological contracts as well as less fairness of treatment. We might expect that this finding would be linked to gender; however, men report a broader content but poorer fulfilment of their psychological contracts than women, ruling out this explanation. Older workers report more fulfilment and somewhat higher levels of fairness of treatment than younger workers. Education level shows no significant association with any aspect of the psychological contract. In general, these individual-level factors are relatively unimportant in explaining the state of the psychological contract.

In contrast to factors at the individual level, work-related factors appear to have the major influence on workers' perceptions of their psychological contracts. Much the most important factor is the number of HR practices reported by workers to be either experienced or in place in the organization where they are currently employed. Those who report a higher number of HR practices report a broader contract and a much more positive state of their psychological contract, reflected in greater fulfilment, less violation, higher fairness, and higher trust. A second important work-related variable is the level of involvement in work; those reporting more work involvement also report that all aspects of the state of their psychological contract are much more positive than those with lower involvement. Measures of work involvement can sometimes tap individual differences in propensity to be involved. In this case, we assessed something more akin to experience of involvement. Two other work-related variables had a consistent impact. Those working longer hours and those with a longer tenure reported a poorer state of their psychological contract. The findings on working hours are in line with expectations but the negative association with tenure is less expected. It is reasonable to expect that people stay with an organization because of a positive deal, but these findings lend more support to the adage that familiarity does breed a form of contempt (Clinton and Guest, 2008). Although the size of its impact is rather lower, occupational level is also associated with all the measures of the state of the psychological contract, with those at more senior levels having significantly more positive psychological contracts. The only other factor that has an impact across more than one aspect of the state of the psychological contract is union membership which is associated with lower fulfilment and lower fairness, but in both cases the associations are relatively weak.

Table 6.1 reveals that organization-level factors, while sometimes statistically significant, are relatively unimportant in explaining workers' psychological contracts. However, it is interesting to note that in organizations employing a higher proportion of temporary workers, the results are generally more negative, particularly with respect to trust and violation of the psychological contract. There is also a tendency for the various features of the psychological contract to be more positive among those working in the private compared with the public sector. These results are not quite confirmed when the specific sectors are taken into account. In most countries, the public sector workers will be found in education. Those in education have narrower psychological contracts but they are more fulfilled compared with those in the retail sector. There are no other sectoral differences.

In contrast to sector, there are quite marked differences at the national level. The German workers are highly positive; although they have narrower psychological contracts than those in some other countries, they are more fulfilled, less violated, and associated with higher trust and fairness. At the other extreme, Israeli workers have contracts that are both narrower and less fulfilled, as well as being more highly violated than in other countries and associated with lower trust and less fairness of treatment. The other country in which workers tend to be rather negative in their evaluation of the psychological contract is the United Kingdom. UK workers report broader psychological contracts than average but also higher violation, and lower trust and fairness. Swedish workers also tend to be more negative than average with lower fulfilment and lower perceptions of trust and fairness. Spanish and Belgian workers are more positive than average while workers from the Netherlands report above average levels of trust and fairness. The relative importance of country effects compared to workplace and other factors is explored in more detail in Chapter 9.

The final item in Table 6.1 is the employment contract. Even after taking account of all the other possible background influences, the nature of the employment contract still has a strong influence on all aspects of the state of the psychological contract. Permanent workers report significantly broader but less fulfilled and more violated psychological contracts as well as reporting lower levels of trust and fairness. This is the key result from this stage of the analysis and it confirms the importance of the type of employment contract.

Table 6.1 Associations between background variables, employment contracts, and the psychological contract variables

	Content of psychological contract	Fulfilment of psychological contract	Violation of psychological contract	Trust	Fairness
	$n = 3,878$	$n = 3,675$	$n = 3,823$	$n = 3,890$	$n = 3,896$
Country					
Sweden	−0.04*	−0.10***	0.03	−0.08***	−0.08***
Germany	−0.08***	0.19***	−0.10***	0.11***	0.13***
The Netherlands	0.00	−0.03	−0.02	0.07***	0.07***
Belgium	−0.02	0.02	−0.10***	0.09***	0.10***
Spain	0.12***	−0.01	−0.08***	0.05**	0.05**
Israel	−0.11***	−0.08***	0.18***	−0.15***	−0.18***
UK	0.13***	−0.01	0.09***	−0.09***	−0.10***
Sector					
Manufacturing	−0.02	0.03	−0.03	0.01	0.03
Education	−0.07***	0.07**	−0.02	0.01	−0.01
Organization variables					
Number of employees	0.02	−0.05**	0.02	−0.04*	0.00
% of non-permanent employees	−0.03	−0.04*	0.05**	−0.06***	−0.03*
Private-sector organization	0.01	0.05*	−0.05**	0.05**	0.04*
Independent/HQ organization	−0.03*	−0.01	0.00	0.01	0.00
Individual variables					
Age	−0.03	0.07***	−0.03	0.03	0.05**
Gender (male+)	0.05**	−0.05*	0.00	0.01	−0.01
Education level (ISCED)	0.00	−0.01	−0.01	0.00	0.00
Domestic situation	0.03	0.03	−0.01	0.02	0.01

(*continued*)

Table 6.1 Continued

	Content of psychological contract	Fulfilment of psychological contract	Violation of psychological contract	Trust	Fairness
Domestic financial contribution	0.00	0.02	0.00	0.01	0.04*
Dependency on household income	−0.04**	−0.01	−0.01	0.02	0.02
Domestic responsibility	−0.01	−0.07***	0.05**	−0.02	−0.03*
Work-related variables					
Work involvement	0.14***	0.06***	−0.10***	0.15***	0.12***
Occupational level	0.06**	0.05*	−0.05*	0.04*	0.07***
Work hours	0.02	−0.07***	0.09***	−0.06***	−0.09***
Night shifts	0.01	0.01	−0.01	0.00	0.02
Tenure	−0.02	−0.07***	0.10***	−0.10***	−0.06**
Supervision	0.06***	0.02	−0.01	0.00	−0.01
Union membership	0.03	−0.06**	0.03	−0.02	−0.04*
Additional job(s)	0.01	0.00	0.02	−0.01	0.00
Core HR practices	0.37***	0.34***	−0.39***	0.41***	0.39***
Permanent contract	0.09***	−0.08***	0.12***	−0.09***	−0.13***
Adjusted *R*-square	0.26	0.19	0.26	0.28	0.26

*$p < .05$, **$p < .01$, ***$p < .001$

It raises the question of whether the state of the psychological contract mediates the relationship between the employment contract and worker well-being. We return to this issue later in the chapter.

Workers' perceptions of their promises and obligations to their employer

The next set of results explores the background factors associated with the promises and obligations made by workers to their employing organization and the extent to which workers believe they have fulfilled these. The results are shown in Table 6.2. One important preliminary finding to note is that the various background factors are able to explain only a small amount of the variation in responses. The adjusted R-squared statistic shows that background variables explain 16 per cent of the variation in responses on the content and only 10 per cent of the variation in fulfilment of the psychological contract. This suggests that there are other important influences that we have not included in the background factors.

The results in Table 6.2 show that none of the individual variables is associated with the number of promises and obligations reported by workers. In contrast, work-related factors are again important. Specifically, those reporting that they experience more HR practices and greater work involvement report that they make more promises. So, too, do those in supervisory positions. Some other factors are marginally significant but the size of any effect is small. Organizational factors have no significant association with the number of worker promises and obligations, but sector and country are important. Those working in retail services report that they make more promises than those in the manufacturing and education sectors. There are also significant country differences with workers in Sweden and the Netherlands reporting fewer promises and obligations and those in Spain and the United Kingdom reporting more.

Turning to contract fulfilment, at the individual level, older workers are more likely than younger workers and women are more likely than men to report that they meet their promises and obligations to their organization. Those experiencing more HR practices and higher work involvement report that they fulfil more of their promises and obligations, suggesting some sort of exchange process involving reciprocal obligations. In contrast, those with longer tenure report less fulfilment of their promises and obligations, reinforcing the poorer perception of the exchange among longer serving staff. No organizational or sector factors are associated with fulfilment of workers' promises and obligations, but there are some national differences. German

Table 6.2 Association between background variables, employment contract, and employee obligations to their employer

	Content of psychological contract	Fulfilment of psychological contract
	$n = 3,889$	$n = 3,816$
Country		
Sweden	−0.14***	−0.11***
Germany	0.01	0.14***
The Netherlands	−0.17***	−0.15***
Belgium	0.01	−0.06***
Spain	0.16***	0.03
Israel	−0.05*	0.12***
UK	0.18***	0.03
Sector		
Manufacturing	−0.11***	0.01
Education	−0.15***	−0.02
Organization variables		
Number of employees	0.01	0.01
% of non-permanent employees	−0.01	0.01
Private-sector organization	−0.03	0.02
Independent/HQ organization	−0.03	0.00
Individual variables		
Age	−0.01	0.13***
Gender (male+)	−0.03	−0.07***
Education level (ISCED)	−0.01	0.01
Domestic situation	0.01	0.04
Domestic financial contribution	0.03	0.01
Dependency on household income	0.01	−0.01
Domestic responsibility	−0.03	0.02
Work-related variables		
Work involvement	0.15***	0.10***
Occupational level	−0.04*	0.02
Work hours	0.04*	0.00
Night shifts	0.04*	0.03
Tenure	0.02	−0.10***
Supervision	0.06***	0.04*
Union membership	0.04*	0.01
Additional job(s)	0.00	0.01
Core HR practices	0.16***	0.09***
Permanent contract	0.06***	−0.09***
Adjusted *R*-square	0.16	0.10

*p < .05, **p < .01, ***p < .001

and Israeli workers are more likely to report that they fulfil their promises and obligations while those in Sweden, the Netherlands, and Belgium are less likely to make this claim.

After taking account of the influence of all these background variables, the type of employment contract still makes a significant difference. Those on permanent contracts report that they make more promises and have more obligations but they also report that they are less likely to fulfil them. Results therefore confirm the importance of the employment contract and again show that those on permanent contracts report a more negative psychological contract than those in temporary employment. This again implies some process of exchange but this time it is a negative one with those on permanent contracts reporting that both they and their employer are less likely to keep their promises and commitments. This pattern also holds true for those with longer tenure, raising further interesting questions about the potentially negative consequences of greater familiarity with life in a particular organization. The results for both organizational as well as employee promises confirm the important influence of human resource practices and employee involvement. Both may be associated with a consistently applied exchange between worker and organization. Despite the interesting issues raised by some of these findings on workers' promises and obligations, we should be cautious about reading too much in to them since, as we have already noted, we are explaining only a relatively small amount of the variation in responses.

THE PSYCHOLOGICAL CONTRACT AND WORKERS' OUTCOMES

The section has two aims. The first is to determine the impact of the various dimensions of the psychological contract on workers' attitudes, behaviour, and well-being. The second is to consider whether the type of employment contract has any impact on workers' outcomes and more particularly whether it retains any impact after taking into account the psychological contract. In effect, we are conducting an evaluation of the role of the various elements of the psychological contract as mediators of the link between employment contracts and workers' outcomes. However, mediation is only possible if we can first show that employment contracts are significantly associated with workers' outcomes. Some information about this was presented in Chapter 4 and is considered again here but, this time, in the context of the psychological contract.

The statistical process is an extension of the analysis presented in Tables 6.1 and 6.2. First we enter all the background variables that were presented in these tables. Then, as a second step in the regression analysis, we add in the seven psychological contract variables (content, fulfilment, and violation of employer obligations, trust, fairness, and content and fulfilment of workers' obligations). The background variables are not presented again in the tables that follow although they are taken into account and controlled for in the analyses.

In practice, the psychological contract might mediate relationships between several of the background factors (e.g. the number of HR practices) and outcomes (e.g. job satisfaction). However, we restrict our analysis in this chapter to focus on the impact that the psychological contract has on worker outcomes and in particular on how it affects any relationships between the employment contract and these outcomes.

Work-related well-being

The role of the psychological contract in shaping employee well-being is one of the major issues of interest in our study, and we therefore included a range of measures of aspects of well-being. In Table 6.3, we present the results for five of these measures. They are occupational self-efficacy, the positive influence of work on life outside work, the measures of anxiety–contentment and depression–enthusiasm, and a measure of irritation. The first point to note about the results in Table 6.3 is that for each of the indicators of well-being, the background variables, including the type of employment contract, explain a sizeable amount of the variation in the results. This is reflected in the adjusted R-squared score in Step 1 although in the table, only the beta weight for the employment contract variable is actually presented. When we add in the psychological contract variables, the adjusted R-squared score increases, showing that the psychological contract measures explain between 5 and 21 per cent of the additional variation in well-being, depending on which well-being measure is being considered. This would appear to confirm the importance of the psychological contract for employee well-being.

Having shown that the psychological contract makes a significant difference to well-being, the next step is to determine which elements of the psychological contract are having the greatest impact. Two stand out. The first is experience of violation of the psychological contract, which is strongly associated with each of the measures of well-being and is particularly strongly associated with the measures of anxiety, depression, and irritation. The second is workers' fulfilment of their promises and obligations to their employer. Those reporting that they fulfil them display more positive out-

Table 6.3 The role of the psychological contract in work-related well-being

	Occupational self-efficacy		Positive work-life influence		Affective well-being: anxiety		Affective well-being: depression		Irritation	
	Step 1	Step 2	Step 1	Step 2	Step 1	Step 2	Step 1	Step 2	Step 1	Step 2
Permanent contract	−0.03	0.01	−0.04*	−0.02	0.11***	0.03	0.13***	0.05**	0.12***	0.07***
Employer obligations										
Content of PC		0.02		0.08***		0.02		0.01		0.01
Fulfilment of PC		0.01		0.03		−0.04		−0.03		0.01
Violation of PC		−0.09***		−0.13***		0.32***		0.37***		0.26***
Trust		0.04		0.01		−0.06*		−0.07**		0.00
Fairness		0.00		0.04		−0.11***		−0.08***		−0.08**
Employee obligations										
Content of PC		0.10***		0.11***		0.00		−0.01		0.00
Fulfilment of PC		0.33***		0.05***		−0.08***		−0.13***		−0.06***
Adjusted R^2	0.14	0.27	0.20	0.25	0.13	0.30	0.19	0.40	0.13	0.21
F-value for R^2 change		87.22		35.27		123.20		172.58		50.22
$n =$		3,573		3,564		3,562		3,551		3,563

N.B. Background variables are controlled for but not presented

*$p < .05$, **$p < .01$, ***$p < .001$

All F values for R^2 change are significant at the $p < .001$ level comes on each of the indicators of well-being and there is a particularly strong association with occupational self-efficacy. In addition to these two key components of the psychological contract, there is also some indication that perceived fairness of treatment is associated with lower levels of anxiety, depression, and irritation. Finally, those who make more promises to their employer report higher self-efficacy and a more positive spillover from work to life outside work. Two of the measures of the psychological contract most frequently reported in the literature, the content of the psychological contract, which measures the number of items on which a promise has been made by the employer, and the fulfilment of the psychological contract, reflecting workers' perceptions of the extent to which their employers have kept their promises and commitments, are not generally associated with any of these measures of well-being.

A further major question in our study is whether the psychological contract mediates the relationship between employment contract and worker well-being. The relevant evidence can be found by comparing Steps 1 and 2 in Table 6.3. The first point to note is that prior to taking into account the psychological contract, shown in Step 1 in Table 6.3, there is a strong association between being on a permanent employment contract and higher levels of anxiety, depression, and irritation. There is also a weak but significant association between having a permanent employment contract and more negative spillover from work to life outside work. When we add in the psychological contract measures, the association between employment contracts and anxiety disappears while the association with depression and irritation remains significant but declines considerably. The weak association with negative spillover also disappears. This supports the view that the psychological contract fully or partially mediates the relationship between the employment contract and workers' well-being. In other words, permanent workers report poorer well-being partly because they have poorer psychological contracts. However, since the associations between being employed on a permanent contract and higher levels of depression and irritation remain significant in Step 2, we have to look beyond the psychological contract for a full understanding of these associations. Nevertheless, by considering the role of the psychological contract, we have gone some of the way towards explaining the puzzling and unexpected association between having a permanent employment contract and reporting poorer work-related well-being.

In summary, the results in this section show that the type of employment contract and the psychological contract are both associated with the measures of well-being. The elements of the psychological contract that have the strongest association with well-being are violation of the psychological contract (a negative association) and employees' perception of their fulfilment of

their own promises and obligations to the organization (a positive association). Interestingly, these are more important than the more widely used
measures of the content and fulfilment of the employers' side of the psychological contract. The psychological contract either fully or partially mediates
the relation between employment contracts and well-being, providing some
explanation for why permanent employees report poorer well-being.

Sickness behaviour and incidents at work

The next set of worker outcomes concern experiences of sickness and of
incidents that might be associated with lower work-related well-being. Specifically, they cover sickness absence and presence, in other words, the experience of attending at work even though unwell, accidents, and experience of
harassment and violence at work. In each case, workers were asked to report
their experiences in the previous year on a single item measure providing a
count of the number of incidents. The results are shown in Table 6.4.

For these experiences, the background factors explain only a small proportion of the variation in results. This ranges between only 3 per cent of the
variation in experience of harassment and violence up to 10 per cent of the
variation in sickness presence. Adding the psychological contract measures
only helps to explain a further 2–5 per cent of the variance. This suggests that
the psychological contract has a limited, albeit significant, impact on these
outcomes.

Bearing in mind its limited impact, we can nevertheless see which aspects of
the psychological contract exert most influence. The most consistent influence is fulfilment of the psychological contract by the employer. Those who
report that their employer has fulfilled more of their promises and obligations
report less harassment and violence, fewer accidents, and lower levels of
presence at work during sickness. They also report marginally less sick
leave. Violation of the psychological contract and fairness of treatment are
associated with three of the four outcomes but not with accidents. Those who
report a higher number of promises and obligations to their employer report
more presence at work while sick and greater experience of harassment and
violence. This measure of employee promises may tap a form of behavioural
commitment reflected in a determination to attend work even when unwell
and perhaps to get more involved in incidents. Those who report that they
have fulfilled their own promises and obligations report fewer sick leaves and
more attendance at work while unwell. This lends further support to the
possibility that some element of behavioural commitment is involved. It
should be noted that for these more behavioural outcomes, the frequently

Table 6.4 The role of the psychological contract in sickness behaviour and incidents at work

	Sick leave		Sick presence		Accidents		Harassment and violence	
	Step 1	Step 2	Step 1	Step 2	Step 1	Step 2	Step 1	Step 2
Permanent contract	0.11***	0.08***	0.11***	0.07***	0.03	0.01	0.05*	0.01
Employer obligations								
Content of PC		0.03		0.05*		0.05*		−0.02
Fulfilment of PC		−0.05*		−0.06**		−0.07**		−0.14***
Violation of PC		0.07**		0.11***		0.05		0.10***
Trust		0.01		0.01		−0.03		0.02
Fairness		−0.07**		−0.12***		−0.04		−0.06*
Employee obligations								
Content of PC		−0.02		0.09***		0.00		0.06**
Fulfilment of PC		−0.07***		0.07***		0.02		0.03
Adjusted R^2	0.09	0.11	0.10	0.15	0.06	0.08	0.03	0.08
F-value for R^2 change		14.00		29.52		9.06		23.74
$n =$		3,556		3,550		3,560		3,551

N.B. Background variables are controlled for but not presented
*$p < .05$, **$p < .01$, ***$p < .001$
All F values for R^2 change are significant at the $P < .001$ level

used measure of fulfilment of the promises contained in the psychological contract, which had very little influence on well-being, is the most important of the various indicators of the psychological contract, suggesting that different elements of the psychological contract matter depending on the type of outcome under consideration

The results in Step 1 in Table 6.4 show that those on permanent contracts report more sick leaves and more presence at work when sick. They also report a greater experience of bullying and harassment although this association is only marginally significant. When the psychological contract measures are introduced in Step 2, the association between permanent contracts and both sick leave and sickness presence drops slightly, as reflected in the change in beta weights, but remains strong. The already weak association with experience of harassment and violence ceases to be significant. These results indicate that the psychological contract offers some partial mediation at best to the relationship between type of employment contract and sickness behaviour and therefore is not an explanation for the association between permanent contracts and sickness. It is quite possible that permanent workers may have greater sickness entitlements which affect their level of sick leave while they may also feel more obliged to attend work, bearing in mind their wider range of reported obligations, which equally explains their presence at work when unwell. A more contentious explanation, which we will explore more fully in Chapter 8, is that the demands of work among those with permanent contracts can lead to higher levels of sickness compared with those on temporary contracts.

In summary, although the psychological contract explains a significant amount of the variation in sickness behaviour and incidents at work, both the background factors and the psychological contract can explain only a rather small proportion of the overall variation. Permanent workers report significantly more sickness absence, sickness presence, and experience of harassment and violence. For these outcomes, fulfilment of the psychological contract by employers is the most consistently important dimension of the psychological contract. The psychological contract does not appear to mediate the association between employment contracts and this set of outcomes, although there is some indication of partial mediation.

Work attitudes and performance

Table 6.5 presents the results obtained when we analyse the effect that the psychological contract has on a number of central work-related attitudes, namely job satisfaction, commitment to the organization, intention to quit, and a measure of self-rated performance. The background factors, including the employment contract, explain quite a large amount of the variation in the three attitudinal measures but have a rather weaker effect on self-rated performance. The psychological contract adds a large amount of explained variation—between 13 and 19 per cent to all four measures—confirming its importance for these outcomes.

Turning to the specific elements of the psychological contract that appear to have an impact, the results in Table 6.5 show that all the dimensions of the psychological contract, with the exception of the content of employers' promises and obligations, display highly significant associations. Job satisfaction is notably lower among those reporting violation of their psychological contract but is strongly and positively associated with greater fulfilment of the employer's promises and obligations and employees' fulfilment of their own promises and obligations. Organizational commitment is strongly associated with workers' fulfilment of their own promises and obligations, confirming our earlier speculation about how this indicates an exchange process. It is also strongly associated with higher levels of trust and fairness, and lower levels of violation of the psychological contract by the employer. Intention to quit is significantly associated with almost all the measures of the psychological contract but the role of violation of the psychological contract stands out as being the key influence. Finally, self-rated performance is very strongly associated with fulfilment of promises and obligations to the employer, a finding that is in line with what we might expect since performance is likely to be a key indicator of this fulfilment. Performance is also associated with lower violation by the employer and, more surprisingly, lower levels of perceived fairness of treatment. This latter finding perhaps suggests that those who believe they are performing well do not always feel that their contribution is sufficiently recognized and therefore question whether the exchange that lies at the heart of the psychological contract is fair.

The beta weights in Step 1 in Table 6.5 confirm that type of employment contract is strongly associated with job satisfaction and with intention to quit but not with commitment or performance, those on permanent contracts reporting lower job satisfaction and higher intention to quit. We should be cautious when considering the intention to quit since this may have a different meaning for permanent and temporary workers, although our adjusted measures did seek to accommodate this. Adding in the psychological contract has an unexpected result. Largely in line with expectations, it reduces the strength of the association between the type of employment contract and both job satisfaction and intention to quit so that while a significant association remains it is now much weaker. In other words, the measures of the psychological contract partially mediate the relationship between type of employment contract and both job satisfaction and intention to quit. How-

Table 6.5 The role of the psychological contract in relation to work attitudes and performance

	Job satisfaction		Organizational commitment		Intention to quit		Perceived performance	
	Step 1	Step 2	Step 1	Step 2	Step 1	Step 2	Step 1	Step 2
Permanent contract	−0.12***	−0.05**	−0.02	0.05**	0.11***	0.04*	0.00	0.03*
Employer Obligations								
Content of PC		0.03		0.02		0.01		0.03
Fulfilment of PC		0.10***		0.07***		−0.06**		0.01
Violation of PC		−0.30***		−0.13***		0.32***		−0.12***
Trust		0.06**		0.14***		−0.07***		0.04
Fairness		0.05*		0.11***		−0.08***		−0.10***
Employee Obligations								
Content of PC		0.05***		0.11***		−0.08***		0.06***
Fulfilment of PC		0.13***		0.22***		−0.08***		0.36***
Adjusted R^2	0.30	0.48	0.25	0.48	0.23	0.40	0.12	0.25
F-value for R^2 change		180.41		175.98		148.01		92.95
n =		3,573		3,573		3,572		3,557

N.B. Background variables are controlled for but not presented

*$p < .05$, **$p < .01$, ***$p < .001$

All *F* values for R^2 change are significant at the $p < .001$ level ever, with respect to organizational commitment and self-rated performance, where initially there had been no association, once the psychological contract variables are introduced, the association between employment contracts and both commitment and performance becomes significant. Therefore, after taking into account the psychological contract, while permanent employees still report marginally lower job satisfaction and slightly higher intention to quit, they also report marginally higher commitment to the organization and slightly higher performance. Why this should occur is hard to explain. Indeed, the enhanced beta weights remain small in size; therefore we recommend that little emphasis be placed upon these particular findings.

In summary, this section shows that the psychological contract is associated with some key work-related attitudes and with self-rated performance, and that this plays some part in accounting for the association between being on a permanent contract and reporting lower job satisfaction and higher intention to quit. Despite this, even after taking into account the role of the psychological contract, the type of employment contract retains a significant influence on these outcomes.

General health and life satisfaction

The last two outcomes look beyond work to consider whether the employment contract and the psychological contract are associated with general health and general satisfaction with life as a whole. The relevant results are presented in Table 6.6. The first thing to note is that the background variables explain only 4 per cent of the variation in ratings of general health and 10 per cent of the variation in life satisfaction. The various elements of the psychological contract increase the amount of variation that can be explained, approximately doubling it in size. However, we can still explain only 10 per cent of the variation in levels of general health and 19 per cent of the variation in life satisfaction. We should not be surprised by this since many important influences are likely to lie outside the workplace.

None of the specific elements of the psychological contract has a particularly strong association with the two outcomes. Those who report that they have fulfilled their promises and obligations to the organization report better health, while those who have had their psychological contract violated report poorer health. The same pattern emerges with respect to life satisfaction except that those reporting fairness of treatment at work also report significantly higher life satisfaction.

Before taking the psychological contract into account, those on permanent contracts reported poorer health and lower life satisfaction. Once we include the psychological contract, the association between employment contract and general health becomes weaker and the association with life satisfaction disappears. This suggests that the negative impact of permanent employment contracts can be partly accounted for by the psychological contracts of permanent workers. Furthermore, it appears that the evaluation of experiences at work associated with the psychological contract has some bearing on general health and more particularly on life satisfaction. In other words, there are important spillovers from work to life outside work.

In summary, although the psychological contract is significantly associated with general health and life satisfaction, neither it nor the background factors exert a strong influence. This is in line with expectations. The association between permanent employment contracts and both poorer general health and lower life satisfaction is significant before the introduction of the psychological contract variables but weakens in the case of health and disappears in the case of life satisfaction once they are introduced suggesting, respectively, partial and full mediation. This reinforces the role of a poorer psychological contract as an explanation for the unexpected finding that permanent workers report poorer health and lower life satisfaction than those in temporary employment.

Table 6.6 The role of the psychological contract in relation to general health and life satisfaction

	General health		Life satisfaction	
	Step 1	Step 2	Step 1	Step 2
Permanent contract	−0.08***	−0.04*	−0.05**	0.00
Employer obligations				
Content of PC		0.01		0.04
Fulfilment of PC		0.06**		0.03
Violation of PC		−0.13***		−0.14***
Trust		−0.02		−0.02
Fairness		0.05		0.17***
Employee obligations				
Content of PC		0.06**		0.06**
Fulfilment of PC		0.13***		0.12***
Adjusted R^2	0.04	0.10	0.10	0.19
F-value for R^2 change		30.19		51.73
$n =$		3,567		3,564

N.B. Background variables are controlled for but not presented
*$p < .05$, **$p < .01$, ***$p < .001$
All F values for R^2 change are significant at $p < .001$

Summary

This section has explored the role of the psychological contracts of employees on a range of employee outcomes. There are several findings worth noting. Firstly, in considering the background factors that help to determine the psychological contract, the number of human resource practices that employees say they have experienced and their reported involvement in work are strongly associated with all seven measures of the psychological contract. Tenure and working hours are also consistently associated with a poorer state of the psychological contract. These background variables confirm the particular importance of work-related factors in shaping the psychological contract. However, even after all these background factors have been taken into account, those on permanent contracts continue to report more negative psychological contracts.

The second major and consistent finding is that all of the aspects of the psychological contract included in this study have a significant influence on some of the outcomes. While violation of the psychological contract often has the strongest influence on outcomes, all the other measures of the psychological contract are significantly associated with at least some outcomes. These include in particular the employees' reports of their own promises and obligations to the organization and the extent to which they have been fulfilled, supporting evidence of the operation of an exchange process. It is also notable that employees' reports of their own promises and their fulfilment of them often seems to display a stronger association with outcomes than the more widely used measures of employer promises and their fulfilment, supporting the case for a more extensive measurement of the psychological contract.

The third major finding, reinforcing the evidence presented in Chapter 4, is that prior to considering the psychological contract, the employment contract is significantly associated with many of the outcomes. The conditions are therefore met for a test of the role of the psychological contract as a mediator of the relationship between type of employment contract and the outcomes (Baron and Kenny, 1986). The results show that when the psychological contract is taken into account, the association between the employment contract and the various outcomes changes and tends to reduce. In about half the cases, the association ceases to be significant, suggesting that full mediation is taking place. However, in the other cases, the association remains significant, indicating only partial mediation. Therefore, while this analysis has confirmed the important role of the psychological contract, there is a need to look further for a full explanation of why workers on permanent contracts report poorer outcomes than those on temporary employment contracts.

This will be the focus of Chapter 8. However, we first explore the psychological contract as reported by representatives of employers and the part it plays in explaining outcomes of relevance to employers.

THE CAUSES AND CONSEQUENCES OF THE PSYCHOLOGICAL CONTRACT AT THE EMPLOYER LEVEL

A distinctive feature of the Psycones study is the collection of data about the psychological contract from both workers and their employers. In this section, we explore the role of the psychological contract as reported by employers, conducting a somewhat similar analysis to that undertaken at the employee level. In doing so, we should be aware of the challenges that this presents. Most notably, we have responses from a single employer representative, albeit usually a manager in a senior human resource role with some responsibility for oversight of relevant policy and practice. That person is likely to be aware of the standard deals and some of the positional deals but is much less likely, using Rousseau's terms (2005), to be aware of the more local idiosyncratic deals that may be particularly important to some workers.

A second challenge is the nature and size of the management sample. In Chapter 2 we described the characteristics of this sample. It consists of 206 organizations employing an average of 538 workers. However, on a number of variables, more particularly those relating to outcomes and to the psychological contract, not all respondents answered all the questions. Therefore, in the analysis that follows, the sample ranges between 147 and 93. This presents some problems for a regression analysis where a large number of variables are used. We wanted to retain those variables that might be associated with outcomes and therefore took a decision for this analysis to exclude the national and sectoral control variables. As a result, the findings in this chapter are not directly comparable with those in Chapter 3 where a fuller sample was available for many of the analyses and where these controls were retained. There are two other ways in which the analysis in this chapter differs somewhat from Chapter 3. Firstly, we have excluded consideration of the motives for employing temporary workers since this was not central to the present analysis; secondly, we have separated some of the human resource variables on the basis of the way in which the data were collected. Specifically, some items required a dichotomous answer to indicate whether a practice was present while others asked for the proportion of workers to whom a practice applied.

The core aim of this analysis of employers' responses is to identify factors that influence a range of outcomes that are likely to be of particular interest to employers. In many ways, these parallel the employee-focused outcomes explored in the previous sections with respect, for example, to performance, sick leave, and accidents. However in this case, the results are inevitably aggregated for the two groups of permanent and temporary employees. The particular interest lies in exploring the effect of the psychological contract on the outcomes. Among employees, we have shown that it has an important role to play; do we find the same for employers? First we explore the psychological contracts reported by employers and the background factors that might influence these. The relevant information is summarized in Table 6.7, which is concerned with permanent staff, and Table 6.8, which covers temporary staff. The related tables of correlations together with the means and standard deviations are presented in the appendix to this chapter.

Permanent staff

Employers' perceptions of the content and fulfilment of their organization's promises and obligations to permanent workers

The average number of promises made by employers to permanent staff is 11.51 out of a possible 15 listed. This is our measure of the breadth of content of the employers' psychological contracts. The first column of Table 6.7 analyses the background factors that influence this measure of the content of employers' psychological contracts with permanent workers. It reveals that only three background factors are significantly associated with the number of promises made. Where there are more HR practices in place, including, as a specific practice, more extensive coverage of performance-related pay, more promises are likely to be made; but where there is a growing temporary workforce, fewer promises are made to permanent staff. This raises the question of whether permanent staff are disadvantaged by a growing presence of temporary workers.

Managers rate the fulfilment of their promises and obligations to employees as averaging 3.99 on a scale ranging from 1 to 5, where 1 represents 'promise not kept at all' and 5 represents 'promise fully kept'. This suggests that the typical employer has a broadly positive view of the extent to which they fulfil their promises and commitments. The second column of Table 6.7 shows the factors associated with fulfilment of employers' promises and obligations. They are less likely to be fulfilled in organizations employing a relatively higher proportion of temporary workers and, unexpectedly, in organizations where more HR practices are in place. One interpretation of

Table 6.7 Employers' psychological contracts with permanent workers

Permanent	Employers' obligations		Employees' obligations		Performance satisfaction		Voluntary quit rate		Dismissal rate		Sick leave rate		Accident rate	
	Content beta	Fulfilment beta	Content beta	Fulfilment beta	Step 1 beta	Step 2 beta	Step 1 beta	Step 2 beta	Step 1 beta	Step 2 beta	Step 1 beta	Step 2 beta	Step 1 beta	Step 2 beta
Organization size	0.06	−0.09	0.01	−0.17*	−0.03	0.01	0.22*	0.22*	−0.08	−0.05	−0.12	−0.11	0.57***	0.57***
% temporary employees	0.02	−0.22**	0.03	−0.20*	−0.12	−0.08	0.29**	0.25**	0.13	0.12	0.02	0.04	−0.05	−0.05
Form (+independent)	−0.03	0.02	−0.12	0.14	0.11	0.07	−0.21*	−0.20*	0.10	0.09	−0.16	−0.15	0.04	0.05
Ownership (+private)	0.03	0.25**	−0.03	0.28**	0.06	−0.03	0.01	0.04	0.11	0.12	−0.13	−0.14	0.03	0.04
Growing workforce	0.10	−0.06	−0.08	0.03	0.12	0.09	0.07	0.09	−0.34**	−0.33**	0.03	0.05	0.11	0.13
Growing temporary workforce	−0.24**	0.15+	−0.08	0.12	−0.06	−0.06	−0.22*	−0.22*	0.06	0.03	0.07	0.04	−0.05	−0.06
Expected growth	0.00	0.16+	0.10	0.02	0.05	0.05	0.22*	0.23*	0.10	0.11	−0.02	−0.04	−0.18*	−0.18*
Union influence	0.08	−0.07	−0.14+	0.14+	−0.01	−0.07	0.01	0.03	0.03	0.03	0.15	0.17	0.03	0.04
Ease of filling vacancies	0.04	0.12	0.09	0.13+	0.30***	0.25**	−0.06	−0.05	0.05	0.05	−0.10	−0.11	−0.07	−0.07
HR practices	0.27**	−0.27**	0.11	−0.23**	0.03	0.05	−0.02	−0.02	0.18+	0.21*	0.02	0.05	0.08	0.10
Training coverage	−0.07	0.05	0.06	0.18*	−0.07	−0.11	−0.04	−0.05	−0.15	−0.17+	0.09	0.09	0.10	0.09
Performance appraisal coverage	0.14	0.12	−0.01	0.09	0.18+	0.13	0.04	0.07	0.05	0.08	−0.28*	−0.27*	−0.11	−0.10

(continued)

Table 6.7 Continued

Permanent	Employers' obligations		Employees' obligations		Performance satisfaction		Voluntary quit rate		Dismissal rate		Sick leave rate		Accident rate	
	Content beta	Fulfilment beta	Content beta	Fulfilment beta	Step 1 beta	Step 2 beta	Step 1 beta	Step 2 beta	Step 1 beta	Step 2 beta	Step 1 beta	Step 2 beta	Step 1 beta	Step 2 beta
Performance-related pay coverage	0.17*	0.07	0.20*	0.05	0.02	−0.01	0.00	0.02	0.16+	0.18+	0.11	0.12	0.03	0.04
Employers' obligations content						0.13		−0.16		−0.15		−0.07		−0.10
Employers' obligations fulfilment						−0.03		−0.11		−0.08		0.10		0.01
Employees' obligations content						0.00		0.08		0.04		−0.03		0.05
Employees' obligations fulfilment						0.31**		−0.03		0.07		−0.06		−0.02
Adj R^2	0.13	0.14	0.04	0.15	0.08	0.14	0.15	0.15	0.11	0.10	0.05	0.02	0.31	0.30
	$n = 147$	$n = 147$	$n = 147$	$n = 147$	$n = 145$		$n = 130$		$n = 130$		$n = 115$		$n = 127$	

+ $p < .10$, * $p < .05$, ** $p < .01$, *** $p < .001$

these results is that a growing temporary workforce is associated with fewer promises to permanent workers and there is some indication that when fewer promises are made, alongside fewer HR practices, they are more likely to be fulfilled. This fits with the results shown earlier in the chapter in the section on the workforce where temporary workers reported receiving fewer promises but also reported that they were more likely to be kept. The same may apply to permanent workers. This appears to support the view, identified in previous research on the management side of the psychological contract (Guest and Conway, 2002*b*) that it is most unwise to make promises you cannot keep. The other significant result in the second column of Table 6.7 reveals that promises are more likely to be kept by private sector employers, possibly because they have greater autonomy to do so.

Employers' perceptions of permanent workers' promises and obligations to the organization

Managers identify an average of 13.23 promises and obligations out of a list of 17 that they believe permanent workers make to the organization. An inspection of column 3 in Table 6.7 reveals that the only background factor positively associated with more perceived workers' promises and obligations is a wider coverage of some form of performance-related pay while a union presence is marginally associated with a perception of fewer promises and obligations on the part of the permanent workforce. It may be that employers believe that performance-related pay induces employees to extend their promises and obligations and that unions discourage them from doing so. Perhaps not surprisingly, organizational and policy-related factors explain very little of the variance in responses.

Managers' perceptions of the extent to which permanent workers fulfil their promises and obligations receives an average rating of 3.65 on the scale from 1 to 5 which is broadly positive but some way below the rating they give for the level of fulfilment of promises by the organization. Higher employee fulfilment is found in privately owned organizations, and there is some tendency for it to be found in unionized settings and where it is easier to fill vacancies. In contrast, employee promises are less likely to be fulfilled in larger organizations, in organizations employing a higher proportion of temporary workers, and where more human resource practices are in place.

Most of these findings are plausible. They confirm again the management perceptions of problems associated with a higher proportion of temporary staff. They also suggest that a trade union presence may help to ensure that workers fulfil their promises and obligations. The unexpected finding concerns the human resource practices. The set of five practices covering the presence of practices such as performance appraisal and policies such as prevention of bullying and harassment are associated with lower fulfilment by both the employer and employees. This is a clear contrast to the reports from employees. To add a further complication, the specific practice of greater provision of training and development is associated with greater perceived fulfilment of promises by workers. The correlation table in the appendix to this chapter confirms that there is no significant association between the set of five HR practices and any of the three additional practices covering training, appraisal, and performance-related pay, to which a different kind of response was provided. Although the response format may have influenced the nature of the results, this does suggest that there may be no coherence to the HR practices in place in many of these organizations. It is less easy to explain why employers' representatives, most of whom are senior HR managers, believe that the presence of more HR practices is associated with lower fulfilment of the promises and obligations made by permanent workers and also those made by employers with respect to permanent workers. It is possible that employers are interpreting the results in terms of an exchange and taking the view that where there are more HR practices in place, more is implied in return, yet they believe permanent workers are not contributing that extra element to the exchange and thereby failing to fulfil the norm of reciprocity (Gouldner, 1960).

Temporary staff

Employers' perceptions of their organization's promises and obligations to temporary workers

The parallel results for temporary workers are set out in Table 6.8. The first column again shows the factors associated with the breadth of the content of the psychological contract, in other words, the number of promises made by the organization to temporary workers. The average score of 10.48 promises out of a possible 13 is a little below the average number made to permanent workers. More promises are likely to be made if there is a growing workforce and if there is a more extensive coverage of performance-related pay among temporary staff. It is also somewhat more likely where there is more extensive use of performance appraisal. In contrast, the regression results strongly suggest that fewer promises are made when there is a growing temporary workforce. This is somewhat puzzling since there is a quite a high positive correlation ($r = 0.40^{***}$) between a growing workforce and a growing temporary workforce; but the correlations in the appendix to this chapter also confirm that the two aspects of growth may be associated in different ways with the number of promises made. By implication, managers get cautious

Table 6.8 Employers' psychological contracts with temporary workers

Temporary	Employers' obligations		Employees' obligations		Performance satisfaction		Voluntary quit rate		Dismissal rate		Sick leave rate		Accident rate	
	Content beta	Fulfilment beta	Content beta	Fulfilment beta	Step 1 beta	Step 2 beta	Step 1 beta	Step 2 beta	Step 1 beta	Step 2 beta	Step 1 beta	Step 2 beta	Step 1 beta	Step 2 beta
Organization size	−0.06	−0.11	−0.05	−0.26**	−0.01	0.01	0.36***	0.35***	0.32***	0.34***	−0.08	−0.04	0.36***	0.31**
% temporary employees	0.03	−0.19*	0.04	−0.14+	−0.05	−0.03	−0.12	−0.14	−0.06	−0.04	−0.03	0.00	0.09	0.03
Form (+independent)	−0.01	−0.01	−0.10	0.15+	0.06	0.05	0.08	0.08	0.10	0.09	−0.16	−0.18	−0.01	−0.01
Ownership (+private)	0.07	0.25**	0.07	0.14	0.05	0.02	−0.01	0.02	−0.04	−0.08	−0.19+	−0.22+	0.17+	0.21*
Growing workforce	0.22*	−0.13	0.01	0.01	0.11	0.12	0.12	0.11	0.04	0.01	0.00	0.03	0.05	0.01
Growing temporary workforce	−0.31**	0.20*	−0.03	0.08	−0.04	−0.05	−0.10	−0.08	−0.10	−0.07	−0.10	−0.14	0.15	0.22*
Expected growth	0.08	0.13	0.06	−0.03	0.07	0.05	0.06	0.07	−0.01	−0.03	0.04	0.05	−0.06	−0.03
Union influence	0.13	0.00	−0.07	0.04	−0.04	−0.05	0.20*	0.19*	0.00	−0.02	0.21+	0.24+	0.04	0.05
Ease of filling vacancies	0.05	0.10	0.01	0.09	0.34***	0.32***	−0.03	−0.03	−0.02	−0.05	−0.12	−0.10	−0.06	0.00
HR practices	0.05	0.23**	−0.10	0.22*	0.03	0.00	0.00	0.02	−0.11	−0.16+	−0.04	−0.04	0.06	0.14
Training coverage	0.02	−0.02	0.11	0.12	−0.09	−0.08	0.17+	0.18+	−0.11	−0.12	0.12	0.09	0.03	0.00
Performance appraisal coverage	0.15+	0.07	0.01	0.14	0.05	0.03	0.08	0.09	0.30**	0.26**	−0.18	−0.18	−0.15	−0.16+
Performance-related pay coverage	0.18*	0.18*	0.07	−0.02	−0.05	−0.08	0.01	0.02	−0.01	−0.06	0.20+	0.24+	0.10	0.13
Employers' obligations content						0.06		0.00		0.18+		−0.13		0.02
Employers' obligations fulfilment						0.11		−0.08		0.10		−0.05		−0.18
Employees' obligations content						−0.04		−0.03		0.01		0.09		0.15
Employees' obligations fulfilment						0.03		−0.02		0.05		0.17		−0.11
Adj R^2	0.11	0.14	0.00	0.12	0.06	0.04	0.06	0.05	0.09	0.10	0.05	0.03	0.11	0.17
	n = 135	n = 135	n = 135	n = 135	n = 133	n = 133	n = 117	n = 117	n = 133	n = 133	n = 93	n = 93	n = 114	n = 114

+$p < .10$, *$p < .05$, **$p < .01$, ***$p < .001$

about the number of promises and commitments they make to temporary workers when the temporary workforce is growing.

Employers report that they are just as likely to fulfil their promises and obligations to temporary as to permanent workers. The factors associated with greater fulfilment are also broadly similar. Fulfilment is more likely to be reported in private sector organizations and where there is a growing temporary workforce; but less likely where there is already a high proportion of temporary workers. The exception to the pattern for permanent workers is that with temporary workers, greater use of HR practices is associated with higher fulfilment. This is reinforced by the positive association with greater use of performance-related pay among temporary workers.

Employers' perceptions of the promises and obligations of temporary workers to the organization

Managers report that temporary workers provide an average of 14.2 out of the provided list of 17 possible promises and obligations to the organization, a figure only marginally below that for permanent workers. The analysis shown in the third column of Table 6.8 reveals that none of the background factors shows any significant association with the number of promises made and the combined set of background factors is unable to explain any of the variation in management estimates of the number of promises and obligations made by temporary workers.

Managers report that temporary workers are just as likely to fulfil their promises and obligations as permanent staff. Column 4 in Table 6.8 indicates that managers believe that temporary workers are less likely to keep their promises in larger organizations and somewhat less likely where there are higher proportions of temporary workers in the organization. They are somewhat more likely to report that promises are kept in independent organizations and clearly more likely where more of the five HR practices are in place. The results therefore differ from those of permanent workers mainly with respect to the role of human resource practices. The results with respect to temporary workers are more in line with those reported by the workers themselves and it is the management responses with respect to permanent workers that appear to be the exception.

Summary

In summary, the results of the analysis of factors associated with employer perceptions of the psychological contract are complex and even appear contradictory. The amount of variation explained is consistently fairly low, never rising above 15 per cent as reflected in the adjusted R-squared scores. A growing temporary workforce appears to be associated with fewer promises made to both permanent and temporary workers by employers but also with more fulfilment of those that are made. Private ownership appears to be associated with greater fulfilment of promises, possibly because in the private sector managers have more autonomy and control over factors determining fulfilment. In contrast, managers working in larger organizations report less fulfilment of the promises and obligations by both permanent and temporary workers.

The main puzzle in these results concerns the HR practices. The employee results reported earlier in this chapter revealed a strong association between reports of more HR practices and both a broader content and more fulfilment of the psychological contract. The employers' responses convey a much less consistent picture. Firstly, only the wider application of performance-related pay is associated with more promises on the part of the employers and also permanent workers. The set of five HR practices are associated with more promises to permanent but not to temporary workers. In the case of temporary workers, employers report that more HR practices are associated with more fulfilment of promises and obligations by both employers and employees. However, with respect to permanent workers, more HR practices are associated with poorer fulfilment by both employers and employees. The logic behind this difference is hard to see. One possible interpretation, hinted at earlier, may be found in the employment exchange and the implication that it is more likely to break down with permanent employees. There is some support for this in the negative association in the employee data between tenure and some of the outcomes. This may also help to explain the poorer psychological contracts, wider dissatisfaction, and lower well-being reported by permanent workers.

THE ROLE OF THE PSYCHOLOGICAL CONTRACT IN DETERMINING MANAGEMENT REPORTS OF OUTCOMES

This final main section of the chapter explores the role of the psychological contract, as reported by employers, and other factors in determining a range of outcomes, namely satisfaction with workers' performance, voluntary quits, dismissals, sick leave, and accidents. The results of the regressions, first without the psychological contract variables and then with them added in, are shown in Tables 6.7 and 6.8.

Outcomes for permanent workers

Columns 5–14 in Table 6.7 show the results of the regressions; in each case the first column shows the influence of the background factors and the second column shows the results when the psychological contract variables are added. The key general finding is that the psychological contract variables do not generally add to the level of explanation of the outcomes. Indeed, with respect to some of the variables, the results in Table 6.7 show that the percentage of the variance explained, reflected in the adjusted R-squared, is actually reduced when the psychological contract is introduced into the analysis. The one exception is satisfaction with the performance of permanent staff. Where managers report that employees are more likely to fulfil their promises and obligations, satisfaction with performance increases. This seems entirely plausible since there is a performance element implicit in the fulfilment of some of the promises and obligations.

No background factors have a consistent influence on outcomes either before or after the psychological contract variables are introduced. Larger organizations report a higher voluntary quit rate and more accidents. Organizations with a higher proportion of temporary workers and those with expected future growth report higher rates of voluntary quits, again suggesting that permanent workers may feel disadvantaged by the presence of temporary staff; on the other hand, those reporting growing numbers of temporary workers report fewer quits. Where there is a growing workforce, there are much lower rates of dismissals among permanent staff. Managers believe unions have no significant influence on any outcomes and human resource practices have only a limited influence. The set of five HR practices are associated with a higher dismissal rate and fuller performance appraisal coverage is associated with lower levels of sickness absence. Both may reflect the consequences of closer monitoring of the workforce.

Outcomes for temporary workers

The results in columns 5–14 of Table 6.8 show the influences on outcomes for temporary workers, as reported by managers. They reveal that managers' assessments of the psychological contract have no significant association with any of the outcomes. The effect on the adjusted R-squared, revealing the amount of variation in responses explained by the psychological variables, is limited and inconsistent. Only in the case of accidents does it show a clear increase but even then, none of the psychological contract items are significantly associated with accident levels.

Looking more broadly at the background factors, the impact of size of workplace is more marked in the case of temporary than permanent workers and among temporary workers it is associated with higher levels of voluntary quits, dismissals, and accidents. The size and growth of the temporary workforce has less effect on managers' perceptions of the outcomes of temporary workers. The only association is between a growing temporary workforce and a higher accident rate, which is plausible given their lower levels of familiarity with the workplace. A union presence is associated with a higher quit rate among temporary workers. It is more common to find unions associated with a lower quit rate, and it is possible that in protecting the permanent staff they may actively discourage the presence of temporary staff. Unions are also associated with management reports of somewhat higher levels of sick leave among temporary staff. Ease of filling vacancies is associated with higher satisfaction with the performance of temporary staff. This is similar to the findings for permanent staff and presumably reflects the opportunity to be more selective. Human resource practices have no significant impact on the outcomes. The main exception to this is a positive association between managers' assessments of the coverage of appraisal schemes among temporary workers and a higher dismissal rate. There is also a tendency for higher coverage of performance-related pay to be associated with higher rates of sick leave. Reflecting these limited and disparate associations, the amount of variance explained is generally low, reaching a maximum of 11 per cent on accident rates, much of which seems to be accounted for by size of organization.

Drawing together these results focusing on determinants of outcomes as reported by managers, the core finding is that employers' reports on the psychological contract have very little significant influence. The single exception is the strong association between employers' perceptions of permanent workers' fulfilment of their promises and obligations to their organization and satisfaction with their performance. This association is not found with respect to temporary workers. Despite this isolated association, we can conclude from this evidence that employers' accounts of a positive psychological contract, and by implication a positive exchange between the organization and its employees, is not reflected in employees' performance, as reflected in the range of outcomes considered. In this context, it is worth noting that these outcomes were selected because, with the exception of satisfaction with performance, they could provide reasonably objective indicators.

Leaving aside the psychological contract, other factors do have some influence on outcomes. For example, larger organizations report generally more negative outcomes. A larger proportion of temporary workers in the workforce is associated with higher levels of quits among permanent employees while a growing temporary workforce is associated with lower voluntary quits. Organizations finding it easier to fill vacancies are more satisfied with the performance of both permanent and temporary workers. Human resource practices have no consistent impact on the various outcomes, even though many are related to the behaviour of the organizations' human resources.

In the final analysis, these results are very different to those reported by employees and question any role for employer accounts of the psychological contract, at least when they are collected from a single representative of the employer, in explaining a range of employee-related outcomes.

Summary of management perceptions of the psychological contract

The general pattern of results is one of inconsistent associations and a limited role for the management assessment of the psychological contract. It has been possible to identify some background policy, employment, and structural factors associated with a broader content and a greater fulfilment of the psychological contract. But there is very little association between the psychological contract measures and any of the outcomes. In short, introducing the psychological contract into explanations for management assessments of a range of performance outcomes does not add to our understanding of their views about what influences these outcomes. More generally, as noted in Chapter 3, while we can find some significant associations between features of the organization and the various employment outcomes, the analysis at this organizational level is consistently much weaker than the analysis at the employee level.

We should not be surprised by these results. As we noted at the outset of this section, the managers who provided the information are single respondents, often working in large organizations. They may have had only a hazy idea of both the background factors and the performance outcomes. They are likely to have had an even less clear basis for sound judgements about the psychological contract of the organization, in so far as it is sensible to think of a psychological contract in organizational terms; and even less idea about the psychological contracts of workers. What the survey might provide is an indicator of a normative psychological contract; in other words, an assessment of what senior managers think the employees ought to promise.

However we interpret the management responses, they do not affect the outcomes.

OVERALL SUMMARY AND CONCLUSIONS

The main aims of this chapter have been to assess the role of the psychological contract in determining a range of outcomes and to explore its role as a mediator in the context of the association, reported in earlier chapters, between type of employment contract and a range of employee attitudes and behaviours. The data are distinctive in covering several different aspects of the psychological contract and in providing both an employee and employer perspective. The associations reported in this and earlier chapters confirm that the data fit the standard criteria for tests of mediation.

The employee results show that experiences in the workplace have the major influence on employees' psychological contracts. In line with earlier research by Guzzo and Noonan (1994) and Rousseau and Greller (1994), the presence of more human resource practices has a positive influence on various aspects of the psychological contract. So, too, does the level of work involvement. Although factors at the workplace level are the most important, there are a number of issues at other levels, ranging from the individual to the national level that are also significantly associated with features of the psychological contract.

The analysis of employee outcomes revealed that all seven dimensions of the psychological contract have a significant association with one or more outcomes. Violation of the psychological contract generally has the strongest association with outcomes but an interesting finding is the importance of employees' perceptions of their own promises and obligations. This fits with the exchange framework that informs psychological contract theory (Coyle-Shapiro and Kessler, 2002*b*; Coyle-Shapiro and Neuman, 2004).

When the psychological contract is included in the analysis, the association between employment contracts and outcomes tends to decline. In some cases the association ceases to be significant, in others it remains significant but at a weaker level. There is therefore evidence of full or partial mediation. However, even after taking into account the full range of measures of the psychological contract as well as the extended concept of the state of the psychological contract, including fairness and trust, workers on temporary contracts still report significantly lower levels of depression, irritation, sick leave, and presence at work when sick as well as higher job satisfaction. We have therefore gone some way to explaining the unexpected finding that temporary workers report higher levels of well-being and more positive attitudes and behaviour than their permanent counterparts. The partial explanation lies in the more fulfilled, less violated, and generally better state of the psychological contracts of temporary compared with permanent workers. But we still need to look further for a full explanation. We will pick this issue up again in Chapter 8.

The data from employers reveals a much weaker role for the psychological contract; indeed there are almost no significant associations between dimensions of the psychological contract reported by employers and outcomes. This is to be expected, given the location of respondents at a senior position in their organizations. It is likely that they can only give answers concerning what Rousseau (2005) terms standard deals and positional deals relating to permanent and temporary workers. These managers are not able to consider the more local, idiosyncratic deals that might matter most to employees. However, one way of checking the validity of the management responses is to compare them with those of employees. This is the focus of the next chapter.

Appendix 6.1 Intercorrelations of employers' responses for permanent workers

	n	Mean	SD	1	2	3	4	5	6	7	8	9	10	11	12	13	14	15	16	17	18	19	20	21
1 Organization size	199	514.9	1,397.0																					
2 % temporary employees	194	30.92	25.86	−0.13																				
3 Form (+independent)	194	1.51	0.50	0.17*	−0.01																			
4 Ownership (+private)	199	0.68	0.47	0.00	0.09	−0.03																		
5 Growing workforce	194	2.34	0.79	−0.07	0.04	0.17*	0.15*																	
6 Growing temporary workforce	193	2.23	0.73	0.06	0.02	0.09	0.01	0.40***																
7 Expected growth	193	2.16	0.70	0.05	0.03	0.14*	0.06	0.40***	0.11															
8 Union influence	191	2.51	0.95	0.15*	0.04	−0.20***	−0.11	−0.07	−0.05	−0.03														
9 Ease of filling vacancies	191	3.31	0.84	−0.02	−0.03	−0.02	0.02	−0.07	−0.20*	−0.19**	0.00													
10 HR practices	202	0.61	0.97	0.04	−0.03	0.07	0.16*	−0.08	−0.03	0.11	0.09	−0.10												
11 Training coverage	178	61.04	32.88	−0.04	0.03	−0.02	−0.17*	−0.02	−0.08	0.04	0.05	0.06	0.13											
12 Performance appraisal coverage	190	67.58	43.71	−0.02	0.23***	−0.13	0.09	0.03	−0.02	0.08	0.06	0.05	0.06	0.27***										
13 Performance-related pay coverage	192	26.38	34.98	0.05	0.01	0.00	0.09	−0.08	−0.15*	−0.04	−0.06	0.11	−0.04	0.14	0.24***									
14 Employers' obligations content	188	11.51	5.38	0.01	0.13	−0.10	0.22***	−0.04	−0.15*	0.00	0.08	0.09	0.24***	−0.01	0.28***	0.24***								
15 Employers' obligations fulfilment	187	3.99	0.55	−0.05	−0.16*	0.03	0.20***	0.15*	0.13	0.11	−0.11	0.10	−0.20**	0.06	0.13	0.04	−0.12							
16 Employees' obligations content	202	13.23	5.22	−0.05	−0.04	−0.15*	0.12	−0.05	−0.04	0.08	−0.02	0.14	0.18***	0.04	0.14*	0.23***	0.60***	−0.04						
17 Employees' obligations fulfilment	183	3.65	0.57	−0.08	−0.12	0.09	0.17*	0.18*	0.11	0.04	0.08	0.07	−0.15*	0.16*	0.12	0.06	−0.01	0.63***	−0.09					
18 Satisfaction with performance	188	5.30	0.92	0.00	−0.15*	0.08	0.05	0.14	0.01	0.05	0.01	0.19*	0.01	0.01	0.06	0.07	0.05	0.28***	0.00	0.38***				
19 Voluntary quit rate	158	6.40	12.26	0.18*	0.30***	−0.12	0.10	0.05	−0.08	0.17*	0.05	−0.08	0.00	0.00	0.17*	0.07	0.09	−0.10	0.00	−0.12	−0.01			
20 Dismissal rate	158	2.09	4.69	0.02	0.17*	0.07	0.15	−0.21**	−0.07	0.03	0.02	0.04	0.18*	−0.02	0.14	0.17*	0.04	0.00	−0.04	0.02	0.04	0.33***		
21 Sick leave rate	139	7.06	8.48	−0.10	−0.04	−0.13	−0.04	−0.04	0.05	−0.05	0.12	−0.10	0.02	0.04	−0.18*	0.00	−0.10	0.01	0.05	−0.03	−0.11	0.02	0.00	
22 Accident rate	154	7.07	19.59	0.55***	−0.08	0.02	0.08	0.01	−0.02	−0.06	0.08	−0.03	0.13	0.06	−0.11	0.02	0.04	−0.03	0.05	−0.04	−0.10	0.06	0.04	−0.01

*$p < .05$, **$p < .01$, ***$p < .001$

Appendix 6.2 Inter-correlations of employers' responses for temporary workers

	n	Mean	SD	1	2	3	4	5	6	7	8	9	10	11	12	13	14	15	16	17	18	19	20	21
1 Organization size	199	514.9	1,097.0																					
2 % temporary employees	194	30.92	25.86	0.13																				
3 Form (+independent)	194	1.51	0.50	0.17*	−0.01																			
4 Ownership (+private)	199	0.68	0.47	0.00	0.09	−0.03																		
5 Growing workforce	194	2.34	0.79	−0.07	0.04	0.17*	0.15*																	
6 Growing temporary workforce	193	2.23	0.73	0.06	0.02	0.09	0.01	0.40***																
7 Expected growth	193	2.16	0.70	0.05	0.03	0.14	0.06	0.38***	0.11															
8 Union influence	191	2.51	0.95	0.15*	0.04	−0.20**	−0.11	−0.07	−0.05	−0.03														
9 Ease of filling vacancies	191	3.31	0.84	−0.02	−0.03	−0.02	0.02	−0.07	−0.10	−0.19**	0.00													
10 HR practices	202	3.31	1.38	0.05	−0.11	−0.05	0.00	0.04	−0.01	0.03	0.08	0.05												
11 Training coverage	168	50.60	37.28	−0.06	0.10	0.04	−0.10	0.06	−0.04	−0.04	−0.10	0.17*	−0.05											
12 Performance appraisal coverage	185	57.35	43.74	0.01	0.10	−0.01	0.00	0.16*	0.09	0.10	0.01	0.03	0.17*	0.20**										
13 Performance-related pay coverage	187	17.83	35.09	0.07	0.04	0.02	0.04	−0.02	−0.05	−0.03	−0.09	0.10	0.09	0.09	0.13									
14 Employers' obligations content	186	10.48	3.67	−0.06	0.14	−0.10	0.20**	0.09	−0.14	0.07	0.02	0.11	0.13	−0.01	0.13	0.22**								
15 Employers' obligations fulfilment	184	3.98	0.54	−0.07	−0.14	0.01	0.25***	0.09	0.18*	0.11	−0.11	0.11	0.23**	−0.04	0.14	0.14	−0.07							
16 Employees' obligations content	202	12.69	5.48	−0.08	0.01	−0.19**	0.13	0.00	−0.02	0.08	0.01	0.11	0.24***	0.04	0.05	0.09	0.52***	−0.07						
17 Employees' obligations fulfilment	180	3.66	0.58	−0.19*	−0.12	0.13	0.08	0.17*	0.10	0.02	−0.06	0.04	0.24***	0.13	0.20**	0.00	0.04	0.49***	−0.09					
18 Satisfaction with performance	188	5.30	0.92	−0.03	−0.02	0.15*	−0.03	0.03	0.02	0.04	−0.12	0.10	0.11	0.03	0.18*	0.07	0.05	0.24***	0.01	0.36***				
19 Voluntary quit rate	154	9.00	23.31	0.37***	−0.12	0.06	0.04	0.03	0.01	0.14	0.17*	0.04	0.02	0.09	0.05	0.10	0.10	0.00	0.03	−0.09	−0.13			
20 Dismissal rate	193	47.48	50.43	0.26***	−0.03	0.09	0.02	−0.01	−0.04	0.02	0.03	−0.01	−0.13	−0.10	0.19**	0.03	0.09	0.07	−0.18*	−0.03	0.07	0.05		
21 Sick leave rate	121	6.02	9.98	−0.03	0.03	−0.17	−0.07	−0.04	−0.05	−0.07	0.15	−0.07	−0.11	0.05	−0.14	0.09	0.02	0.02	0.06	−0.02	−0.06	0.13	−0.03	
22 Accident rate	151	1.89	4.27	0.24***	0.13	−0.11	0.18*	0.10	0.11	−0.03	0.08	−0.03	0.04	−0.02	−0.04	0.02	0.03	−0.11	−0.04	−0.25***	−0.26*	0.06	−0.11	0.17

*p < .05, **p < .01, ***p < .001

7

Mutuality and Reciprocity in the Psychological Contracts of Temporary and Permanent Workers

Kerstin Isaksson, Francisco J. Gracia, Amparo Caballer, and José Maria Peiró

INTRODUCTION: THE NATURE AND ROLE OF MUTUALITY AND RECIPROCITY

The previous chapters have explored the role of the psychological contract from the perspective of either the employer or the employee. However, the core of psychological contracts is the mutual exchange of contributions from the employer and the employee. Building on social exchange theory (Blau, 1964), earlier research on the topic more or less took notions about mutuality and reciprocal contributions for granted. Furthermore, most of the early research has followed Rousseau's definition (1995) concentrating on one side of the employment relationship—*employees'* perceptions of the content of the psychological contract with their employer. Recent years, however, have seen an increase in studies focusing on both parties to the psychological contract (e.g. Coyle-Shapiro and Kessler, 2000*b*, 2002; Dabos and Rousseau, 2004), thereby broadening the focus of theory and research from the individual to the employment relationship. Nevertheless, there is still a need for a fuller investigation of the basic assumptions underlying the relationship such as mutuality and reciprocity, and the functioning of these principles across various employment situations.

This chapter aims to contribute to our understanding of the employment relationship that lies at the heart of the psychological contract by operationalizing the concepts of mutuality and reciprocity as two forms of agreement between employees and their managers. Mutuality is defined as agreement on the promises and commitments shaping the content of the psychological contract. Reciprocity on the other hand is defined as agreement on the fulfilment of the mutual commitments. The chapter also explores any differences in degrees of mutuality and reciprocity between permanent and temporary workers.

This chapter aims to expand earlier research in the area by investigating a set of indicators of the quality of the employment relationship. Firstly, we introduce and describe mutuality and reciprocity as two critical dimensions of the employment relationship, describe levels of mutuality and reciprocity in our samples, and identify possible differences associated with permanent and temporary employment contracts. Secondly, we consider additional indicators of the quality of the relationship including levels of agreement on the more explicit issues of the presence of HR practices employed by the organization. Thirdly, we investigate the role of the measures of mutuality and reciprocity and additional indicators of the quality of the relationship, namely employees' perceptions of fair treatment and perceived violations of the psychological contract, in explaining the well-being and attitudes of employees. In doing so, we will explore how far mutuality and reciprocity help to explain some of the differences in the well-being and attitudes of permanent and temporary workers.

MUTUALITY: AGREEMENT ON THE PROMISES
AND OBLIGATIONS OF BOTH PARTIES

Mutuality describes agreement between parties about the promises and obligations that employer and employee have made as part of the employment relationship (Dabos and Rousseau, 2004). Thus, mutuality exists when both parties agree, for example that the employer has promised to allow employees to participate in decision making or to provide reasonable job security. Furthermore, agreement should exist about employees' obligations, for example that the employees are obliged to work extra hours when it is necessary, and show loyalty towards the organization.

Mutuality provides both parties with the basis to align behaviours with the actual commitments made and accepted in the context of the relationship. Frequent communication, shared information, and common frames of reference (e.g. implicit theories and mental schemata regarding employment) are likely to give rise to high levels of perceived and objective agreement (Engle and Lord, 1997; Rousseau, 2001). Nonetheless, research has shown that workers and employers often have different understandings regarding specific terms of the exchange (Porter et al., 1998; Coyle-Shapiro and Kessler, 2000).

Potential discrepancies in each party's beliefs regarding what was promised can lead to a perception that there has been a breach of contract (Morrison and Robinson, 1997), with negative consequences for both individuals and organizations. Conversely, an employment relationship is more likely to have positive consequences when parties have developed shared understandings regarding the existence and meanings of specific contract terms (Rousseau, 1995, 2001).

An early attempt to investigate similarities between employer and employee perceptions by Herriot, Manning, and Kidd (1997) reported generally similar sets of obligations identified by employers and employees. Shore and Barksdale (1998) conducted one of the few studies with a focus on the meaning of balance, using data about the number of obligations in the psychological contract. They defined a balanced contract as one where the levels of employee and employer obligations are similar. Based on the norms of reciprocity, both parties are assumed to seek to establish a balance. These researchers reported empirical support for a two-by-two typology of patterns of exchange between employer and employee based on measures of content of the psychological contract reported by employees. The four patterns of agreement were mutually high, mutually low, employees over-obligated, and employees under-obligated. Results indicated that a high level of perceived agreement on mutual obligations was positively related to commitment and other outcomes. However, results for the other three patterns were mixed, but generally there was a tendency that a balanced pattern was more positive than an unbalanced one. The measure of balance in their studies is obtained by matching responses from employees only and thus the employers' perspective is missing. Using both employer and employee reports about the psychological contract and specifically the extent to which there is a match in responses about content and fulfilment will provide a fuller test of the nature and consequences of different patterns of exchange.

The impact of shared perceptions of the specific promises made has seldom been investigated with measures from both parties. Exceptions are studies by Coyle-Shapiro and Kessler (2002b) and Dabos and Rousseau (2004). However, both use samples drawn from a single organization; here, in contrast, we broaden the samples used to include data from a large number of organizations. Moreover, we adopt a new operationalization of mutuality based on agreement obtained by matching of identical responses from managers and their employees. This is clearly distinguished from a general, nonspecific *perception* that the parties agree and from a count of items on which promises have been made which can reveal agreement about breadth but not necessarily about content. Agreement about the content of the psychological contract should cover both organizational or employer promises and obligations and workers' promises and obligations. The implicit hypothesis is that a high level of agreement on both sides of the psychological contract will have a positive impact on work-related well-being and other outcomes.

Taking the analysis a step further, it is possible to distinguish the match between promises made (positive match) and promises not made (negative match). The psychological contract would generally consist of only the promises actually made, that is, positive match. Investigating differences related to employment contracts, however, it may also be relevant to investigate agreement that a promise was not made. Among temporary workers, for example, mutuality could also mean that both parties agree that a certain promise, perhaps on career guidance, is clearly *not* part of the deal.

Our analysis builds on the opportunities provided by the extensive data on the psychological contract in the Psycones study. To explore mutuality, we analyse the general levels of agreement between employers and employees about employers' promises and then employees' promises. We then draw the results together by exploring the positive and negative matches and levels of agreement on each for both permanent and temporary workers. It is important at this point to bear in mind that the agreement we are exploring is between an often senior manager with responsibility for employment relations and a range of often junior and temporary staff. It may therefore be unrealistic to expect that levels of agreement will be high.

Agreement on employers' promises

Agreement on promises made by the organization (employer promises) in Table 7.1[1] is shown both for permanent (P) and temporary (T) employees. Employees have reported their perceptions of the promises and commitments made by their employing organization from a list of fifteen possible promises presented in our questionnaire. These have been matched with reports from the management respondent, usually an HR manager acting as a representative of the employing organization. The result of this match is presented as the proportion of managers and workers reporting identical promises made (positive match, represented as 'yes' in column 1 of Table 7.1), but also the proportion agreeing that a certain promise was *not* made (negative match, represented as 'no' in column 2 of Table 7.1). Column 3 adds positive and negative matches to give a score showing percentage of total agreement. The second part of the table shows mismatches between the parties and takes two forms. In column 4, the workers say yes and employers no promise was made (Wyes–ERno) while in column 5, employers say yes and workers say no promise was made (Wno–ERyes). In column 6, both disagreement values are

Table 7.1 Percentages of matches and mismatches on each of the employer promises for permanent (P) and temporary (T) staff

		Agreement			Disagreement		
		(1)	(2)	(3)	(4)	(5)	(6)
		Positive	Negative	Total % agree	Wyes–ERno	Wno–ERyes	Total % disagree
1. Safe work environment	P	68	4	72	13	15	28
	T	53	9	62	16	22	38
2. Good working atmosphere	P	61	5	66	11	23	34
	T	52	9	61	18	21	39
3. Ensure fair treatment by	P	59	5	64	10	26	36
managers and supervisors	T	47	10	57	16	27	43
4. Provide possibilities to work	P	55	7	62	15	23	38
together in a pleasant way	T	51	9	60	18	22	40
5. Provide an environment free	P	53	8	61	14	25	39
from violence and harassment	T	42	13	55	15	30	45
6. Reasonably secure job	P	60	6	66	17	17	34
	T	29	25	54	21	25	46
7. Provide them with opportunities	P	52	8	60	12	28	40
to advance and grow	T	29	23	52	23	25	48
8. Good pay for the work they do	P	44	18	62	17	21	38
	T	34	26	60	17	23	40
9. Challenging job	P	40	15	55	17	28	45
	T	28	24	52	19	29	48
10. Participate in decision making	P	42	13	55	14	31	45
	T	22	30	52	16	32	48
11. Be flexible in matching	P	34	17	51	19	30	49
demands of non-work roles	T	26	26	52	24	24	48
with work							
12. Interesting work	P	31	24	55	20	25	45
	T	27	25	52	20	28	48
13. Provide them with a career	P	28	24	52	18	30	48
	T	14	45	59	15	26	41
14. Improve their future	P	24	28	52	24	24	48
employment prospects	T	18	36	54	23	23	46
15. Help them deal with problems	P	23	28	51	15	34	49
they encounter outside work	T	13	40	53	17	30	47

Note: W = worker, ER = employer, P = permanent workers, T = temporary workers.

added to give a total score of mismatch. Differences larger than 3 per cent are statistically significant.

The table shows some promises and commitments with a very high percentage of positive matches, that is, where both managers and employees report that the organization has made a certain commitment. The promises with the highest percentages of positive agreement both for permanent and temporary employees are a safe working environment, a good working atmosphere, ensuring fair treatment by managers and supervisors, and providing possibilities to work together in a pleasant way. The lowest percentages of positive agreement between managers and both temporary and permanent workers are found for the promises related to the future of their careers and to providing help with problems outside work. Employees having a permanent contract generally seem to have higher levels of positive agreement with their managers compared to those on temporary contracts; indeed, differences between permanent and temporary workers are significant on all items in the list. On the other hand, negative matches (agreement that a certain promise was not made) seem to be more common among temporary workers, so too are both kinds of mismatch.

Negative matches are less common than positive matches and on most of the specific promises and obligations temporary workers are more likely to report agreement with their employer that a promise was not made. The highest score is found for temporary workers (45%) agreeing with their employers that they have not been promised a career by their employers. Among permanent workers, 24 per cent of them agree with their manager that this promise was *not* made. Adding positive and negative agreements to provide a total score then naturally leads to decreasing differences between the permanent and temporary workers. However, differences in overall levels of agreement remain, with permanent employees reporting significantly higher overall levels of agreement on most items.

The more common form of mismatch shown in Table 7.1 is that employers report that they have made a promise, whereas the employee does not perceive that the promise was made (Wno–ERyes). Thus, it seems to be more common for employers to report a promise has been made and for employees to fail to acknowledge it than the other way around. The promises with high scores of *mismatches of both types* are those items relating to long-term commitments such as improving future employment prospects, or those with a more discretionary interpretation such as flexibility in matching demands of non-work roles with work. Employers also more often report that they feel obliged to help workers with problems outside work, while both permanent and temporary workers are more likely to report that no such promise was made.

In summary, the general conclusion to be drawn from these results is that perceptions of managers and their workers about promises and commitments made by the organization do not match very well. Agreement scores are lower than 60 per cent for almost half of the items on the list and the mean number of items agreed upon is relatively low. The match is greater for permanent employees. Given their longer time with the organization and the greater opportunities this provides to become familiar with the mutual promises and obligations, we should not be surprised by this finding. It is less predictable that employers seem more often to report that they made a promise than their employees acknowledge. This is especially the case with respect to providing future employment prospects and flexibility in matching demands of work and non-work, where employers perceive much more often than their employees that they have made promises and commitments. Next we look at agreement on promises and commitments of employees towards their employing organization in a similar way.

Agreement on employees' promises

Table 7.2 provides an overview of positive matches, negative matches, and mismatches for a list of promises and obligations made by employees towards their organization. Responses from permanent and temporary workers have been matched with those of the manager in their employing organization.

The results in Table 7.2 reveal generally high levels of agreement that a promise has been made but also a wide range of responses. There are higher levels of agreement among permanent than among temporary workers; more specifically, there is a positive agreement among over half the permanent employees and their managers on fourteen out of the seventeen items, while among temporary workers, over half agree with their manager on ten out of the seventeen items. Corresponding levels of agreement that a promise has not been made or disagreement about whether a promise has been made are inevitably somewhat reduced. Very high levels of positive agreement (>75%) were found for employee obligations such as respect and punctuality. If we compare the general level of agreement in Table 7.2 with that in Table 7.1, we find higher levels on employee promises and obligations.

When it comes to negative agreement, where both parties agree that no promise was made, Table 7.2 shows relatively low figures and again relatively small differences between permanent and temporary workers. 'Going to work even if you don't feel particularly well' is the item with the highest level of negative agreement. However, this item also has the highest level of total disagreement, where one party thinks this is a promise while the other party

Table 7.2 Percentages of matches and mismatches on each of the employee promises and obligations

		Agreement			Disagreement		
		(1)	(2)	(3)	(4)	(5)	(6)
		Positive	Negative	Total % agree	Wyes–ERno	Wno–ERyes	Total % disagree
1. Respect the norms	P	80	1	81	13	6	19
and regulations of the company	T	74	2	76	17	7	24
2. Be a good team player	P	77	2	79	13	8	21
	T	67	4	71	20	8	28
3. Be punctual	P	78	2	80	13	7	20
(prompt)	T	70	2	72	20	8	28
4. Meet the performance	P	77	2	79	14	7	21
expectations for their job	T	70	3	73	20	7	27
5. Assist others with	P	75	2	77	15	8	23
their work	T	60	6	66	24	10	34
6. Show loyalty to the	P	66	4	70	16	14	30
organization	T	49	9	58	23	19	42
7. Work overtime or	P	66	4	70	17	13	30
extra hours when required	T	54	8	62	22	16	38
8. Work enthusiastically	P	65	5	70	16	14	30
on jobs they would prefer not	T	50	10	60	23	17	40
to be doing							
9. Develop new skills	P	64	5	69	15	16	31
and improve their current skills	T	48	10	58	21	21	42
10. To develop their	P	64	4	68	22	10	32
competencies to be able to	T	52	7	59	28	13	41
perform efficiently in their job							
11. Volunteer to do	P	64	4	68	18	14	32
tasks outside their job	T	49	9	58	25	17	42
description							
12. Be polite to customers or	P	64	5	69	17	14	31
the public even when they are being	T	53	9	62	22	17	39
rude and unpleasant							
13. Protect their company's	P	62	5	67	16	17	33
image	T	48	10	58	21	21	42
14 To take the responsibility	P	52	9	61	25	14	39
for their career	T	40	15	55	29	15	44
15. Provide the organization	P	48	20	68	12	20	32
with innovative suggestions for	T	28	25	53	23	24	48
improvement							
16. Accept an internal transfer	P	37	19	56	15	29	44
if necessary	T	34	23	57	17	26	43
17. Go to work even if they	P	27	22	49	30	21	51
do not feel particularly well	T	22	26	48	26	24	52

Note: W = worker, ER = employer, P = permanent workers, T = temporary workers.

does not. 'Accepting an internal transfer' is another example of an item on which there is a higher level of disagreement. An interesting finding is that mismatches on employee promises seem to occur more frequently in the form that employees think an obligation exists, whereas employers do not. The other form of mismatch, where employers report a promise and employees do not, is less common. One example is 'accepting an internal transfer', where employers report a higher degree of perceived obligation on the part of employees than employees do themselves. On the basis of these results, it appears that both employers and employees report that they have made more promises than the other party acknowledges. This raises interesting questions about the way in which these promises and obligations are communicated and tends to contradict a popular assumption that employees in particular are likely to perceive that a promise has been made by the employer when in practice it has not.

The differences between permanent and temporary workers with respect to employees' obligations are generally quite small. We typically find higher levels of positive matches between permanent employees and their managers and higher levels of negative matches for the temporary workers while temporary workers, with only a few exceptions, tend to report higher levels of both types of mismatch. Despite this, the gaps between permanent and temporary workers are mostly smaller regarding employees' obligations compared with the results for employer's obligations shown in Table 7.1. Only one item shows a difference as large as 20 per cent between permanent and temporary workers; this item reveals that a requirement to make innovative suggestions is accepted as an unusual agreement between temporary workers and managers. We also find generally lower levels of negative match with respect to employee obligations. This is another indication that positive agreement is easier to obtain regarding the promises and obligations of employees.

Summarizing agreement on mutuality

Table 7.3 summarizes the results, showing the mean number of items on which there is positive agreement, negative agreement, and the total agreement scores for both permanent and temporary workers. Both employer and employee promises and obligations are shown in the table.

Table 7.3 confirms the pattern of results seen in earlier tables. Compared with temporary workers, permanent employees have significantly higher levels of positive mutuality reflected in agreement with their employer on both employer and employee items that a promise has been made. Neverthe-

Table 7.3 Summarized agreement on the content of the psychological contract for permanent and temporary workers

	Permanent workers	Temporary workers	Test of significant difference
Promise was made by employer (1–15)			
Positive agreement	6.4 (4.5)	5.1 (4.4)	$F = 116.7^{***}$
Negative agreement	2.3 (2.8)	3.2 (3.4)	$F = 105.1^{***}$
Total	8.7 (3.5)	8.2 (3.5)	$F = 23.4^{***}$
Promise was made by employee (1–17)			
Positive agreement	10.4 (5.6)	8.8 (5.9)	$F = 98.4^{***}$
Negative agreement	1.1 (2.1)	1.7 (2.9)	$F = 77.1^{***}$
Total	11.6 (4.7)	10.6 (4.8)	$F = 55.8^{***}$

Note: Values are means of promises agreed and the figures in brackets are standard deviations.
*** $p < .001$

less, the number of positive employer promises agreed upon is still relatively low, six out of fifteen (40%), while the number is higher on employees' promises (ten out of seventeen or 58%). The table also confirms that temporary workers have higher levels of negative mutuality, reflecting agreement that no promise was made. Despite this, the overall level of agreement or mutuality is still significantly higher among permanent than among temporary workers. Next, we turn to agreement on fulfilment of the promises implied in the psychological contract used here as an indicator of reciprocity.

RECIPROCITY: BALANCE IN THE FULFILMENT OF PROMISES AND OBLIGATIONS

Commitments made by one party to the contract obligate the other to reciprocate because both parties are expected to strive for balance in their exchange (Blau, 1964). Under the general norm of reciprocity (Gouldner, 1960), recipients of help, contributions, or beneficial treatment not only increase their liking for the giver but also seek to reciprocate as a means of restoring the balance in the relationship (e.g. DePaulo, Bittingham, and Kaiser, 1983; Eisenberger et al., 1986; Greenberg, 1980). An employment relationship is more likely to endure and meet its goals when parties reciprocate their commitments and obligations to one another (Rousseau, 1989, 1990; Wayne, Shore, and Liden, 1997).

A critical issue in the discussion about changing employment relations and new deals at work is whether the norm of reciprocity operates in temporary relationships. There is an obvious need for empirical testing of ideas about what constitutes a fair balance in this context and whether reciprocity seems to be a leading principle also for the psychological contracts of temporary workers. Reciprocation can be described as a process starting with individual expectations and preferences that leads them to accept an employment contract and develop an interdependent relationship with an employer where each party behaves in ways that fulfil the other's needs (Conway and Briner, 2005). The core assumption is that fulfilling obligations towards each other is part of reciprocation and should be related to generally positive attitudes for both parties.

In one of the few relevant empirical studies, Coyle-Shapiro and Kessler (2002b) showed that the principle of reciprocity seems to be a norm. Dabos and Rousseau (2004) investigated employer and employee beliefs about their exchange agreement and reported positive effects of both mutuality and reciprocity. They recommended that future research investigates factors that impede or contribute to mutuality. Both these studies were conducted in a single organization and there is a need to broaden the context and focus of the research. In the present study, we have a wide range of contexts and in addition can explore the question of whether reciprocity operates in temporary employment relationships.

Several different forms of measurement of reciprocity have been used and the optimal choice of approach is far from clear (see Conway and Briner, 2005; Dabos and Rousseau, 2004; Coyle-Shapiro and Kessler, 2002*b*). In this study, employers' reports of how far they had fulfilled their promises and commitments were matched with employees' reports of how far they had fulfilled their promises and obligations using a five-point scale in both cases. The sample was divided based on mean scores of fulfilment on all items into high and low fulfilment using a split at the midpoint of the fulfilment scale (1–3 were used as indicators of low fulfilment and 4–5 as high fulfilment). The four types resulting from the cross-tabulation of employer and employee responses are shown in Table 7.4.

The table shows results for all employees since no significant differences were found between permanent and temporary employees. The most interesting result in the table is that the form of reciprocity, whereby both parties report high levels of fulfilment of promises and obligations towards the other party, is the most common pattern in the exchange relationships between employers and employees. About 40 per cent of workers and their corresponding employers report high fulfilment of their promises and commitments. It was also interesting to find that differences between reports regarding permanent and temporary workers generally are very small and statistically non-significant. The other form of balance—that both parties admit not fulfilling their part of the deal—is clearly much lower; in only 12 per cent of cases do both sides agree that they have failed to fulfil their promises and obligations. The second most common result is an unbalanced

Table 7.4 Four patterns of exchange in fulfilling the psychological contract

Employees' reports of fulfilment of their promises and obligations to the organization (%)	Employers' reports of fulfilment of organizational promises and obligations to employees (%)	
	Low	High
Low	12	11
High	36	40

pattern of responses regarding reciprocity in which employees report high fulfilment while their employers report low fulfilment of their promises and obligations. Thus, employers are not reciprocating their employees' fulfilment of their promises. About 36 per cent of all exchanges belong to this group and confirm evidence from earlier chapters indicating that both parties to the psychological contract agree that employers are less likely than employees to keep the promises they make.

So far in this chapter we have shown that the employment contract seems to make a clear difference for agreement on the content of the psychological contract, and that having permanent employment seems to be related to a higher level of mutuality. This difference does not extend to reciprocity which seems to operate independently of the formal type of employment.

Agreement on HR practices

HR practices can be an important way for organizations to articulate the relationships with their employees. The practices within an organization can differ for different groups of employees and it might be expected that they would differ for temporary and permanent workers. If temporary workers are viewed as peripheral employees within the Atkinson (1984) model, then employers might be less eager to apply HR practices to them compared with permanent 'core' workers. However, alternative models have emphasized that temporary employers may not necessarily be peripheral workers, removing the rationale for different application of HR practices. Empirical data are needed to clarify these issues.

As we described in Chapter 3, we asked both employers and employees to report the HR practices used in their organization. Thus, it was possible to obtain a measure of agreement or shared perception on this issue between employers and their employees. In the discussion of the quality of the employment relationship, it is interesting to compare the possible effects of agreement on the HR practices, which are usually quite concrete and explicit, to agreement on the content of the psychological contract which can be much more implicit. Agreement on HR practices was calculated as follows: we asked the employers about the use of a set of five core HR practices for permanent and temporary employees and matched their answer to the responses of their respective employees to the equivalent question. Agreement was defined as existing if both sides confirmed that a certain HR practice was in use for the group of employees under consideration (temporary or permanent workers). Table 7.5 shows the level of positive agreement between the employers and employees.

Table 7.5 Percentage of agreement between the employees and the employers on the HR practices in use in the organization, by employment contract

	Agreement employers– permanent workers (%)	Agreement employers– temporary workers (%)	Test of significant difference (%) Chi square
Opportunities to express views	73	70	ns
Interesting and varied jobs	33	33	ns
Support with non-work responsibilities	23	18	18.9***
Equal opportunities practices	36	29	25.9***
Preventing harassment or bullying	40	28	87.8***

*** $p \leq .001$

The item most often agreed upon as being in use by permanent workers and their managers concerned the opportunity to express views (73% agreement) followed by steps to prevent harassment and bullying (agreed by 40% of permanent employees and managers). For temporary workers, the order between items is slightly different. The results show a large variation across the HR practices in the levels of agreement; for permanent workers, the range is 73 to 23 per cent, and for temporary workers, the range is 60 to 18 per cent. There are significant differences between permanent and temporary workers on three of the five items with temporary workers less likely to report agreement with their manager in each case. The average number of HR practices on which there was agreement about their presence was 2.2 for permanent and 2.0 for temporary workers ($F = 15.1$, $p < .001$).

CONSEQUENCES OF MUTUALITY, RECIPROCITY, AND FAIRNESS FOR EMPLOYEE WELL-BEING

The final section of this chapter tests the effects of mutuality and reciprocity of the psychological contract on the well-being of employees and a range of related attitudes and compares their relative effect with three indicators of what we broadly define as fairness of treatment.

Chapter 5 revealed that temporary workers reported higher levels of perceived fulfilment of organizational promises and commitments but the content of their psychological contract was on average more limited in its range, comprising fewer promises made by the employer than those made to permanent employees. This could make it difficult to compare the different types of psychological contact without including some evaluation of fairness and the state of the psychological contract (Guest, 1998, 2004b). If the deal for some reason was considered as unfair, for example because the psychological contract was too narrow or the promises received covered unimportant rather than valued issues, a high level of fulfilment would not have the same positive effect. Therefore, to evaluate the consequences of mutuality and reciprocity, we decided to include some indicators of fairness. We have already suggested that the number of HR practices in place is an indicator of the willingness of an organization to invest in the relationship and that the number of practices that both parties agree as being in place is a useful indicator of this. This therefore constituted our first measure of fairness. The second was the specific measure of perceptions of fairness of treatment that was reported in Chapter 6 as part of the extended set of measures of the state of the psychological contract. A third important indicator of the quality of the relationship and of fairness is whether or not the promises and obligations are perceived by employees to have been violated. We therefore, as a further step in the analysis, added in these three broad measures of the quality of the relationship. This will provide an opportunity to determine whether it is the content of the relationship, reflected in mutual agreement about the content and fulfilment of promises or its quality, reflected in measures of HR investment, fairness of treatment, and violation of the psychological contract by the organization, that have the main influence on well-being and related outcomes.

The general assumption based on earlier theory and the research of Shore and Barksdale (1998) would be that a balanced contract in terms of a high level of agreement would be beneficial and have a positive effect on employees' well-being and attitudes towards the job. Furthermore, Porter et al. (1998), in their study of employer and employee perceptions of organizational inducements, concluded that gaps between the parties appeared to be a significant factor explaining a variation in satisfaction with the organization. Dabos and Rousseau (2004) used matched data from both sides and concluded that both mutuality and reciprocity were positively related to productivity and career advancement. We therefore expect that high levels of mutuality and reciprocity, as defined in this chapter, will be associated with positive outcomes. We also expect that positive indications of fairness of treatment will contribute significantly to positive attitudes and behaviour, since there was already some evidence of this reported in Chapter 6.

For the analysis of the role of mutuality and reciprocity, we amended the original model used in Chapter 6, designed to test the role of the psychological contract as a mediator between type of employment contract and employee well-being, attitudes, and behaviour. In the model tested here, we replace the measures of the content and fulfilment of the psychological contract with the measures of mutuality and reciprocity. We add in the three indicators of fairness, namely agreement on the presence of the five core HR practices, general perceptions of fairness of treatment, and perceptions of violation of the psychological contract, as a third step in the regression.

The influence of mutuality, reciprocity, and fairness on work-related well-being

The findings regarding the association between mutuality and reciprocity of the psychological contract and work-related health are presented in Table 7.6. Step 1 (not shown in the table) introduces the same set of individual and organizational control factors (including country and sector) used in Chapter 6 including the type of employment (temporary or permanent). The indicators of mutuality (mean value of items agreed on for employer and employee promises) and reciprocity (reports of high fulfilment from both parties) are entered in Step 2 and in the final step the three additional indicators of fairness, namely agreement on HR practices, perceptions of fairness, and violation of the psychological contract are entered. Results of the regression for four different well-being indicators are presented.

The results in Table 7.6 show that at Step 2, when mutuality and reciprocity are entered, mutuality with respect to employer promises is significantly associated with all four outcomes. However, mutuality concerning employee promises is much less important and generally statistically insignificant. Reciprocity, the indicator of agreement about high levels of fulfilment of promises and obligations, is also significantly associated with all four outcomes. These findings are very much in line with the previous research cited above. We should also note that a permanent employment contract is significantly associated in each case with poorer outcomes.

The picture changes when we add in the fairness measures at Step 3. Mutuality concerning employers' promises and reciprocity largely cease to be significant. In each case, one significant association remains. In the case of mutuality concerning employers' promises, it is with anxiety and in the case

Table 7.6 The influence of mutuality, reciprocity, and fairness on work-related well-being

	Occupational self-efficacy		Irritation		Affective well-being: Depression		Affective well-being: Anxiety	
	Step 2	Step 3	Step 2	Step 3	Step 2	Step 3	Step 2	Step 3
	$n = 3,508$		$n = 3,502$		$n = 3,481$		$n = 3,493$	
Permanent contract	−.03	−.00	.14***	.09***	.11***	.03	.11***	.05**
Mutuality, employer promises	.07***	−.01	−.05**	.04	−.17***	.02	−.10***	−.06**
Mutuality, employee promises	.04	.05**	.05**	.04	.00	−.02	.02	.00
Reciprocity	.10***	.08***	−.06**	−.03	−.09***	−.03	−.07***	−.01
Agreement on HR practices		.05**		.00		−.08***		−.05**
Fairness		.08***		−.09***		−.17***		−.18***
Violation		−.13***		.24***		.40****		.33****
Adjusted R^2	0.13	0.16	0.08	0.16	0.11	0.38	0.07	0.27
R^2 change		0.03***		0.08***		0.26***		0.20***

Note: ** $p < .01$, *** $p < .001$

of reciprocity, it is with self-efficacy. Instead, the three measures of fairness are all significantly associated with all four outcomes with the single exception of agreement on HR practices which is not significantly associated with our measure of irritation. The role of violation of the psychological contract is particularly strong. It is also notable that, more particularly in the case of the measures of depression and anxiety, the amount of variance explained increases markedly once the fairness measures are added. Finally, we should note that after the fairness measures are added, there is evidence that they partially mediate the relationship between type of employment contract and irritation and anxiety and fully mediate the relationship between type of employment contract and depression.

In summary, these results initially appear to support previous research in showing a positive influence of mutuality. However, it is mutuality on employer promises and obligations rather than employee promises that matter more as far as employee well-being is concerned. Reciprocity, in the form of a high level of agreement about fulfilment, is also important. However, both cease to be significant once the measures of fairness are introduced. This suggests that the idea of the 'state of the psychological contract' is more important than the agreement on its content or even the fulfilment of that content. Interestingly, all three measures of fairness, including the agreement that certain HR practices are in place, show a significant association with the measures of well-being. Despite their strong influence on well-being, those employed on permanent contracts continue to report significantly higher levels of anxiety and irritation.

The impact of mutuality, reciprocity, and fairness on general health and life satisfaction

The results of the analysis of the influence of mutuality and reciprocity on general health, life satisfaction, and the influence of work on life outside work are shown in Table 7.7.

The results for Step 2 are similar to those for well-being in showing a significant association between mutuality with respect to employer promises, but not employee promises, and each of the outcomes. Reciprocity is only associated with life satisfaction. Workers on permanent contracts report poorer general health and a more negative interference of work on life outside work. Once the measures of fairness are added in Step 3, mutuality on employers' promises ceases to be significant except with respect to the influence of work on life outside work. Reciprocity also ceases to be significant, but mutuality with respect to employee obligations now becomes significantly associated with a more positive influence of work on life outside work. The

Table 7.7 The influence of mutuality, reciprocity, and fairness on general health, life satisfaction, and the influence of work on home life

	General health		Life satisfaction		Positive influence of work on home life	
	Step 2	Step 3	Step 2	Step 3	Step 2	Step 3
	$n = 3,503$		$n = 3,500$		$n = 3,498$	
Permanent contract	−.08***	−.05**	−.02	.02	−.06***	−.02
Mutuality, employer obligations	.08***	.01	.12***	.01	.17***	.06**
Mutuality, employee obligations	.00	.01	.01	.03	.04	.06**
Reciprocity	.03	.01	.07***	.04	.00	.03
Agreement on HR practices		.01		.05**		.10***
Fairness		.06**		.19***		.10***
Violation		−.18***		−.15***		−.16***
R^2	0.04	0.08	0.08	0.16	0.13	0.20
R^2 change		0.04***		0.08***		0.07***

Note: ** $p < .01$, *** $p < .001$

three fairness measures are significantly associated with each of the outcomes with the single exception that agreement on the presence of HR practices is not associated with general health. It therefore appears that once again it is fairness and avoidance of the unfairness associated with violation of the psychological contract that have a greater influence on general health, life satisfaction, and the home–work interface than agreement on the content and fulfilment of the psychological contract.

The impact of mutuality, reciprocity, and fairness on work attitudes and performance

In this subsection, we report the findings for four outcomes that have been reported in the previous chapters and are the subject of investigation in many studies. Two are the core work-related attitudes of job satisfaction and organizational commitment, the third is a behavioural intention, namely intention to quit, and the final one is a measure of self-rated performance. The relevant results are shown in Table 7.8.

In Step 2, mutuality with respect to employer promises and reciprocity are both significantly associated with all the outcomes. Mutuality with respect to

Table 7.8 Effects of mutuality, reciprocity, and fairness on work attitudes and performance

	Job satisfaction		Organizational commitment		Intention to quit		Performance	
	Step 2	Step 3	Step 2	Step 3	Step 2	Step 3	Step 2	Step 3
	$n = 3,510$		$n = 3,509$		$n = 3,507$		$n = 3,503$	
Permanent contract	−.09***	−.02	−.01	.06**	.10***	.02	.01	.04
Mutuality, employer obligations	.21***	.02	.22***	.03	−.18***	.01	.07***	−.01
Mutuality, employee obligations	.03	.05**	.08***	.10***	.00	−.02	.06**	.07***
Reciprocity	.10***	.04	.14***	.08***	−.10***	−.03	.13***	.10***
Agreement on HR practices		.10***		.15***		−.11***		.04
Fairness		.16***		.25****		−.16***		.00
Violation		−.37****		−.22***		.37****		.21***
Adjusted R^2	0.19	0.43	0.21	0.41	0.18	0.41	0.12	0.15
R^2 change		0.24***		0.20***		0.23***		0.03***

Note: ** $p < .01$, *** $p < .001$

employee promises is only significant in relation to organizational commitment and performance. Introduction of the three fairness measures in Step 3 alters the picture. Violation of the psychological contract is strongly associated with all the outcomes. Agreement about the presence of more HR practices and perceptions of fairness of treatment are associated with three of the four outcomes but not with self-rated performance. Meanwhile, mutual agreement about the promises made by employers ceases to be significant in all cases, but mutuality concerning employees' obligations remains significantly associated with commitment and performance and it now becomes significantly associated with job satisfaction. Reciprocity remains significantly associated with commitment and performance, and ceases to be associated with job satisfaction and intention to quit.

These results confirm again the strong influence of the three measures of fairness of treatment and it is reflected in the increase in size of the adjusted *R*-squared measure after they are introduced. This indicates that following their introduction, we are able to explain a much higher proportion of the variation in the differences on the scores for satisfaction, commitment, and intention to quit while for performance they add only a small amount of explanation. We should note the role of mutuality of employee promises and obligations with respect to commitment and performance. A somewhat similar pattern of results was reported in Chapter 6 and perhaps indicates that high commitment and high performance are both a product of, and a reflection of, an extensive number of promises and obligations on the part of employees that are at least partly acknowledged by employers.

The results in Table 7.8 indicate that after the measures of mutuality and reciprocity are introduced, permanent workers are still more dissatisfied and display a higher intention to quit than temporary employees. However, once the fairness items are introduced, there is no longer a significant association. Instead, a significant association now emerges between being on a permanent contract and being more committed to the organization. This reinforces the importance of fair treatment for the commitment of permanent staff.

In summary, when considered in isolation, mutuality and reciprocity seem to be important both for well-being and work-related attitudes. However, their effect is very much reduced by the measures of fairness, reflecting the state of the psychological contract, which seem to fully or partially mediate the effect of employment contract on several work-related attitudes and health outcomes. On the basis of these findings, perceptions of fairness, reflected in our three measures, are more important in explaining work-related well-being and attitudes to work than a shared understanding of the employment relationship. We should perhaps not be too surprised by this since the assessment of the state of the psychological contract is, in effect, an evaluation of the content and nature of the exchange.

CONCLUSIONS

There are several important conclusions to be drawn from this chapter. The first one concerns the level of agreement between employees and their HR managers about the content of the psychological contract. Permanent workers appear to have a generally higher level of agreement compared to temporary workers both regarding the promises they perceive from their employing organization and their own promises as employees. However, the level of agreement is rather low with less than 60 per cent agreement on over half the employers's promises. Mutual agreement appears to be higher concerning the promises and obligations of employees and differences between permanent and temporary workers are lower. These results are the opposite to those of Tekleab and Taylor (2003). In their study, differences were larger on employees' obligations compared to those of the employer. Their study was conducted in a large organization under a situation of restructuring which may limit the generalization of their results.

In the case of reciprocity, we find that a positive, balanced relationship is the most common. Second most common, however, was an unbalanced pattern of workers' overfulfilment where workers reported high levels of fulfilment whereas their managers reported a low level of fulfilment on their part. This result contradicts earlier research (Shore and Barksdale, 1998) based on the content of the psychological contract using employees' reports only. Moreover, no differences were found between permanent and temporary workers on this measure based on fulfilment of promises and obligations. Agreement on HR practices in use was higher for permanent compared to temporary workers. Nevertheless, even for permanent workers, a relatively low number of practices were acknowledged as being in place. This could indicate different ways of understanding the practices or it might reflect the heterogeneity of the workforce and the scope for error when a senior manager has to provide observations about practices applied to the workforce as a whole even though they may not be fully informed about the extent to which line managers implement some of the practices. Indeed, the senior role of many of the managers in our sample of organizations, which included some large organizations, may have seriously limited their ability to provide accurate information on mutual promises and obligations and their fulfilment and also on the application on the ground of specific HR practices.

In the analysis of the impact on outcomes, the regressions show that agreement on employers' promises and obligations are usually more important than agreement on those of employees. In both cases, the individual making a promise is likely to cite more than are perceived by the other party. This may reflect the implicit nature of some promises and obligations; and it raises questions about the way in which they are communicated. Employers are more ready than employees to admit that they do not always fulfil their promises and obligations. This suggests that the norm of reciprocity (Gouldner, 1960), at least when it concerns managers operating at the organizational level, may not be as strong as is sometimes assumed. This may help to explain why perceptions of (un)fairness, and especially violation of the psychological contract, have such a strong influence on the range of outcomes reported in this chapter.

In conclusion, the analyses in this chapter, aiming to understand the consequences of mutuality and reciprocity, have shown that both seem, initially, to have an important and significant influence on outcomes. But once the measures of fairness are introduced, they cease to be so important and often cease to be statistically significant. This suggests that we need to be cautious in interpreting existing studies of mutuality and reciprocity if they do not take account of perceptions of fairness. Indeed, the most important implication of these findings is that it is the state of the psychological contract, reflected in the quality of the relationship in terms of perceptions of fairness of treatment that has the major influence on outcomes.

NOTE

1. Mutuality = total number of positive and negative matches of items reported by both the employees and their employer representative. Positive match = both parties report that a promise was made. Negative match = both parties report that a promise was not made. Range for mutuality on employer promises was 0–15 and for employee promises, it was 0–17.

8

Establishing the Main Determinants
of Worker Well-Being

Michael Clinton and David E. Guest

INTRODUCTION

The main aim of this chapter is to draw together all the evidence about the determinants of worker well-being and related outcomes. We go beyond the previous chapters that have focused mainly on employment contracts and the psychological contract to take into account a range of other possible influences. A second and related aim is to determine whether, even after taking into account all these other factors, the type of employment contract still has a significant association with well-being and other outcomes. At the same time, we will identify what seem to be the most important determinants of well-being. A final aim is to evaluate the model that has informed this research and in particular to assess the role of the psychological contract once the range of other potential influences on well-being and related outcomes have been incorporated into the analysis.

The full model is set out in Figure 1.1, page 10. This serves as a reminder that there are seven main variables that might be expected to have some link to the various outcomes. They are the employment contract; the various elements of the employer's side of the psychological contract as perceived by the employees; the employees' perceptions of their own side of the psychological contract; employment prospects, including job insecurity and employability; volition with respect to contract, profession, and job of choice; job characteristics; and support from the organization and immediate supervisor. The literature providing the rationale for including these variables was outlined in earlier chapters (see also Warr, 2007). In the model, the employment contract serves as the main independent variable, while the other six are viewed as intervening variables. We should also bear in mind that we have included a large number of individual and organizational background factors as control variables in the analyses. The chapter that follows this one will pay particular attention to differences at the national and sector level.

Towards the end of the chapter, we will review the relative importance of each of the main variables in the model and also identify any consistent findings with respect to individual and organizational background factors before drawing the findings together as a basis for a preliminary evaluation of the model and in particular the role of employment contracts and the psychological contract. The first sections of the chapter explore the main influences on each of the outcomes. They are clustered into four groups covering work-related well-being, sickness and incidents, work-related attitudes and behaviour, and wider issues of satisfaction and health in life as a whole. In each case, we will identify the variables that are most strongly associated with each outcome.

The analysis throughout is based on regressions with two main steps. In the first step, the background control variables and the type of employment contract were entered to establish the relative importance of the employment contract. This is identical to the analysis reported in Chapter 6, and the results will not be repeated here. Instead, we will focus on the second step, in which all of the intervening variables were entered together. By comparing them, when they are all entered together, we can begin to gauge their relative importance and significance.

DETERMINANTS OF WORKER WELL-BEING

Determinants of psychological work-related well-being

As noted in the previous chapters, the more psychological aspects of work-related well-being were measured through four items. These are occupational self-efficacy, levels of anxiety–contentment, levels of depression–enthusiasm, and irritation. The findings are presented in Table 8.1. The table shows the beta weights in the regression, and the asterisks indicate levels of significance. Since we find once again that a lot of the variables are highly significant, it is useful to pay some attention to the size of the beta weights.

Occupational self-efficacy

Occupational self-efficacy is very strongly associated with employees' fulfilment of their promises and obligations to the organization, with perceptions of their employability, and with a sense of autonomy in the job. It is also

Table 8.1 Evaluation of the impact of all the variables in the model on work-related well-being

	Occupational self-efficacy		Affective well-being: Anxiety		Affective well-being: Depression		Irritation	
	Step 1	Step 2	Step 1	Step 2	Step 1	Step 2	Step 1	Step 2
Permanent contract (PC)	−0.03	−0.03	0.11***	0.06***	0.14***	0.07***	0.13***	0.09***
Employer obligations								
Content of PC		−0.03		0.03		0.04*		0.01
Fulfilment of PC		−0.02		0.00		0.00		0.03
Violation of PC		−0.01		0.24***		0.29***		0.20***
Trust		−0.05		0.01		0.03		0.05
Fairness		0.01		−0.05*		−0.06**		−0.02
Employee obligations								
Content of PC		0.09***		−0.01		−0.01		−0.01
Fulfilment of PC		0.27***		−0.07***		−0.10***		−0.05**
Employment prospects								
Job insecurity		−0.10***		0.14***		0.11***		0.12***
Employability		0.21***		−0.09***		−0.09***		−0.05**
Volition								
Contract of choice		−0.03		0.03		0.06**		0.03
Job of choice		−0.01		−0.04*		−0.12***		−0.02
Profession of choice		0.01		−0.05**		−0.03		−0.03
Job characteristics								
Role clarity		0.09***		−0.07***		−0.04**		−0.04*
Autonomy		0.16***		−0.08***		−0.06**		−0.04
Skill utilization		−0.01		0.05*		−0.01		0.11***
Workload		−0.03*		0.27***		0.07***		0.25***
Support								
Organizational support		0.08***		−0.03***		−0.08***		−0.07**
Supervisory support		0.10***		−0.04		−0.09***		−0.02
Adjusted R^2	0.15	0.37	0.13	0.40	0.19	0.45	0.13	0.28
F-value for R^2 change		65.56		84.87		89.89		40.79
n =		3,431		3,421		3,413		3,422

Notes: Background variables are controlled for, but not presented.
* $p < .05$, ** $p < .01$, *** $p < .001$.
All F values for R^2 change are significant at the $p < .001$ level.

significantly associated with a larger number of promises and obligations from the employee to the organization, with lower job insecurity, with high role clarity, and with high levels of organizational and supervisor support. It should also be noted that occupational self-efficacy shows no association with the employer's side of the psychological contract or with the employment contract. By including the set of intervening variables, the amount of variation in occupational self-efficacy explained within the model rises from 15 to 37 per cent, reinforcing their importance. This is also a significant increase on the 27 per cent of the explained variance when only the psychological contract variables are included, as reported in Chapter 6.

The results imply that there may be a virtuous circle of positive evaluation by employees of their own contribution, reflected in fulfilment of their extensive promises and obligations and also a belief in their own employability, both of which reinforce self-efficacy. There is also some evidence of an exchange process whereby support within the organization, coupled with perceptions of autonomy, is reciprocated with more extensive employee promises and obligations and greater fulfilment of them. The evidence suggests that occupational self-efficacy is based, to an important extent, on what the individual does, reflecting an internal locus of control, but reinforced by organizational and supervisory support.

Work-related anxiety

Work-related anxiety and, at the other end of the dimension, contentment is an important component of well-being. In the sample as a whole, levels of anxiety are generally fairly low, but there are quite considerable variations. The analysis presented in Table 8.1 indicates that anxiety is likely to be significantly higher among those who have a high workload, who believe that their psychological contract has been violated, and who have a sense of job insecurity. While these are the strongest factors associated with higher anxiety, several other items have a significant association. They reveal that anxiety is higher among those who feel that they have not fulfilled their own side of the psychological contract by meeting their promises and obligations to the organization, those who feel that they have a lower level of support from the organization, and who feel that they are treated less fairly. Anxiety is also higher among those who believe that they are less employable and who are less likely to be employed in their profession and job of choice. Finally, work-related anxiety is higher among those who report lower levels of role clarity, lower autonomy, and lower skill utilization, reinforcing the importance of job characteristics.

The findings confirm that a wide range of factors in the workplace appear to have a bearing on levels of work-related anxiety. The more important are those that we might expect to find, namely what is perceived to be unreasonable treatment by the organization, reflected in a heavy workload and violation of the psychological contract and a sense of insecurity. Taken together, the intervening variables increase the amount of variation in anxiety that is explained from 13 to 40 per cent, confirming their importance. This compares with 30 per cent of the explained variance when only psychological contract variables are included in the analysis, as reported in Chapter 6. Despite this, contract type is still associated with work-related anxiety. The size of the beta weight has reduced but remains highly significant. This suggests that the introduction of the various intervening variables partially mediates the relation between type of employment contract and anxiety, but even after taking all of these into account, workers on permanent contracts report higher anxiety than those on temporary contracts, indicating that this is a robust if unexpected finding from the study.

Work-related depression

The third core psychological measure of work-related well-being is the level of depressive mood, which we have labelled as depression, with, at the other end of the continuum, enthusiasm. Once again, the general level of depression is quite low, but there is considerable variation within the sample. Depression is most strongly associated with violation of the psychological contract. Although none of the other factors shows quite as strong an association, the results in Table 8.1 indicate that several other factors have highly significant associations with depression. These include not being in job of choice, failing to fulfil your own promises and obligations to the organization, a sense of job insecurity, lower employability, and lower levels of support from both the organization and the immediate supervisor. Aspects of job design have a more modest, but still significant impact and reveal that depression is higher among those who report a high workload, lower autonomy, and less role clarity.

The addition of the intervening variables increases the amount of variation in depression that is explained from 19 to 45 per cent, once again confirming their importance. This compares with 40 per cent of the variance that is explained when only psychological contract variables are included and confirms their key role, and particularly that of violation of the psychological contract. Contrary to our initial expectations, those on a permanent contract still report higher levels of depression than those on the various types of temporary contract. The reduction in the size of the beta weight indicates that, as with anxiety, there is evidence of partial mediation. Another interesting if unexpected finding is that those on contract of choice report higher levels of depression. This may be partly because permanent workers are significantly more likely to report that they have their contract of choice, although this association between contract of choice and higher depression occurred after controlling for type of contract. In summary, all the intervening variables as well as the core independent variable of employment contract contribute to the explanation of variations in depression.

Irritation

The final main indicator of psychological well-being at work is a measure of irritation. The pattern of responses is very similar to those for anxiety. Therefore, irritation is higher among those who have a high workload, believe their psychological contract has been violated, report a high level of job insecurity, and, more surprisingly, report a high level of skill utilization. There are also significant but somewhat weaker associations showing that irritation is higher among those who fail to fulfil their promises and obligations to the organization, those reporting lower employability, those with less role clarity and autonomy, and those who believe they receive less organizational support. Workers on a permanent contract continue to show a higher level of irritation, even after the intervening variables have been introduced, although there is some indication of partial mediation. The amount of variation explained has increased from 13 to 28 per cent as a result of introducing the intervening variables; this compares with 21 per cent of the variances when only the psychological contract variables are included, as reported in Chapter 6.

Summary

This section has analysed the determinants of four core measures of psychological well-being. While the average scores reveal generally positive levels of well-being, they also reveal quite considerable variation. A sizeable part of this variation can be explained by the intervening variables that we are considering in this chapter. This is revealed by the generally large increases in the amount of variance explained when these variables are included in the regression analyses. Furthermore, across the four indicators of well-being, all six of the intervening variables exert a significant influence at some point. Some variables consistently emerge as significantly associated with the various measures of psychological well-being. These include employment prospects in the form of job insecurity and perceived employability, fulfilment of the psychological contract by employees themselves, perceived organizational support, and the job characteristics of high role clarity and a manageable workload. Violation of the psychological contract is very strongly associated with three of the four measures.

From this analysis, we can begin to develop a picture of the factors that are likely to promote high levels of well-being. We can identify these factors through the somewhat arbitrary means of selecting variables with a beta weight, or effect size, above 0.10. Given the large sample size and the greater likelihood of statistically significant associations, this may well be a more useful guide. On this basis, occupational self-efficacy is strongly associated with fulfilling your own promises and obligations to your employer, a feeling of employability and job security, a high level of job autonomy, and strong supervisory support. A high level of contentment, the opposite end of the continuum from anxiety, is particularly strongly associated with having a manageable workload, a sense of job security, and not having your psychological contract violated. A high level of enthusiasm, the opposite end of the continuum from depression, is particularly strongly associated with not having your psychological contract violated, fulfilling your own promises and obligations to your employer, being in your job of choice, and feeling secure in your job. Finally, low levels of irritation are particularly strongly associated with a manageable workload, not having your psychological contract violated, utilization of your skills, and a sense of job security.

It is important to bear in mind that we have focused mainly on the negative aspects of well-being, namely anxiety, depression, and irritation. This is because our main focus is on temporary workers and our initial working hypothesis was that these would be characteristic features associated with temporary employment. The results can equally be interpreted as demonstrating that the intervening variables have a significant role to play in promoting contentment, enthusiasm, and an absence of irritation, as well as high self-efficacy.

For three of the four measures of well-being, the relationship to the type of employment contract remains significant, even after the additional variables are considered. While there is some evidence of partial mediation, we are nevertheless left with a clear and unexpected finding that after taking everything into account, temporary workers report higher levels of well-being than permanent workers. This is not what we expected to find.

Determinants of sickness and negative incidents at work

The second set of outcomes is concerned with behaviour and experiences and therefore reflects a more physical side of work-related well-being. The first two deal with behaviour and cover subjective accounts of days lost through sickness and days of sick presence, defined as attending work, even when you are feeling unwell. The second pair of outcomes is concerned with two types of negative experience, namely accidents at work and incidents of harassment. In contrast to the use of established scales to measure aspects of psychological well-being, all these outcomes are measured through single items.

Sickness absence

Only a relatively small proportion of the variation in sickness absence is explained by the model. This may not be too surprising since we would not expect most genuine illness to be primarily attributable to factors at work. It is possible that we might have explained more sickness absence if we had added the psychological well-being measures to the regression analysis. There are, nevertheless, a number of highly significant associations. Sickness absence is higher among those who believe that their psychological contract has been violated by their employer, that their employer has not fulfilled their promises and that they have been treated unfairly. Those in their employment contract of choice report higher sick leave, as do those with higher role clarity and autonomy. These last findings are counter-intuitive unless we want to speculate that autonomy is associated with greater freedom which extends to greater freedom to be absent from work.

The amount of variation in sickness absence explained by the variables in the model is only 12 per cent, with the intervening variables accounting for a mere 3 per cent in addition to the control variables and employment contract. This is only 1 per cent more than the variance explained by the psychological contract variables on their own, as reported in Chapter 6, and reflects the importance of the psychological contract variables compared with the other potential influences on sickness absence. Before the intervening variables are introduced, there is a significant association between being on a permanent contract and more sickness absence. Once they are introduced, the association ceases to be significant, indicating that despite their small impact on sickness absence, the intervening variables fully mediate the relationship.

Sickness presence

Sickness presence is considered to be a potential problem among those who are anxious about their employment security, including those on temporary contracts who might believe that if they miss work they will lose their job or may not receive sick pay. The results in Table 8.2 highlight the important

	Sick leave		Sick presence		Accidents		Harassment and violence	
	Step 1	Step 2	Step 1	Step 2	Step 1	Step 2	Step 1	Step 2
Permanent contract	0.11***	0.04	0.12***	0.10***	0.04	0.01	0.05*	0.02
Employer obligations								
Content of PC		0.03		0.04*		0.04*		−0.02
Fulfilment of PC		−0.05*		−0.06*		−0.06*		−0.13***
Violation of PC		0.09***		0.09***		0.04		0.09***
Trust		0.00		0.01		−0.03		0.05
Fairness		−0.09***		−0.09***		−0.03		−0.04
Employee obligations								
Content of PC		−0.02		0.08***		−0.01		0.05**
Fulfilment of PC		−0.07***		0.06**		0.03		0.03
Employment prospects								
Job insecurity		−0.01		0.00		0.00		0.02
Employability		−0.03		0.00		0.03		0.06**
Volition								
Contract of choice		0.06**		−0.05*		0.01		0.00
Job of choice		−0.01		−0.01		−0.01		0.01
Profession of choice		0.00		−0.02		−0.03		0.01
Job characteristics								
Role clarity		0.05**		0.02		−0.02		0.01
Autonomy		0.06**		−0.02		−0.02		−0.02
Skill utilization		0.01		0.01		0.04		0.03
Workload		−0.04		0.13***		0.04		0.05*
Support								
Organizational support		0.05		0.04		0.01		−0.01
Supervisory support		−0.02		−0.03		0.02		−0.05
Adjusted R^2	0.09	0.12	0.10	0.16	0.07	0.08	0.04	0.08
F-value for R^2 change		7.12		14.81		3.85		9.99
$n =$		3,415		3,410		3,419		3,412

Notes: Background variables are controlled for, but not presented.

*$p < .05$, **$p < .01$, ***$p < .001$.

All F values for R^2 change are significant at the $p < .001$ level.

influence of various aspects of the psychological contract. They also indicate that workload is a key predictor of sickness presence, presumably because those with a heavy workload are more likely to feel compelled to attend work. It is also possible that the high workload makes them more likely to be sick although workload is not related to sickness absence. Sickness presence is associated with a higher violation of the psychological contract, lower fairness of treatment, and a higher number of promises by the employer but less fulfilment of these promises. Sickness presence is also higher among those who say they have made more promises to their employer and have fulfilled these promises. There, therefore, appears to be a sense of inequity and unfair treatment underlying these responses. The only other significant association indicates that those on their contract of choice report less sickness presence; these same people also reported more sickness absence perhaps implying that a feature of contract of choice is being able to take time off rather than feeling obliged to attend when sick.

Contrary to expectations, those on a permanent contract are more likely to report sickness presence. This association was significant prior to introducing the intervening variables and remains significant after they are included, indicating little evidence of mediation. The amount of variation in sickness absence explained by the model remains modest. It rises from 10 to 16 per cent once all the variables are included. Once again, this is only 1 per cent higher than the variance explained by the psychological contract measures alone, confirming the central part they play in explaining presence at work when sick. However, we need to be careful when interpreting these findings. They seem to reflect a sense of obligation which is perceived as unfair and inequitable.

Accidents

The third variable in this section is accidents. We might expect workers on temporary contracts to have more accidents because they are less familiar with their work settings. In the event, workers in the sample report very few accidents and the model is able to explain very little of the variation in levels of accident experience. Table 8.2 reveals that only two items are marginally significant. Accidents are higher among workers whose employer makes more promises, and lower among those who believe their employer keeps their promises and fulfils their psychological contract. There is no association between accidents and the type of employment contract either before or after the intervening variables are included. When all the variables are present, the model explains 8 per cent of the variation in accidents, a modest rise from

7 per cent before the intervening variables are included, and the same as when only the psychological contract variables are taken into account.

Harassment and violence

The final item in this group is the experience of harassment and violence. One assumption is that workers on temporary contracts may be exploited in a variety of ways and these might include experience of harassment and possibly violence from other staff or perhaps certain types of customer. The results in Table 8.2 indicate that only a few of the variables show a significant association. The most important once again are elements of the psychological contract. Specifically, those who say their psychological contract has been fulfilled by their employer report less harassment and violence, while those who have had their psychological contract violated report more. Those reporting a higher workload and higher employability report more experience of harassment and violence. Those who report making more promises to their employer also report higher levels of harassment and violence. While a link between workload and harassment is perhaps understandable, reasons for the link to the number of employee promises made and to employability are not clear.

The full model is able to explain only 8 per cent of the variation in responses, the same as when only the psychological contract variables are included in the analysis. This suggests that there are other more important influences that we have not considered. Prior to the introduction of the full set of variables in the model, there is a significant association between being on a permanent contract and experiencing harassment and violence. However, once all the variables are included, the association ceases to be significant, indicating that they fully mediate the link. Nevertheless, there is no support for our implicit hypothesis that temporary workers would be more likely to experience harassment and violence.

Summary

The results reveal generally low scores on these negative physical aspects of well-being. Indeed, levels of reported accidents and harassment and violence are notably low. The model explains much lower levels of the variation in these physical well-being outcomes compared with the measures of psychological well-being. This is to be expected since it was not designed to capture all the influences on outcomes such as sickness absence or accidents. Furthermore, and in contrast to the measures of psychological well-being, the intervening variables did not add much explanatory value. The low levels of explained variation in these outcomes are reflected in the much lower beta weights in the regression analyses, reducing the ability to identify potential areas of leverage to reduce harmful physical experiences. A scan of Table 8.2 reveals only three beta weights of .10 or above. It also confirms the importance of the psychological contract compared with the other variables. All the psychological contract variables except the measure of trust are significantly associated with at least one of these outcomes. Fairness and violation of the psychological contract are particularly strongly associated with both sickness absence and sickness presence. There is also the interesting finding that more sickness absence is associated with lower fulfilment of employees' promises and obligations to their organization, while more sickness presence is associated with higher fulfilment of their promises and obligations to the organization.

Despite the limited influence of the various intervening variables, there was some evidence of mediation. Prior to their introduction into the regression analyses, there was a significant association between having a permanent contract and levels of sickness absence, sickness presence, and experience of harassment and violence. Once they were introduced, the link between type of employment contract and both sickness absence and experience of harassment and violence ceased to be significant. Only the link between a permanent contract and sickness presence remained highly significant, suggesting that permanent workers feel more obligated or more indispensable and are therefore more likely to go to work even when they are feeling unwell. At the same time, sickness presence is associated with a high workload, violation of the psychological contract, and perceptions of less fair treatment. Our findings suggest that these features are likely to be associated with permanent rather than temporary employees.

Determinants of work attitudes and performance

In this section, we explore the impact of the intervening variables on four outcomes that are of longstanding and central concern in organizations. These are the attitudinal outcomes of job satisfaction and organizational commitment and two outcomes more closely related to behaviour, namely intention to quit and self-rated performance. The results of the regression analyses are shown in Table 8.3. We will again consider each outcome in turn.

Job satisfaction

Job satisfaction is associated with at least one item from all the groups of intervening variables. The strongest 'predictors' of job satisfaction are being in

Table 8.3 Evaluation of the impact of all variables in the model on work attitudes and performance

	Job satisfaction		Organizational commitment		Intention to quit		Perceived performance	
	Step 1	Step 2	Step 1	Step 2	Step 1	Step 2	Step 1	Step 2
Permanent contract	−0.12***	−0.06***	−0.02	0.02	0.11***	0.09***	0.00	−0.02
Employer obligations								
Content of PC		−0.02		−0.04*		0.04**		−0.02
Fulfilment of PC		0.05**		0.02		−0.02		−0.05**
Violation of PC		−0.19***		−0.06***		0.22***		−0.05*
Trust		−0.04*		0.01		0.01		−0.01
Fairness		0.03		0.09***		−0.04*		−0.10***
Employee obligations								
Content of PC		0.05***		0.11***		−0.08***		0.05**
Fulfilment of PC		0.09***		0.18***		−0.05***		0.31***
Employment prospects								
Job insecurity		−0.03*		−0.05**		0.10**		−0.06**
Employability		0.00		0.03*		0.09***		0.06***
Volition								
Contract of choice		−0.02		0.00		0.00		0.01
Job of choice		0.22***		0.08***		−0.20***		0.04
Profession of choice		0.14***		0.04**		−0.09***		0.03
Job characteristics								
Role clarity		0.01		−0.02		−0.04*		0.15***
Autonomy		0.05**		0.04*		0.00		0.23***
Skill utilization		0.12***		0.08***		−0.05*		0.10***
Workload		0.02		0.07***		0.01		0.03*
Support								
Organizational support		0.13***		0.19***		−0.12***		0.09***
Supervisory support		0.08***		0.14***		−0.05**		0.02
Adjusted R^2	0.31	0.61	0.29	0.54	0.23	0.48	0.12	0.37
F-value for R^2 change		147.55		101.46		94.11		76.72
$n =$		3,431		3,431		3,430		3,419

Notes: Background variables are controlled for, but not presented.
* $p < .05$, ** $p < .01$, *** $p < .001$
All F values for R^2 change are significant at the $p < .001$ level.

job of choice, not having your psychological contract violated, being in profession of choice, receiving organizational support, and being able to utilize your skills. Satisfaction is also significantly associated with reciprocal fulfilment of promises and obligations and with making more promises to the organization. As we might expect from previous research, it is associated with having more autonomy, with supervisory support, and with lower job insecurity. The only unexpected result is that higher job satisfaction is associated with lower trust.

Most of the results for job satisfaction are in line with expectations. There is a large body of research that has linked job satisfaction to a positive psychological contract, to perceived organizational support, and to job content (Conway and Briner, 2005). The importance of being in a job and profession of choice is less frequently covered in previous research but emerges here as being more important than being on contract of choice. In terms of our core proposition that these intervening variables will mediate any relation between type of employment contract and outcomes, the findings in Table 8.3 indicate that there is partial mediation. In other words, the link between contract type and job satisfaction remains highly significant but the size of the beta weight has dropped. Less expectedly, the results continue to show that it is the temporary workers who are more satisfied with their jobs, confirming the results initially reported in Chapter 4. Finally, when all the background and intervening variables are included, 61 per cent of the variation in job satisfaction is explained. This is a marked increase from the 41 per cent of the variation explained when only the psychological contract variables are considered and indicates that many of the important influences on job satisfaction have been included in the model.

Organizational commitment

Organizational commitment, like job satisfaction, is again associated with at least one item from each of the clusters of intervening variables. Commitment is most strongly associated with a fuller set of promises and obligations to the organization and greater fulfilment of these and with strong organizational and supervisory support. These variables represent a good example of an exchange process. The results for the other variables reveal significant but rather weaker associations. They show that commitment to the organization is higher among those who report higher skill utilization, higher autonomy, and a higher workload. It is also higher among those in their job and profession of choice. It is higher among those with lower job insecurity and higher employability. Finally, it is higher among those whose psychological contract has not been violated, who feel fairly treated and, more surprisingly, who report that their employer has made fewer promises to them.

With respect to variables such as commitment, we must be careful in making assumptions about causality. The association between commitment and workload, which often extends to working longer hours, is likely to reflect the fact that those who are more committed to the organization willingly accept a higher workload and choose to work longer hours.

Organizational commitment is one of the outcome variables that showed no association with type of employment contract prior to the inclusion of the independent variables and the results remain unchanged once they are added into the analysis. However, the results in Table 8.3 show that the various background variables account for 29 per cent of the variance in scores on organizational commitment and this rises to 54 per cent once the intervening variables have been taken into account. This is only 6 per cent higher than the psychological contract variables on their own, once again confirming their importance. Nevertheless, it appears that the model includes many of the more important influences on commitment.

Intention to quit

Intention to quit, as its name implies, is a behavioural intention rather than a behaviour, but it has been shown in a number of studies to be among the best predictors of whether people will actually leave their job (Griffeth, Hom, and Gaertner, 2000). We have to be a little cautious in using this measure in the present study, since many temporary workers are on short contracts where intention to quit may not have a great deal of meaning. For them, the relevant question is therefore whether they intend to quit before the end of their contract; in other words, to quit when they could have stayed on longer. The results in Table 8.3 show that intention to quit is notably higher among those who report that their psychological contract has been violated, those who are not in their job of choice, and among those who feel that they lack organizational support. It is also higher among those who report more promises and obligations from their employer and those who offer less in return and are less likely to fulfil their own promises and obligations. In this context, it is impossible to determine whether the employers' lower number of promises and lower fulfilment of their own promises and obligations are a cause or consequence of an intention to quit. However, the association with less fair treatment suggests that it reflects a larger problem of the way potential leavers feel treated. This is reinforced by the association with lower supervisory support. Intention to quit is also associated with lower role clarity, lower skill utilization, and less likelihood of being in profession of choice. Finally, it is associated with higher job insecurity, but also higher employability. In other words, those who feel insecure in their present job but believe they can quite easily find another job are more likely to say they plan to quit.

The findings on intention to quit are broadly in line with previous research. Most other research would also report a strong link between low job satisfaction, low commitment, and intention to quit, and if these had been included in this analysis, the amount of variation in responses explained by the model would undoubtedly have been higher. In the event, the background variables account for 23 per cent of the variance in responses on intention to quit and this rises to 48 per cent once the intervening variables are included. This is a marked increase from the 40 per cent of the variance that is explained when only the psychological contract variables are included, confirming the importance of other variables in the model.

Prior to including the intervening measures, there was a positive association between type of employment contract and intention to quit. Once they were included, the association remains and is only marginally reduced. In line with most previous findings in this study, but contrary to initial expectations, those on permanent contracts provide the more negative responses; in other words, they are more likely to report an intention to quit.

Self-rated performance

Measurement of performance is fraught with difficulty and subjective measures carry a high risk of positive bias. However, if we assume that this is a consistent bias across the respondents, then the differences in responses can still provide some useful insights. The results in Table 8.3 show that higher self-rated performance is strongly associated with job characteristics and in particular having more autonomy, role clarity and opportunity to utilize skills. It is also very strongly associated with perceived fulfilment of obligations to the organization. In this context, the causal direction cannot be established, but it seems plausible to assume that high self-rated performance is a key indicator of fulfilling obligations. Performance is also higher among those who receive stronger organizational support, who report less violation of their psychological contract, and who report lower job insecurity and higher employability. However, the pattern of results is more complex because those who rate their performance highly also report less fulfilment of the promises and obligations made by the organization, less fairness of treatment, and a higher workload. Taken together, these results imply that those who believe that they are performing well also believe that they are not being fairly rewarded for their contribution.

The various background variables account for 12 per cent of the variation in self-rated performance and once the intervening variables are included, this rises to 37 per cent, confirming the importance of the full model. This level of explained variance is significantly higher than the 25 per cent when only the psychological contract variables are added. Indeed, the amount of variance explained is rather higher than that found in many reported studies and suggests that we have included some of the key factors in our model. However, as noted above, we must be cautious in our assumptions about cause and effect; furthermore, the association between high self-rated performance and perceptions of a higher workload, less fair treatment, and less fulfilment of promises by the organization suggests that self-rated high performance in organizations is not without its problems. Finally, perceived performance shows no association with type of employment contract. While this finding is out of line with many of the others in this respect, it is still contrary to our expectations, since we might expect that permanent workers, with their longer experience in the organization, would report superior performance.

Summary

This section has reported the results for the analysis of factors associated with four widely used outcomes, namely job satisfaction, organizational commitment, intention to quit, and self-rated performance. The amount of variation in the responses on these measures that is explained by the background and intervening variables included in the model ranges from 37 per cent for self-rated performance to 61 per cent for job satisfaction. These high levels of explanation confirm that we have captured many of the key influences on these outcomes in our model.

An analysis of the larger beta weights (above .10), indicating effect size, helps to identify possible levers for improving attitudes and performance. Higher job satisfaction is strongly associated with being in one's job of choice and profession of choice, with no violation of the psychological contract, with high levels of organizational support, and with an opportunity to utilize skills. High commitment to the organization is particularly associated with strong organizational and supervisor support and fulfilment by employees of their promises and obligations to their organization. Intention to quit is lower among those in their job of choice, with strong organizational support, no violation of their psychological contract, and high job security. Finally, self-rated performance is higher where employees believe that they are fulfilling their promises and obligations to their organization, and where there are high levels of autonomy, role clarity, and skill utilization, but it is also associated with lower perceived fairness of treatment.

The pattern of results confirms the importance of all the variables in the model in understanding this set of outcomes. However, they are unable fully to account for the role of contract of employment. After the control variables are included in the analysis, the results showed that permanent workers have significantly lower job satisfaction and significantly higher intention to quit. After including all the variables in the model, these associations are still significant, although that between employment contract and job satisfaction reduces, indicating partial mediation. We, therefore, still need to explain why permanent workers report lower job satisfaction and higher intention to quit.

Determinants of life satisfaction and general health

The final set of outcomes moves beyond the workplace to take a broader view of well-being by considering measures of work–life balance, general health, and life satisfaction. Since each of these is likely to be influenced by factors outside work, many of which we were not able to take into account in this study, we might expect the variables in our model to explain rather less of the variation in responses. The results of the regression analysis are shown in Table 8.4.

Work–life balance

Work–life balance was measured using a distinctive measure of the extent to which work interfered with life outside work and more specifically, whether it had a positive or negative influence. The results reveal that none of the intervening measures are particularly strongly associated with this indicator of work–life balance. Nevertheless, there are still a number of significant associations. Work is more likely to have a benign influence on life outside work among those who report less violation of their psychological contract, a fuller set of promises and obligations from their employer as well as more promises made by them to their employer and more fulfilment of these promises and obligations. Work is also considered to have a positive influence on non-work life among those who are in their job and profession of choice, who report higher levels of autonomy and skill utilization, and who receive stronger organizational support. Finally, it is higher among those who consider themselves more employable but also, less predictably, higher among those reporting more job insecurity.

In this study, we have not used a conventional measure of work–life balance. However, we suspect that this has not greatly affected the results. Since this issue addresses the border between work and life outside work, we might expect only a moderate amount of the variation to be accounted

Table 8.4 Evaluation of the impact of all the variables in the model on work–life balance, general health, and life satisfaction

	Positive work–life impact		General health		Life satisfaction	
	Step 1	Step 2	Step 1	Step 2	Step 1	Step 2
Permanent contract	−0.04*	−0.02	−0.08***	−0.07**	−0.05*	−0.05*
Employer obligations						
Content of PC		0.05*		−0.01		0.02
Fulfilment of PC		0.00		0.04		−0.01
Violation of PC		−0.09***		−0.09***		−0.07**
Trust		−0.05		−0.05		−0.06*
Fairness		0.03		0.03		0.12***
Employee obligations						
Content of PC		0.10***		0.06**		0.06**
Fulfilment of PC		0.04*		0.11***		0.09***
Employment prospects						
Job insecurity		0.05**		−0.10***		−0.05**
Employability		0.03*		0.07***		0.12***
Volition						
Contract of choice		0.02		−0.02		0.03
Job of choice		0.06**		0.01		0.07***
Profession of choice		0.04*		0.03		0.05*
Job characteristics						
Role clarity		−0.02		0.01		0.05**
Autonomy		0.07**		0.07**		0.06**
Skill utilization		0.09***		0.00		−0.03
Workload		−0.02		−0.09***		−0.15***
Support						
Organizational support		0.12***		0.05		0.12***
Supervisory support		0.04		0.00		−0.02
Adjusted R^2	0.19	0.28	0.04	0.12	0.10	0.24
F-value for R^2 change		22.39		17.40		34.35
$n =$		3,423		3,426		3,423

Notes: Background variables are controlled for, but not presented.
*$p < .05$, **$p < .01$, ***$p < .001$.
All *F* values for R^2 change are significant at the $p < .001$ level.

for by work-related factors. This is indeed the case and the factors included in our study explain 28 per cent of the variation in responses. Background factors play quite an important role, explaining 19 per cent of the variance, and the intervening variables in the model add only a further 9 per cent. This is a modest improvement on the amount of variance explained when only the psychological contract variables are included, with the variance explained as rising from 25 to 28 per cent.

Prior to entering the intervening variables, there was a significant, if fairly marginal association between type of employment contract and the positive influence of work on life outside work, with those on permanent contracts reporting less positive influence and by implication a poorer work–life balance. However, this association ceases to be significant once the full set of variables in the model is introduced, suggesting that they mediate the relationship between type of employment contract and our measure of work–life balance.

General health

General health is likely to be influenced by a range of factors outside the workplace. Indeed, the results in Table 8.4 indicate that the measures in the model account for only 12 per cent of the variation in reported health, although the inclusion of the intervening variables has increased this from 4 per cent, indicating that these are of some importance. This is a marginal improvement on the 10 per cent of variance explained when only the psychological contract variables are added to the background variables. No variables stand out as having a markedly higher influence than others. However, general health is reported to be significantly lower among those who report that their psychological contract has been violated, who have a higher level of job insecurity, and who have a higher workload. In contrast, general health is rated as better among those who report a higher number of promises and obligations to their employer, especially if they also fulfil them. It is also higher among those reporting more autonomy and more employability.

Most of these findings are in line with expectations. Job insecurity and a high workload have been associated with poorer health in previous studies (Sverke, Hellgren, and Naswall, 2002) and violation of the psychological contract reflects a negative emotional response that may well affect general health if it persists.

Prior to considering the intervening variables in the model, type of employment contract was significantly associated with general health. Once the full model is considered, the association remains, albeit at a marginally reduced level of significance. The results indicate that even after taking everything else into account, those on permanent contracts are likely to report poorer health than those on temporary contracts. Given the importance of job insecurity, this is a somewhat surprising finding. However, it is also an important result, confirming that some of the pressures of work, including a high workload and the experience of violation of the psychological contract, both of which are more likely to be reported by permanent workers, are associated with poorer ratings of general health.

Life satisfaction

Life satisfaction potentially embraces a wide range of elements that may include work, depending in part on the extent to which work can be considered a central life interest. It is possible that work might be rather less central in the lives of some of those on temporary contracts. In the event, life satisfaction is significantly associated with at least one item in each of the clusters of intervening variables in the model. The association is strongest with workload, those with a higher workload reporting lower life satisfaction; in contrast, those reporting stronger organizational support, higher fairness of treatment, and higher employability all have higher life satisfaction. Life satisfaction is also higher among those in their job of choice and profession of choice and among those with higher autonomy and higher role clarity. Both 'sides' of the psychological contract are important. Those who make more promises to their employer and fulfil them report higher life satisfaction, while those who have had their psychological contract violated by their employer report lower life satisfaction, as do those with higher job insecurity and, more unexpectedly, those reporting higher trust in their employer.

The analysis in Table 8.4 shows that the background variables account for 10 per cent of the variance in life satisfaction, but the full model accounts for 24 per cent of the variation, confirming the importance of work experiences for overall life satisfaction. This is higher than the 19 per cent accounted for when only the psychological contract variables are included.

Prior to the introduction of all the intervening variables in the model, there was a significant association between being on a permanent contract and lower life satisfaction. After taking account of all the variables in the model, this association remains significant. Therefore, in line with most of the other results, and once again contrary to our hypothesis, those on permanent contracts report lower life satisfaction.

DISCUSSION AND CONCLUSIONS

Now that all the main results have been presented, there is an opportunity to review their implications and provide a preliminary assessment of the core model that we have used in this study. In Chapter 6, we showed that the measures and the state of the psychological contract have an important part to play in explaining the various indicators of well-being and associated attitudes and behaviour. However, it also showed that the type of employment contract remained significantly associated with many of the outcomes, and in particular, it revealed that contrary to expectations, those on permanent contracts generally reported lower levels of well-being. This chapter has presented the results of analyses incorporating a fuller range of variables including many that have been shown in other studies to have an association with well-being and related outcomes. We therefore expected that these, together with the psychological contract measures, would mediate the link between employment contracts and well-being. We are now in a position to review whether this is indeed the case and also to review the key determinants of well-being.

As a preliminary step, we have integrated the findings to provide a summary overview of the most important influences on outcomes. The results are shown in Table 8.5. This analysis omits the variables on sickness behaviours and accidents or incidents presented in Table 8.2 since only a very small amount of the variance was accounted for. The results represent the average variance accounted for by each measure when they are all entered into the regressions for the outcomes shown in Tables 8.1, 8.3, and 8.4. The criterion for inclusion is that the variables account for a greater or equivalent amount of variance in well-being to the employment contract. This reveals that the strongest overall association is with aspects of the psychological contract. Reported violation of the psychological contract accounts for an average of 14 per cent of the variation in well-being and related outcomes. The number of promises and obligations reported by employees and, more importantly, fulfilment of these, feature strongly and, perhaps surprisingly, are more important than the content and fulfilment by employers of their side of the psychological contract. Support, both from the organization (10%) and from supervisors (5%), is also consistently associated with well-being; so too is being in job and profession of choice (8 and 5%, respectively). The job characteristics of autonomy and workload account for 8 and 7 per cent of variance on average. Employee prospects also appear important, with job insecurity and employability accounting for 7 and 6 per cent of the variance in well-being reports, respectively. Age is the only demographic variable included. It is as strongly associated with well-being as type of employment contract, explaining 5 per cent of the variance. Other background variables, such as the number of HR practices, which had quite a strong impact on the measures of the psychological contract, are less important once the full set of measures are included in the analysis. This summary analysis confirms that all the groups of intervening variables contribute to the explanation of variations in well-being, supporting our choice of these measures in the model.

Employment contract alone accounts for between 3 and 12 per cent of the variation in well-being and other outcomes after controlling for background factors and between 1 and 10 per cent after controlling for the background

Table 8.5 Average effect sizes of the strongest associates of well-being[1]

	Average effect size
Violation of psychological contract	−0.14
Fulfilment of PC (employee obligations)	0.12
Perceived organizational support	0.10
Job of choice	0.08
Autonomy	0.08
Workload	−0.07
Job insecurity	−0.07
Employability	0.06
Content of PC (employee obligations)	0.06
Supervisory support	0.05
Profession of choice	0.05
Age	0.05
Permanent contract	−0.05

factors and all intervening variables. The average variance explained by employment contract in the full model is 5 per cent which, as we might expect, is relatively small, more particularly when compared with some of the other variables. Nevertheless, it remains a fairly consistently significant presence and invariably indicates that those on temporary contracts report higher well-being than those on permanent contracts.

Employment prospects are among the key variables that we expected to mediate the relationship between employment contract and well-being. This was measured through job insecurity and employability. Both are associated with the various indicators of well-being. Job insecurity is consistently and quite strongly associated with lower scores on the psychological well-being measures and also has a consistent, significant, but less strong association with lower job satisfaction, organizational commitment, and life satisfaction. As we revealed in previous chapters, job insecurity is also significantly higher among those on temporary contracts. Yet on the evidence in this chapter, it does not have much effect in mediating the positive association between temporary contracts and well-being. Employability is important and is positively associated with psychological well-being and also with life satisfaction and general health. However, it is not associated with job satisfaction and organizational commitment which appear to be more strongly linked to factors related to the current job and organization. Nevertheless, it appears that having attractive alternatives and therefore choices in employment is important for well-being.

In the survey on which this analysis is based, workers on temporary contracts were asked a number of additional questions. These were reported in some detail in Chapter 4. Some of the questions concerned motives for accepting temporary employment and two concerned job prospects. The analysis in Chapter 4 indicated that good job prospects are associated with a variety of positive outcomes, providing further confirmation of the importance of employability within the subgroup of temporary workers. However, we can take this analysis a step further by comparing expectations about the extension of the current temporary contract and the prospect of being offered permanent employment. These have very different results. Expectations of a contract extension is invariably associated with positive outcomes while expectations of a permanent contract is much more neutral or even negatively associated with outcomes, although rarely at a statistically significant level. One interpretation of this is that some of the core features of temporary employment appear to be valued and preferred to permanent employment by many temporary workers. In this context, the attraction of a contract extension is that it may provide an opportunity to reduce job insecurity without taking on the negative elements of a permanent job. Another additional question asked about length of temporary contract. There is some indication that as temporary workers become more like permanent workers, reflected in a longer duration of their temporary contract, they take on some of the attitudes and aspects of the behaviour of permanent employees; and these are predominantly negative. Although our data are far from conclusive, it does begin to appear that the freedom offered by temporary employment more than compensates for the constraints and demands, but also the security of permanent employment.

The variables that have been labelled in the model as 'volition' are, in effect, measures of the extent to which workers are on their employment contract and in their job and profession of choice. The key issue of interest in the present context is the relative importance of job and profession compared with contract. Being in job of choice and to a lesser extent in profession of choice has a consistent association with positive outcomes. This is in line with findings reported in Swedish research by Aronsson and Goransson (1999). Given the kinds of workers in the study, many of whom work in relatively low-level jobs in food production and retail, the concept of profession may hold less significance for them than a job. The positive association is most notable with respect to job satisfaction and intention to quit. More surprisingly, being on contract of choice is seldom significantly associated with outcomes, but when it is, the association is often negative. For example, it is associated with higher depression and higher sickness absence as well as lower sickness presence, which, as noted above, may be an indicator of commitment. Since those in permanent contracts are more likely to be in their contract of choice, this may begin to provide some insights into why they are not more positive.

A further potential explanation for some of the unexpected results may be that those on temporary contracts are more likely to give priority to working in their job and profession of choice rather than in their employment contract of choice. The positive impact of job and profession of choice for temporary workers may also help to mitigate the effects of job insecurity and explain why insecurity seems to have only a minor impact on the well-being of temporary workers. The implied pay-off is that permanent workers give greater priority to job security, but at some cost in terms of job content, while temporary workers opt for job and profession of choice and enjoy great job satisfaction and higher levels of work-related well-being while living with a degree of job insecurity.

There has been a large body of research showing an association between job characteristics and measures of work-related well-being and job satisfaction. These range from the work of Karasek (1979) on job content and stress to the extensive job redesign literature (Parker and Wall, 1998). The results of this study are very much in line with these streams of research. High autonomy has a consistent association with positive outcomes while high workload has an almost consistently negative association. The qualification with respect to workload is that a higher workload is associated with higher commitment, higher performance, and higher sickness presence. In these cases, we need to unravel the causal links. It seems probable that those who are more committed are more likely to accept a high workload and to feel that they must attend work even when unwell. Those who rate their performance highly may use their workload as one indicator of this. In general, however, a high workload is negatively associated with well-being and with life outside work. In this context, it is also worth noting that longer working hours display a similar negative association. The other job characteristics of role clarity and skill utilization are consistently associated with positive outcomes, but the associations are rarely very strong. Nevertheless, they confirm the general pattern of responses highlighting the importance of job content for well-being. The higher workload among permanent workers appears to be one of the key contributory factors in their lower reported levels of well-being.

Support from the organization and from the immediate supervisor is also consistently and significantly associated with positive outcomes. This fits well with the extensive literature on the role of perceived organizational support (Eisenberger, Fasolo, and Davis-LaMastro, 1990) and with the rather more limited literature on perceived supervisor support (Brough and Pears, 2004). Although both organizational and immediate supervisor support are associated with many of the positive outcomes, the measure of organizational support consistently shows the stronger association, reinforcing the potential importance of the organizational climate for which this is a plausible proxy.

Having shown that all the intervening variables in the model are significantly associated with well-being, we might expect the various measures of the psychological contract to become less important. As the results summarized in Table 8.5 reveal, this is not the case. The most important variable in determining well-being and other outcomes is violation of the psychological contract. Importantly for psychological contract theory, the second most important is the measure of employees' fulfilment of their promises and obligations to the organization. Well-being is higher when individuals believe that they are fulfilling their side of the psychological contract. It seems that both 'sides' of the psychological contract matter, suggesting the importance of exchange and reciprocation as well as notions of equity. Violation of the psychological contract by their employer outweighs the role of fulfilment of the psychological contract by the employer with respect to most outcomes. Exceptions to this are experiences of harassment and violence and accidents. In these cases, fulfilment of the psychological contract by the employer is strongly associated with fewer accidents and less experience of harassment and violence.

The other items reflecting the state of the psychological contract, namely fairness and trust, are less important and have inconsistent links with the outcomes. Fairness is associated with organizational commitment, sickness behaviour, and more particularly self-rated performance. However, in the case of performance, the association is negative, pointing once again to the importance of an equitable exchange and implying that some of those who rate their own performance highly are less inclined to believe that they are fairly treated. Somewhat surprisingly, trust has very little association with any outcomes, and where it does have an impact, it is generally negative. Therefore, higher trust is associated with lower job satisfaction and lower life satisfaction. There is no logical reason for this and it may be most sensible to look for explanations in the statistical process. Despite the more limited role for some of the dimensions of the psychological contract, a general conclusion is that certain aspects have a major impact on well-being. In future research, some measures of the psychological contract, with an indicator of violation of the psychological contract as the strongest candidate, should be included in research exploring work-related well-being.

Returning to the evaluation of our model, which was presented once again at the start of this chapter, it is useful to bear in mind that it was originally designed, based on relevant theoretical and empirical literature, to identify factors that might help to explain why workers in temporary employment contracts reported lower well-being and related outcomes. In the event, we have had to use the model for a different purpose, namely to explain why temporary workers report higher well-being than permanent staff. The six sets of variables were included because the literature suggested that they were likely to have an impact on well-being. Our results have confirmed this and, as we have reported in this chapter, all six are consistently associated with well-being and with other outcomes.

The variables included in our model were also selected for their potential role as mediators of the relationship between employment contracts and well-being. The test of this mediating role has been less successful. While there has been some evidence of partial and even full mediation, most of the significant associations remain. For eight of the fifteen indicators of well-being and related outcomes, those on temporary contracts report significantly more positive results than those on permanent contracts. Specifically, permanent workers report more anxiety, depression and irritation, more presence at work when sick, lower job satisfaction, higher intention to quit, poorer general health, and lower life satisfaction. There is evidence that the intervening variables in the model mediated the relationship between type of employment contract and amount of sick leave, experience of harassment and violence, and the influence of work on life outside work. The association between type of employment contract and aspects of well-being is therefore a robust finding that has withstood quite rigorous statistical scrutiny. It may be accounted for by other variables that have not yet been identified in research elsewhere on this topic and which we failed to include in our study. We can find some clues in our study about where to look for an explanation. As we have noted at several points, the combination of a high workload, violation of the psychological contract, and comparatively lower organizational support, which suggest that permanent employees are too often taken for granted, may reflect negative features of contemporary permanent employment. This is an issue we return to in Chapter 10.

So far we have explored the results for the sample as a whole without considering in detail national differences or differences according to sector. Given some potentially important institutional differences between countries, it is possible that a more detailed exploration of country and sector differences might shed further light on the results. They therefore form the focus of Chapter 9.

NOTE

1. Strictly speaking, the actual amount of independent additional variance after taking account of all other factors is the R^2. In order to calculate this, the effect sizes would need to be squared. For example, autonomy, with an average effect size of 0.8 in the table reflects an R^2 of 0.0064 or 0.64% variance explained.

9

International Comparisons of Employment Contracts, Psychological Contracts, and Worker Well-Being

Rita Claes, René Schalk, and Jeroen de Jong

INTRODUCTION

This chapter examines national influences on the role of temporary employment contracts, psychological contracts, and on the influence of employment contracts on well-being and other outcomes. The core issues of interest are whether the national context and the related differences in norms and values affect the adoption and utilization of employment contracts, the content and fulfilment of psychological contracts, and how these relate to workers' well-being.

Country-specific factors are particularly likely to affect the behaviour of employers. For example, aspects of the labour market might influence the reasons for hiring temporary workers as well as the type of temporary workers hired. National norms and values might influence the psychological contracts offered by employers to permanent and temporary workers and their perceived obligations to fulfil the promises they make. This chapter therefore focuses on both employer and employee data.

While the emphasis in this chapter is primarily on national factors, the influence of sector differences is also examined. Our sample covered three sectors: food manufacturing, retail services, and education. These sectors were selected because of availability and accessibility in all participating countries, because of the amount of temporary workers in each sector, and the range of skills and educational levels represented across them. In practice, these sector categories were interpreted quite broadly when the data were collected, so the rationale for expecting differences was potentially compromised. We therefore focus more on country differences.

The chapter is structured as follows. We start by characterizing the country-specific context of the participating countries in terms of six societal dimensions that are relevant for psychological contracts. These societal dimensions can potentially be used to interpret patterns in the findings, but the main reason for considering them is to determine the extent of similarities and differences across countries and therefore the likely influence of national differences. We then examine our data sets to compare national and sectoral influences on reasons for hiring temporary workers and reasons for accepting temporary work. This is followed by an exploration of national and sectoral influences on psychological contracts. Finally, we assess the relative importance of country and sector influences compared with organizational and individual factors on the relationship between type of employment contract and the various outcomes included in the study. The concluding discussion offers tentative interpretations of the findings. For more detailed technical descriptions of the methods, we refer the reader to Chapter 2 of this book, and for a description of the development of the qualitative comparative analysis, outlined in the following section, to the relevant Psycones reports (2004, 2005).

NATIONAL COMPARISONS OF FACTORS THAT MIGHT INFLUENCE EMPLOYMENT CONTRACTS AND PSYCHOLOGICAL CONTRACTS

The European Union has been seeking standardization of various aspects of employment legislation, including legislation affecting the employment of temporary workers. Nevertheless, there is still some scope for national interpretation of such legislation, reflecting the traditions, norms, and priorities of each country. We know that there are persisting differences in the proportions of temporary workers across European countries in general, including those in our sample. We might expect even more scope for national differences in psychological contracts, and national factors seem likely to have a bearing on the way psychological contracts function in the interplay between employers and employees (Schalk and Soeters, 2009). We agree with Rousseau and Schalk (2000a, b), Schalk and Rousseau (2001), Thomas, Au, and Ravlin (2003), and Westwood, Sparrow, and Leung (2001) that we need to explore the cross-national contexts of psychological contracts, particularly bearing in mind the expansion of multinational firms and labour markets and the need to understand any key national influences on psychological contracts and on their consequences. Rousseau and Schalk's book *Psychological Contracts in Employment: Cross-National Perspectives* (2000) showed that there are differences in psychological contracts between the thirteen countries that were examined. However, the data were not strictly comparable across all countries, and in this respect, the present study may provide a more rigorous comparison and analysis of country differences.

The study of country differences

'Country' is a potentially broad proxy for a range of different and complex influences on behaviour. A number of researchers, such as Hofstede (2001) and Schwartz (1999), have attempted to measure characteristics of national cultures and then to identify clusters of countries with similar cultures. In doing so, they imply that in important respects the similarities between countries within a cluster may outweigh the differences. Others have adopted what is typically described as an 'institutional' approach (Whitley, 1999) to national comparisons in which the role of key institutional factors that are likely to have a bearing on national systems and behaviour are identified and compared.

In this study, we were particularly interested in factors that might explain national differences in the role of employment contracts and psychological contracts. We therefore adopted a more institutional approach but also sought to take some account of the national cultural context. Our aim was to seek factors that might lead us to expect differences in the role of employment contracts and psychological contracts across the seven countries included in our research. Following a thorough literature review and after the consultation with experts from different disciplines in each of the countries, described in Chapter 2, six societal dimensions were identified as being likely to have a major influence on the content and impact of employment contracts and, more particularly, psychological contracts. Specific indicators for each of the dimensions were suggested by experts. In total, twenty-seven indicators were selected for the six dimensions. The most reliable comparative data with which each of the indicators could be measured were identified and used. In cases where no comparative data could be found, the experts were asked to provide an appropriate rating. This body of information was then used as a basis for cross-country comparisons.

Country comparisons on key national dimensions

Below we describe the six dimensions. In addition, we point out the potential impact of each dimension on employment contracts and psychological contracts. We then use these dimensions to describe any distinctive national characteristics for the seven countries included in the study based on information available for the period at the start of data-collection (i.e. 2003–4).

Laws and regulations include legal facilitators and constraints that shape the conditions for both the formal employment contract and the psychological contract. Firstly, laws and regulations define the zone of negotiability, the bargaining space for employer and employee (Rousseau and Schalk, 2000a). The zone of negotiability is determined by state laws and regulations, and by any (central) agreements between unions and employers. A narrow zone of negotiability may constrain both the circumstances under which temporary workers can be employed and the scope for variability in the content of the psychological contract. Secondly, sanctions for violation incorporated in laws and regulations may inhibit breach of the rules concerning the employment of temporary workers and breach of the psychological contract. Thirdly, laws and regulations help to define the issues that may be, or in some cases must be, either agreed in contracts of employment or bargained over by representatives of employers and employees.

The industrial relations system is 'the system by which workplace activities are regulated, the arrangement by which the owners, managers and staff of organizations come together to engage in productive activity. It concerns setting standards and promoting consensus. It is also about the management of conflict' (Pettinger, 2000, p. 1). The industrial relations system shapes employer–employee exchanges at various levels (societal, industry, organizational, and workplace) and in so doing may affect the psychological contract at the individual level as well. The level of trade union power, for which trade union density can be used as an indicator, may be brought to bear on an organization's policy concerning the employment of temporary workers.

The labour market and the economic system. The labour market refers to the exchange of labour supply and demand within the broader economic system. The current and anticipated labour market is likely to influence the use of temporary workers. The degree of welfare support in a society, as an outcome of the economic system, may also influence the content of both the employment contract and the psychological contract.

The educational system (the provision of education, development, and training for children, young people, and adults) affects the employment contract and the psychological contract in at least three ways. Firstly, the educational system constrains or facilitates an organization's ability to obtain employees with the skills they need. Secondly, the educational system affects the individual's market power, including power to negotiate both the type of employment contract and the content of the psychological contract (Rousseau, 2005). Thirdly, the educational system establishes school-to-work pipelines, prepares people for employment, and helps to create norms and expectations about the nature of work and employment.

Family orientation refers to family structure and family ties. The family structure (e.g. large family, single-parent, or dual-earners household) and family ties can influence both the type of employment contract and the content of the psychological contract that employees seek in order to satisfy their family obligations. Depending on the societal attitude towards their role, parents, and in particular mothers, may seek employment contracts and psychological contracts that can accommodate family obligations.

Cultural values, according to Schwartz (1999, p. 25), are 'implicitly or explicitly shared abstract ideas about what is good, right, and desirable in a society'. These values are likely to influence employment contracts and the psychological contract. In the first place, they can facilitate or constrain one's ability to enter into agreements (Rousseau and Schalk, 2000b; Schalk and Rousseau, 2001). Secondly, cultural values can influence the kind of exchanges that are considered to be negotiable. Thirdly, cultural values can give different meanings to whether promises and obligations have been kept. Fourthly, cultural values can influence perceptions of the nature and meaning of fairness and trust, which, we have argued, help to determine the state of the psychological contract. To assess the cultural values in the different countries, we used Schwartz's cultural map of the world (Schwartz, 1994a).

The current study collected data in six member states of the European Union (covering countries in the north, south, and west of Europe) and in Israel. Rousseau and Schalk (2000a) argue that psychological contracts can only develop in countries that comply with two key requirements, namely a minimum level of personal freedom and a minimum degree of social stability. The countries we examined fulfil Rousseau and Schalk's key requirements for studying psychological contracts.

Cross-country differences on the six comparative dimensions

The main purpose in identifying core societal dimensions and developing operational measures for each of them was to establish the degree of similarity or difference between the seven countries. This in turn would help to predict whether country-level factors are likely to make a significant contribution in explaining the use of temporary employment, the nature of the psychological contract, and the relationship between employment contracts and outcomes. Furthermore, where major national differences emerge, the analysis of the specific dimensions might help to explain the nature of the country effect.

In the event, both the available data and expert feedback revealed only a few often relatively minor differences between the countries. We found significant outlier countries on twelve of the twenty-seven societal indicators we included in our analysis, with five countries revealing at least one distinctive and relevant societal characteristic. The Netherlands is characterized by a particularly high percentage of part-time employment. Sweden has a particularly favourable attitude towards working mothers. The United Kingdom combines a very large zone of negotiability with very few sanctions for violations; further, it has very weak family ties. Spain combines very low rates of part-time employment, fertility, and divorces with very strong family ties and highly egalitarian cultural values (i.e. 'transcendence of selfish interests in favour of voluntary commitment to promoting the welfare of others', Schwartz, 1994b, p. 111). Israel has a very limited welfare state, a very high fertility rate, and a very high score on educational expenditure. Additionally, Israel's cultural values are characterized by low harmony (i.e. 'fitting harmoniously in the environment', Schwartz, 1994b, p. 111), high embeddedness (i.e. 'maintenance of status quo, propriety, and restraint of actions or inclinations that might disrupt the solidarity group or the traditional order', Schwartz, 1994b, p. 111), and low egalitarianism. Belgium and Germany are very similar to the other Psycones countries with no outlying characteristics.

Despite some apparent differences on elements of Schwartz's cultural dimensions, all seven countries fall in two adjacent regions of values on Schwartz's cultural map of the world (1994a) and are thus rather similar in their scores on cultural values. Belgium, Germany, the Netherlands, Spain, and Sweden are in the 'West Europe' region of values, which is characterized as attributing a high level of importance to egalitarianism and intellectual autonomy. 'These are cultures in which individuals are viewed as autonomous but subject to legitimate expectations to concern themselves voluntarily with the welfare of their fellow citizens' (Schwartz, 1994b, p. 111). Israel and the United Kingdom are in the 'English-speaking' region of values, which emphasizes the importance of affective autonomy and mastery. 'These are entrepreneurial cultures in which mastering and controlling the environment are central goals' (Schwartz, 1994b, p. 111).

On the basis of this broad analysis of societal dimensions, we expect more similarities than differences among the seven countries in the likely impact of employment contracts on well-being and other outcomes and in the content and consequences of psychological contracts across the countries studied.

THE RELATIVE IMPORTANCE OF COUNTRY AND SECTOR FOR PSYCHOLOGICAL CONTRACTS

In this section, we use our data to examine the role of countries and sectors in explaining variations in the various aspects of psychological contracts and, more briefly, well-being. Ideally, we would use multilevel analysis but with only seven countries and three sectors, it is not possible to undertake conventional multi-level analysis. We therefore included the country and sector level indicators in our regression analyses reported in Chapters 3, 6, and 8. The regressions show the amount of overall variation in the dependent variable explained by the range of independent variables and also indicate which specific variables had a significant influence on the outcome. The analyses reveal that the country variables were often significant. The next step is then to determine the relative proportion of explained variance attributable to different levels of aggregation, namely individual, organization, sector, and country. For example, in the employee sample, all the independent variables explain 26 per cent of the variation in breadth of content of the psychological contract. The question we are particularly interested in, in this chapter, is what proportion of that 26 per cent can be attributed to country or sector level. The results of these analyses are presented below, first for the employer data, and after that for the employee data.

Employer data

Table 9.1 shows the proportion of the variation in responses of employers that can be explained by the national, sector, and organizational levels. In a regression analysis, the adjusted R-squared score tells us the percentage of total variation in responses on a dependent variable that can be explained by the items included in the analysis. If these items explain 20 per cent of the variation in responses, then we are interested in the proportion of that 20 per cent that can be explained by country or sector differences. This proportion might range from 0 to 100 per cent. Table 9.1 reveals that the major part of the variation in employers' reports of the psychological contract can be explained by factors at the organizational level, a minor part is attributable to the country level, and a very small part is explained by the sector. More specifically, organizational-level factors account for between 84 and 89 per cent of the variation, national factors account for

Table 9.1 Percentage of variance explained by different levels of analysis for psychological contracts in the employers' data set

	Employers (*n*)	Organization (%)	Sector (%)	Country (%)
Permanent workers				
Content of employers' obligations	188	89	1	10
Content of employees' obligations	202	84	1	15
Delivery of employers' deal	187	88	2	10
Delivery of employees' deal	183	86	1	13
Temporary workers				
Content of employers' obligations	186	86	2	12
Content of employees' obligations	202	84	0	16
Delivery of employers' deal	184	88	1	11
Delivery of employees' deal	180	86	2	12

between 10 and 16 per cent, and sector-level factors account for between 0 and 2 per cent. This is the case for psychological contracts of employers with respect to both temporary and permanent employees.

Additional analyses revealed only two significant country-specific differences. Belgian employers reported a significantly narrower content of the psychological contract (i.e. lower number of employer and employee promises and obligations) for both permanent and temporary workers compared to most countries. Spanish organizations reported a significantly broader content of temporary workers' promises and obligations, as judged by employers, compared with most other countries.

In summary, it appears from these results that it is organizational policies and practices that explain most of the variation in employers' views of psychological contracts with national characteristics playing only a minor part while sector has almost no influence.

Employee data

With the employee data, we can compare four levels by adding the individual level to country, sector, and organization. Analysis of the employee responses again confirms the limited impact of country differences. As Table 9.2 reveals, around 90 per cent of the variance was explained at the individual level. The variance explained by the country level varied between 3 and 5 per cent. This was somewhat lower than the variance explained by the organizational level (3–7%), but higher than the variance explained by the sector level (0–2%).

Table 9.2 Percentage of variance explained by different levels of analysis for psychological contracts in the employees' data set

	Employees n	Individual (%)	Organization (%)	Sector (%)	Country (%)
Content of employers' promises and obligations	5,271	91	6	1	3
Content of employees' promises and obligations	5,284	88	6	2	5
Fulfilment of employers' promises and obligations	4,999	92	6	0	3
Fulfilment of employees' promises and obligations	5,188	92	3	0	5
Trust	5,285	89	7	0	4
Fairness	5,294	89	6	0	5
Violation of the psychological contract	5,183	90	7	0	4

In considering the results in Table 9.2, we must take into account the dominance of the individual level in the analysis. This category included variables such as hours, occupational level, and tenure. It is therefore an amalgam of individual characteristics, such as age and family responsibilities and current employment experiences. The organizational level was restricted to size, public–private sector, proportion of temporary workers employed, and type of establishment; it did not include potentially important features such as organizational culture, leadership style, and strategy which were beyond the scope of this study. The analysis of employee responses may therefore underplay the significance of organizational factors. Nevertheless, this does not affect the key finding which is the limited impact of the country and sector levels.

With respect to employee well-being and related outcomes, similar analyses and tests as above were performed and showed that the major part (87–97%) of worker well-being was explained by the individual level. A minor part was explained by the organization (1–7%) and by the country (2–8%). A barely existent part (0–1%) was accounted for by the sector. The conclusion is that country factors also appear to have a limited impact on variations in employee well-being.

Country differences in psychological contracts

Although the country level accounts for only a small proportion of the variation in psychological contracts, there are, nevertheless, some significant differences between countries on each of the psychological contract measures. The data presented in Chapter 6, and more specifically in Tables 6.1 and 6.2, provide information with which to compare the psychological contracts across the seven countries. Here, we summarize how each country differs from the average across the seven countries in the sample on the basis of data provided by employees about both the employers' promises and obligations and their own.

Sweden has a smaller content of employer promises and obligations, lower fulfilment of employer promises, and a smaller content and lower fulfilment of employee promises.

Germany has a smaller content of employer promises and obligations, lower fulfilment of employer promises, lower violation of the psychological contract reported by employees, and higher fulfilment of employee promises.

The Netherlands is close to the average with respect to employer promises and obligations and has smaller content and lower fulfilment of employee promises.

Belgium has lower violation of the psychological contract reported by employees and a lower fulfilment of employee promises.

Spain has a broader content of employer promises and obligations, lower levels of violation of the psychological contract reported by employees, and a larger content of employee promises.

Israel has a smaller content of employer promises and obligations, lower fulfilment of employer promises, more violation of the psychological contract reported by employees, and higher fulfilment of employee promises.

The United Kingdom has a broader content of employer promises and obligations, more violation of the psychological contract reported by employees, and a smaller content of employee promises.

The analysis in Table 6.1 also reveals significant country effects with respect to levels of trust and fairness. Both are significantly higher in Germany, the Netherlands, Belgium, and Spain and significantly lower in Sweden, Israel, and the United Kingdom.

With respect to sector, compared with the retail services sector, education has a smaller content and higher fulfilment of employer promises and obligations, and both food manufacturing and education have a smaller content of employee promises and obligations.

This section has shown that there are some significant differences between countries with respect to the psychological contract. However, it has also shown that national characteristics play only a minor part in explaining the overall variation in psychological contracts. We should therefore not give much weight to national differences.

COUNTRY INFLUENCE ON REASONS FOR HIRING TEMPORARY WORKERS AND UNDERTAKING TEMPORARY WORK

Psychological contracts and well-being reflect individual perceptions and experiences and we might therefore expect them to be largely determined by factors at the individual and workplace or organizational levels. On the other hand, reasons for hiring temporary workers or for seeking to become a temporary worker may be more strongly influenced by societal factors such as legislation and the state of the labour market. In this section, we therefore explore country differences in the use of temporary employment, reasons offered by employers for hiring temporary workers, and motives outlined by employees for accepting temporary work.

Proportion of temporary employees in the sample

The overall ratio of permanent to temporary employees in our sample is about 60:40. We should bear in mind that the sample was deliberately biased to ensure a sizeable proportion of temporary workers and it proved easier to gain access to organizations employing large numbers of temporary workers in some countries than in others. As a result, there are quite marked differences in the proportion of temporary workers in the national samples ranging from approximately 20 per cent in the United Kingdom to 50 per cent in Belgium. These figures bear no direct relation to the actual proportion of temporary workers in each country which, in 2005, ranged between 5.5 per cent in the United Kingdom and 33.3 per cent in Spain (OECD, 2006).

We used a technique (Chi-squared automatic interaction detection) on the employee data set to identify any national differences in the personal and work-related characteristics of permanent and temporary employees. This revealed both similarities and differences between countries. Organizational tenure, sector, and supervisory position were the main factors associated with the type of employment contract. In all countries, longer organizational tenure predictably corresponded with having a permanent contract. In most countries, respondents employed in the manufacturing sector were more likely to have permanent contracts. In Israel, the Netherlands, and Spain, having a position as supervisor was related to having a permanent contract. In Sweden, being a union member and not having an additional job were also associated with having a permanent contract. In the UK education level and in Israel age were associated with permanent employment. Gender, living conditions, household contribution, hours worked per week, and night shifts showed no association with the type of employment contract in any of the seven countries. We should emphasize again that these results are specific to our sample and should not be generalized to the wider national populations of permanent and temporary workers in these countries.

Employers' reasons for employing temporary workers

Table 9.3 highlights the influence of country and sector in explaining employers' reasons for using temporary workers. The results show that most of the variation (between 76 and 96 per cent according to the reason) is explained by the organization. Country-level factors explain between 2 and 20 per cent, while the sector level explains between 0 and 9 per cent. Country influence is the strongest with respect to the use of temporary workers to cover for unfilled vacancies, followed by limiting the recruitment of core workers, testing out new employees, and covering long-term absence. Spain, in particular, makes more extensive use of temporary workers to cover unfilled vacancies.

These results are plausible in suggesting that labour market factors at the national level exert some influence on employers' motives for hiring temporary workers. Similarly, sectors feature more strongly with respect to the influence of peaks in production and the requirement for specialist skills, both of which might quite plausibly be sector-specific issues.

Table 9.3 Percentage of variance explained by different levels of analysis for employer motives for using temporary workers

	Employers (n)	Organization (%)	Sector (%)	Country (%)
Peaks in production	185	87	9	4
Replace due to short absence	188	94	0	6
Replace due to long absence	187	84	4	12
Unfilled vacancies	182	76	4	20
Specialized skills	184	91	5	4
Limiting core workers	183	83	3	14
Improving performance	182	96	2	2
Testing new employees	185	84	2	14
Working unusual hours	185	89	3	8
Saving salary costs	184	93	1	6
Saving training costs	185	92	4	4
Saving benefits costs	184	90	0	9

Workers' reasons for choosing temporary employment

When we turn to reasons why workers accepted temporary employment, the findings reveal that, when the total explained variance is put to 100 per cent, the major part (more than 81%) is explained by the individual level or the workplace level, up to 15 per cent by the organization level, a lesser part by the country (up to 9%), and a very minor part (up to 2%) by the sector. A more detailed inspection of the country data reveals an almost total lack of country differences.

In summary, the results presented so far suggest that country and sector levels play only a rather minor part in explaining variations in psychological contracts, even though there are some statistically significant albeit small country differences with respect to specific dimensions of the psychological contract. We also found some evidence of national differences in employers' reasons for hiring temporary workers, but again the influence of the national level remains relatively small. The differences between sectors are consistently smaller and able to explain only a very minor proportion of the overall variance. In considering the wider significance of these results, we need to take into account some consideration of how much national variation we might expect and more specifically, what proportion of the explained variance we might reasonably expect to attribute to country-specific factors. Our comparison based on the six identified dimensions suggested that we should expect relatively little variation between countries and analysis of our data has confirmed that this is indeed the case.

COUNTRY AND SECTOR INFLUENCES ON RELATIONSHIPS BETWEEN EMPLOYMENT CONTRACTS, PSYCHOLOGICAL CONTRACTS, AND WORKER WELL-BEING

In this section, we take the comparison of country differences a step further by examining whether country and sector have an influence on employee well-being and, in particular, on the relationships between employment contracts, psychological contracts, and employee well-being.

The influence of country and sector on the relationships between type of employment contract, the psychological contract, and well-being was examined by exploring the interaction effects of countries and sectors. With respect to the countries, Israel was used as the comparison country, and for sectors, retail services was the comparison sector. In other words, we explored whether the associations between type of employment contract, aspects of the psychological contract, and employee well-being reported in previous chapters were affected by country or sector; and we did this by comparing each country in turn with Israel and each sector with retail services to provide standard bases for comparison. We tested country interactions and sector interactions for each of fifteen outcomes related to worker well-being; that is, a total of 1,050 interactions. Given the very large number of tests of interactions, we only considered an interaction significant when its standardized regression coefficient had a low chance of occurring ($p < .01$). On this basis, there were significant country or sector differences in only 18 out of 1,050 interactions (thus, not even 2%). This is only a little above what we might expect by chance, indicating once again that national- and sector-level factors have only a very minor influence.

Because any significant results might be a product of chance effects, we should view them with considerable caution. With this in mind, we briefly review some of the significant associations. First, we explore the effect of country and sector on the relationship between type of employment contract and employee outcomes; then, we explore their impact on the relationship between the psychological contract variables and employee outcomes.

There are only six significant interactions where either country or sector affected the relationship between the type of employment contract and worker outcomes. Compared with Israel, which served as the reference or comparison country in all cases, occupational self-efficacy and organizational commitment in Belgium were lower among permanent workers. In Germany, workers in permanent employment reported more interference of work on home life. In Sweden, occupational self-efficacy was lower among permanent workers. In the United Kingdom, permanent workers reported lower perceived performance than temporary workers, as compared to Israel. Moving on to sector differences, compared with retail services, permanent employees from the manufacturing sector displayed lower job satisfaction than temporary employees.

When we explore the effect of country and sector on the relationship between the psychological contract variables and employee outcomes, there are twelve significant interactions. In Belgium and Germany, higher fairness is more likely to be associated with higher life satisfaction. In Spain, presence at work when sick increases slightly with higher fulfilment of promises and obligations by employees, whereas in Israel there seems to be a non-linear relation, with higher fulfilment of employee promises and obligations associated with either low or high sickness presence. In Spain, a broader content of the employer's psychological contract is associated with higher job satisfaction, and higher fairness is associated with higher organizational commitment and lower perceived performance. In Sweden, there is a significant interaction effect for sickness presence but it is very hard to interpret. In the United Kingdom, higher fulfilment of promises and obligations by employees is associated with lower presence at work when sick. Also, in the United Kingdom, higher fulfilment of employees' promises and obligations is associated with higher perceived performance, while the relationship is non-linear in Israel. Turning again to the effects of sector, compared with retail services, employees from the manufacturing sector who report a broader content of their own promises and obligations also report higher irritation and lower trust. Among employees from the education sector, a broader content of employee promises and obligations is associated with poorer general health.

In this section, we have reported the different relationships between the type of employment contract, psychological contract variables, and worker well-being variables, across countries. There are only a few significant inter-actions and, moreover, there is no coherent pattern to them implying that they may reflect random findings. The overall conclusion from this section supports the view that there is considerable similarity between the countries included in this study with respect to the effects of type of employment contract and features of the psychological contract on employee well-being and other outcomes.

DISCUSSION AND CONCLUSIONS

The results presented in this chapter have revealed some minor country effects and some minor, albeit statistically significant, differences between countries with respect to a range of issues associated with psychological contracts. In particular, we found some country differences in employer motives for hiring temporary workers, and in employee reports of their psychological contracts. However, compared to the contribution of the individual and organization levels in explaining variations in psychological contracts and worker well-being, the role of the country level is limited. The sector level has an even smaller effect. The absence of noteworthy country effects was reinforced when we explored interactions between country, psychological contracts, and worker well-being and found very few significant results.

The same pattern of results was found when we explored the relationships between type of employment contract and worker well-being and other outcomes. These relationships are similar in each of the countries we have examined. Our testing of the effect of country on the relationships between type of employment contract and worker well-being outcomes yielded only a few significant interactions. Furthermore, the results displayed no coherent or easily explained pattern.

In the Introduction to this chapter, we outlined a range of societal dimensions that might be expected to affect the employment relationship. Our preliminary conclusion, on the basis of the literature and the feedback from a number of experts, was that the similarities between the seven countries in our sample outweighed the differences. Analysis of the results from our seven-country study has confirmed this conclusion. We should not be surprised by this since one of the aims of the European Union is to promote harmonization of employment relations systems. Israel provided a comparator country but it, too, is similar in many relevant respects. Perhaps if we are to identify national differences, a more heterogeneous sample of countries will be needed.

Despite the limited impact of country differences in this study, it is important not to ignore them. We know that important differences exist between the countries in our sample in the proportion of workers employed on temporary contracts and in the proportion of part-time workers. Spain and Sweden provide interesting comparisons in this respect. In the analyses reported in this chapter, country effects have accounted for about 10 per cent of the explained variation in employer responses and about 5 per cent for employees; the figure is sometimes a little higher, and sometimes rather lower. This raises the question of what proportion of the variance we might expect to be accounted for by country factors. Evidence from other studies of relatively homogeneous countries, such as the Eurobarometer and European Social Surveys of worker satisfaction suggests that the country effect is generally low. In this context, we should perhaps not be surprised by the findings we have reported.

In summary, our answer to the questions 'Does country matter in explaining the role of type of employment contract in shaping worker well-being?' and 'Does country matter in explaining the role of the psychological contract in shaping worker well-being?' is 'not much'. A negative answer can be provided even more emphatically with respect to sector differences. As such, the current chapter's findings support the use of the total sample across countries presented in previous chapters. At the same time, we cannot afford to ignore the country effects altogether. In this study, country factors appear to have at least as much influence as in some other work-related pan-European studies. Set against this, the analysis reported in this chapter of the effects of different levels—individual, organization, sector, and country—confirms the importance of workplace experiences for work-related outcomes. Indeed, despite reference to the 'individual' level, it is work experiences, rather than individual factors that operate independently of work, that matter most. The analysis of the employer data reduces the levels of analysis but confirms the importance of what happens at the organizational rather than the sector or national level in considering employment policy and practice. To reiterate, despite its explicit comparative framework, the Psycones study confirms that worker well-being is largely determined by experiences at work. The onus therefore lies on the social partners and in particular the employers, to ensure that appropriate policies and practices are in place.

10

Conclusions

Kerstin Isaksson, David E. Guest, and Hans De Witte

INTRODUCTION

The main aim of this large international study was to explore the impact of temporary employment on workers' satisfaction and well-being. A second major aim was to investigate whether the psychological contract had a role in explaining this relationship. The research was conducted in the context of a policy debate and a series of European legislative activities that have been based on the assumption that those on temporary contracts are significantly disadvantaged. Indeed, this was the basis of our initial hypothesis. However, the main conclusion of this book must be that the results failed to support this assumption and the related hypothesis. Instead, those on permanent employment contracts reported lower levels of satisfaction and well-being on almost all our measures. This is even more surprising, considering the additional finding that permanent employees were far more likely than temporary employees to indicate that they had their contract of choice. This result proved robust even after controlling for a range of possible confounding factors, both individual and work-related. It is important at this stage to emphasize that 'lower' levels of satisfaction and well-being do not necessarily imply 'low' levels. While there are significant differences between permanent and temporary workers, both are more positive than negative on most outcomes. Therefore, we are left with the unanticipated and counter-intuitive but quite consistent finding that those on permanent employment contracts report lower levels of satisfaction and well-being than those on temporary contracts. The aims of this concluding chapter are to review these unexpected results, set them in the context of current research, consider some possible explanations for the findings, and discuss their implications for organizations, workers, and policy makers.

A literature review conducted at the outset of our project (De Cuyper, Isaksson, and De Witte, 2005) clearly indicated that results from studies comparing permanent and temporary employees were very heterogeneous.

Some studies characterized temporary employment as casual, precarious work and highlighted its disadvantages, but other studies showed no difference between permanent and temporary workers; and a few studies even reported more positive outcomes among temporary workers. The review also highlighted a range of methodological issues that we sought to address in this study. A more recent and updated review by De Cuyper et al. (2008) confirms that researchers are still reporting mixed results. There was, therefore, a clear need for more controlled comparative studies within a coherent analytic framework. For example, the initial review had identified a range of possible intervening variables, largely unexplored at that time, and an inability to determine whether any differences between the experiences, attitudes, and behaviour of permanent and temporary workers could be due to differences in individual factors or job characteristics. This review of research studies formed the background for our theoretical model and the rigorous design presented in the early chapters of this book.

The issue of differences between countries was also an important starting point for the project. The literature review (De Cuyper, Isaksson, and De Witte, 2005) presented a rather diverse picture with varying levels of temporary employment and flexible working across the European countries. Most countries have been promoting flexibility because of its anticipated positive impact on employment rates (e.g. Belgium and the Netherlands) and in fighting unemployment (e.g. Spain, the Netherlands, and Germany). For example, in Germany, there has been a series of legal changes aimed at making temporary employment more attractive to employers and employees. Efforts to achieve 'flexicurity', aiming to meet both employers' and employees' concerns by highlighting the need for flexibility and security, have become a major European issue. Nevertheless, compared to permanent employees, temporary workers are likely to be more vulnerable in the labour market: they are generally younger, less educated, and less skilled. This vulnerability is reflected in the wage gap between workers on different contract types (OECD, 2002). This evidence about the greater disadvantage and vulnerability of temporary workers helped to inform our initial assumptions that they would experience lower levels of satisfaction and well-being compared to their permanent counterparts.

The Psycones project was designed to address and, where possible, overcome many of the weaknesses in previous studies in this field. It has given us comparable data from more than 5,000 permanent and temporary workers employed in over 200 organizations across six European countries and Israel. Three sectors are included in the study: food manufacturing, retail services, and education. This allowed us to explore the experiences of temporary employment among workers in different types of work, with a focus on relatively low skilled blue-collar workers in food manufacturing, intermediate white-collar workers in retail services, and professional workers in education. By comparing permanent and temporary workers undertaking the same or very similar work in each context, we were able to provide a more direct comparison of their experiences than has often been possible in previous studies. We also collected data from senior managers in over 200 organizations. This provided insights into employment policy as it relates to temporary work, permitted some matching of employer and employee responses, and also allowed us to gain distinctive insights into the mutuality of the psychological contract. Indeed, this is the first large-scale European study of the psychological contract. It provides data from a multifaceted measure and permits analyses of the relative importance of different features of the psychological contract for outcomes such as satisfaction and well-being.

A critical question is, of course, the generalizability of these results. Although our sample of temporary workers was large ($n = 1,981$) and heterogeneous, a majority (62%) had fixed-term contracts. This seems to be broadly representative of practices across the countries in our study (De Cuyper, Isaksson, and De Witte, 2005). The fact that mean tenure on the job was relatively long (more than two years for temporary workers) and that weekly working hours were as high as thirty-six for the temporary workers (significantly lower, but with a larger variation than the permanently employed) give indications of relative stability. The most frequently reported reason cited by employers for hiring temporary workers was that they needed substitutes during longer absence of permanent workers. Although the sample includes all types of temporary contract, it has relatively few workers in highly casual work at the most precarious end of the employment continuum. When we compared the responses of the different categories of temporary worker, including those on casual, on-call, and agency contracts, the attitudes and levels of well-being were broadly similar. The within-group differences were invariably smaller than those between temporary and permanent workers. It was for this reason that we treated the temporary workers in our sample as a single group for the purposes of analysis. On this basis, we would argue that it should be possible to generalize our results. Having said this, some caution is warranted regarding generalizations across sectors and organizations. The sample was deliberately selected from a restricted range of sectors and from organizations that employ more than the normal proportion of temporary workers, and the results may therefore not be generalizable to all sectors and organizations.

Having argued that the research was carefully designed to address many of the weaknesses in previous studies and can potentially be generalized, what are the key findings? The following section explores these and relates them to some of the existing literature.

THE CORE FINDINGS

Temporary workers report higher satisfaction and well-being than permanent workers

In Chapter 4, we compared the attitudes, well-being, and behaviour of permanent and temporary workers and showed that temporary workers were significantly more positive on several of these outcomes. These differences could not be explained by demographic differences or job characteristics, which were controlled for in the analyses. These findings clearly challenge our initial assumptions that temporary workers will be disadvantaged and this will be reflected in their attitudes and well-being.

The analysis in subsequent chapters revealed that other factors seem to be more important for well-being than the formal employment contract. Several of these factors were identified in our initial literature review and incorporated into our analytic model; and they mostly concern relations between managers and their subordinates in the workplace. Factors consistently associated with lower worker well-being are violations of the psychological contract, low levels of fulfilment of perceived promises and commitments made by the organization, lack of support from supervisors and managers, and, last but not least, a heavy workload. These factors apply to workers on permanent employment contracts more than to those on temporary contracts. One conclusion is that although the employment contract has a significant effect on worker well-being, a number of other factors are more important determinants.

Our core conclusion that temporary workers, irrespective of the type of temporary employment, report higher well-being than permanent workers needs to be set in the context of the existing literature, since it differs from many, though not all, previous studies. One of the major European reviews, incorporating twenty-seven studies and drawing heavily on Finnish research (Virtanen et al., 2005), concluded that there was higher psychological morbidity among temporary as compared to permanent workers. According to the authors, the health risk associated with temporary work seemed to be dependent on the level of instability of the temporary contract. In other words, the most unstable contract forms such as agency and on-call contracts had more negative health consequences than other forms of temporary contracts. Other studies, such as Bernhard-Oettel, Sverke, and De Witte (2005) and another Finnish study (Saloniemi, Virtanen, and Vahtera, 2004), comparing permanent employees with relatively stable temporary staff in the health-care sector, reported similar results to ours with the same or higher levels of well-being among temporary workers.

Our study is cross-sectional and it has generally been difficult to conduct longitudinal studies or studies over time of temporary workers because of the high rate of attrition. The European Survey of Working Conditions uses repeated representative samples. Using this data set, Benach et al. (2002) explored the job satisfaction of temporary workers comparing results from ES1995 and ES2000 and reported similar results from both years. Temporary workers (including those on fixed-term and temporary agency contracts) reported high percentages of dissatisfaction with their jobs, but low levels of stress.

A longitudinal study is reported by Bardasi and Francesconi (2004) based on a British panel from 1991 to 2000. Looking at the impact of temporary employment (seasonal, casual, and fixed term) on individual well-being, they conclude that temporary employment does not seem to have adverse health effects over time for either men or women. This was true even controlling for a range of background characteristics. However, there was evidence that job satisfaction was lower among seasonal and casual workers. A longitudinal study of continuous temporary employment reported that it does not lead to unfavourable outcomes over time and that there are no differences in the impact of changes between those who move from permanent to permanent, temporary to temporary, or temporary to permanent jobs (De Cuyper, Notclaers, and De Witte, 2009).

In summary, although the more recent evidence remains somewhat inconsistent, there is evidence from some of the longitudinal research and from other carefully conducted studies supporting the conclusion that temporary work is not damaging to individual well-being. Our study goes further in suggesting that temporary workers report higher well-being than permanent workers. One distinctive point to note is that most of the other reported studies have been conducted in a single country and often with temporary agency workers. The results of the Psycones study are very similar across the seven countries and emerge after controlling for a large number of potentially confounding variables. We can therefore be confident that across these countries, at the time the data were collected in the middle of the decade, the experience of work was more positive for temporary than for permanent workers; or, to put it another way, in a period of increasing work intensity, it was more negative for permanent workers. This is a point we return to later in the chapter.

The psychological contract affects the relationship between employment contract and well-being

The conceptual model that informed the Psycones project assumed that the psychological contract would play a key role affecting the relationship between the type of formal employment contract and well-being, as it might be crucial in shaping employees' attitudes and behaviour (Anderson and Schalk, 1998). More specifically, as McLean Parks, Kidder, and Gallagher (1998) have noted, the subjectivity inherent in psychological contracts might be more useful in assessing the impact of temporary versus permanent employment than a classification based on objective criteria such as contract duration, hours of work, or type of temporary contract. This view is strongly supported in our results (Chapter 6). Aiming to capture the full richness and complexity of the psychological contract, we used a range of different measures based on reports by both managers and their employees. In addition to content and fulfilment, we also captured perceived violations to the contract as well as fairness and trust, two more basic concepts underlying the idea of a contract. The matched data from employees and managers also provided an opportunity to measure mutuality and reciprocity in the psychological contract.

Based on our conceptual framework, the second broad hypothesis that guided the research was therefore that the psychological contract, measured in a variety of ways, would affect the relationship between the employment contract and the range of outcomes. The analysis reported in Chapter 6 showed that there was some support for this hypothesis in the evidence of full or partial mediation of a number of relationships. In this context, it was the measure of violation that appeared to be most strongly associated with outcomes. The breadth of the content of the psychological contract had relatively little association with outcomes. On the other hand, workers' views on their own promises to their organization and the degree to which these had been fulfilled did have rather more impact. This aspect of the psychological contract has been relatively neglected in most research and these are interesting findings that merit more analysis.

Our initial review of the area (De Cuyper, Isaksson, and De Witte, 2005) indicated that permanent workers would have different psychological contracts with more extensive, more complex, and more ambiguous or relational reciprocal obligations, expectations, and promises than temporary workers. These will be positive to the extent that they offer greater breadth and depth but may be more difficult to fulfil. Our findings confirm that permanent workers do, on average, have broader psychological contracts than temporary workers, as reported by both the employees themselves and their employers. But they also show that they were significantly less likely to be fulfilled and this was accompanied by higher levels of violation of the psychological contract and lower reported levels of fairness and trust in management.

Despite some mediation by the psychological contract measures, there was still evidence that type of employment contract was significantly associated with a number of outcomes and in most cases this showed that those on permanent contracts reported more negative outcomes than those on temporary contracts. Since the psychological contract only acts as a full mediator on four of the thirteen dependent variables, this leaves much to be explained. The third implicit hypothesis in the study, again reflected in the conceptual model outlined in Chapter 1, was that four other classes of variables—employment prospects (including perceived job security), volition, job characteristics, and support—would act as additional mediators. However, the results reported in Chapter 8 showed very little support for this hypothesis. The variables were chosen because the literature review suggested they would have an impact on well-being and this was confirmed in our analyses. But they did not add to the explanation of how employment contracts relate to well-being. Given the quite extensive literature emphasizing, for example, the importance of being on contract of choice, this was a surprising finding. We had expected that the psychological contract would be the most important mediator and, given the limited impact of the other variables, this view was supported. As the analysis in Chapter 8 reveals, violation of the psychological contract, followed by fulfilment of the psychological contract had the largest effect sizes. These were followed by perceived organizational support, being in job of choice and autonomy.

The different psychological contracts of permanent and temporary workers reflect different treatment by employers

A major advantage of this study was the collection of data about employment policy and perceptions of the psychological contract from over 200 employers. A small majority of them (53%) claimed that there was no difference in the treatment of workers on different employment contracts. This reply seems to be the official policy, whereas the more detailed reports about the promises and obligations made to permanent and temporary workers gave an impression of more widespread inequality. Despite this claim, managers on average reported that their organization made significantly more promises to permanent than to temporary workers, and this is reinforced by the responses from the workers themselves. Also, the permanently employed themselves report a wider responsibility towards their organization compared to the temporary workers. The matching of employer and employee descriptions of the content of the psychological contract and how it relates to the employment contract clearly confirms that both parties have higher expectations of mutual contributions for permanent as compared to temporary workers and this is matched with higher expectations of returns. Beyond the exchanges in the psychological contract, all parties agree that on average, permanent workers experience more HR practices than temporary workers.

Employment of temporary workers seems to make employers more cautious about the promises they make since our evidence shows that organizations that report that the size of their temporary workforce is growing report making fewer promises to both permanent and temporary workers. Employees in organizations with a larger temporary workforce, reflected in the proportion of the workforce they represent, seem to have more difficulty managing their permanent staff since they report that they are less likely to keep their promises to permanent workers who, in turn, are less likely to keep their promises to them. But this increase in the failure to keep mutual promises does not arise with temporary workers in this kind of context.

Employers' accounts of the psychological contract have little influence on employer outcomes

Despite the evidence of greater investment in permanent workers, most managers were satisfied with the performance of both permanent and temporary staff and, if anything, were marginally more satisfied with the performance of their temporary staff. Despite this, levels of voluntary turnover and more particularly dismissals of temporary staff were high. Given the high levels of satisfaction with performance, we must assume that the dismissals relate to removing temporary workers when they are no longer required. The recent financial crisis has shown that this assumption holds, with temporary workers being dismissed in high numbers as one of the first reactions at the onset of the crisis. A closer look at the reasons for employing temporary workers showed that numerical flexibility seemed to be in operation to provide cover where necessary but, contrary to assumptions in sections of the literature, not primarily to reduce costs. In the context of the financial crisis and associated cutbacks, priorities may have changed.

As we have already noted, a growing temporary workforce was associated with a lower content of the psychological contract for both permanent and temporary workers. A higher proportion of temporary employees in the workforce was associated with management perceptions of less fulfilment of the psychological contracts of permanent employees, raising interesting questions of cause and effect. However, the employer reports of the various aspects of the psychological contract were not associated with any outcomes. The single exception, noted above, was that where employers perceived that permanent employees fulfilled their promises and obligations to the organization, employers were more satisfied with their performance. This did not hold true for temporary workers. The lack of association between employers' accounts of the psychological contract and outcomes may be at least partly explained by the broader, more generalized, and more objective outcome measures collected from employers.

Mutuality has only a limited association with outcomes

Data on the psychological contracts of employers allowed us to explore the issue of mutuality and determine whether agreement between the employer representative and workers about the content of the psychological contract affected outcomes. The relevant findings were reported in Chapter 7. Levels of agreement about promises and their fulfilment were generally rather low, perhaps reflecting the use of a senior manager as the employer representative when such managers may not always be in close contact with the workers who participated in the survey and therefore not in a good position to know how these workers perceived the promises and obligations. Agreement was higher for permanent workers and higher on the content of employee rather than employer promises. There was a general tendency for the person making promises to report more than they were perceived to be making by the other party. The analysis of fulfilment of promises and obligations revealed that the most common pattern was a positive balance, with both parties reporting high fulfilment. But the next most common pattern was one in which workers kept their promises while employers failed to keep theirs, raising questions about the strength of the norm of reciprocity among employers. While an initial analysis indicated that mutuality had a positive impact on employee outcomes, when the measures of fairness and violation of the psychological contract were introduced into the analysis, these easily outweighed any influence of mutuality. This finding raises questions about the importance of mutuality in the psychological contract and reinforces the importance of taking into account issues of fairness of treatment in assessing outcomes.

Type of employment contract is not the most important predictor of well-being

Contrary to our initial expectations, the type of employment contract continued to be significantly associated with a range of well-being and other outcomes even after we included a number of potential mediating variables that the literature had indicated as likely to be important. However, this finding needs to be set in context. While most of the potential mediators failed to operate in this role, they were still strongly associated with a number of the outcomes and in so doing were more influential than the nature of the employment contract. If we take the average variance accounted for in work-related well-being, general health, and work attitudes as an indicator of relative importance, then twelve variables were more important, or at least as important as the employment contract. The results, set out in Chapter 8, show that these included components of all the potential mediating variables including the psychological contract, organizational and supervisory support, features of job content such as autonomy and workload, aspects of volition such as job and profession of choice, and employment prospects, including employability and job insecurity.

In short, most of the mediating variables are significantly associated with at least some of the outcomes and are often more strongly associated with them than type of employment contract. While these results provide a wider basis for understanding the factors associated with worker satisfaction and well-being, they do not detract from the significance of the findings highlighting the negative role of being in permanent as opposed to temporary employment. Despite all the different variables controlled for and investigated, permanent workers still report poorer outcomes on several of the health and well-being variables compared with temporary workers.

Organizational or workplace experiences have a greater influence than country and sector differences

A critical and novel feature of the Psycones study was the exploration of differences between countries and sectors. The aim was to increase the relevance of results on a European level by estimating country effects and by using carefully defined societal dimensions and indicators to compare countries. Interpretations about country differences, however, must be made bearing in mind the non-representative samples. Six societal dimensions were identified and are described in Chapter 9. These emerged from a review of earlier research as well as interviews with national experts in order to identify dimensions relevant for the psychological contract. The resulting dimensions were laws and regulations, the industrial relations system, the labour market and economic system, the educational system, family orientation, and cultural values.

Our conclusion is that the similarities between the seven countries in our sample outweighed the differences. This is the case with respect to the comparison of the six societal dimensions and also with respect to the pattern of survey findings. The sample consisted of old member states in the European Union, with Israel as a comparator, but it, too, is similar in many relevant respects. A comparison of the three sectors also revealed far more similarities than differences, despite the different types of workers selected within each sector.

We conducted a form of multilevel analysis, reported in Chapter 9, to investigate how the different levels contributed to explaining variation in individual attitudes and job perceptions. The first part of this analysis explored how far the different levels explained variations in the psychological contract variables. The second explored the interaction between first the country and then the sector on the relation between employment contracts and the psychological contract variables and the various individual outcome measures. Using the employee data, the analysis revealed that variations in the psychological contract were largely explained by individual and workplace or work experience factors. These accounted for about 90 per cent of the explained variation. Organizational factors such as size accounted for about 6 per cent, leaving about 4 per cent that was explained by country factors and almost nothing explained by sector level. In the employer sample, where there were no individual or workplace variables, organizational-level factors accounted for about 90 per cent of the variation, leaving the remainder to be explained at country or sector level. What both sets of results reveal is that country and more particularly sector have very little influence on individual or even organizational outcomes. This was confirmed by the analysis of the interactions; almost none of them was statistically significant. We can therefore conclude that employee well-being and satisfaction is largely affected by individual characteristics and workplace experiences and the country and sector in which people work has relatively little direct effect on this. Furthermore, the workplace experiences, positive or negative, appear to have a similar impact on outcomes in each country.

HOW CAN WE EXPLAIN THE HIGHER LEVELS OF
WELL-BEING AMONG TEMPORARY WORKERS?

The central and unexpected finding in our study is that temporary workers report higher levels of well-being and satisfaction than permanent workers. While this is not the first study to report such findings, it seems to be the first to report them across all types of temporary employment, even including casual and on-call workers. These findings therefore require some explanation.

The first point to consider is that the results might be an artefact of the research method and the sample. With respect to the sample, we deliberately selected organizations that employed a sizeable number of temporary workers. This was partly a matter of research convenience to limit the number of organizations we had to approach to gain access. It is possible that in settings where there are more temporary staff, the sheer number requires management to consider more carefully how they should be managed. It may also mean that the demands on permanent workers are greater while at the same time, management may neglect the interests of permanent workers (see e.g. De Cuyper et al., 2009). One of the findings from the employer survey was that organizations with a higher proportion of temporary staff had higher levels of quits among permanent, but not temporary staff. While we cannot disentangle cause and effect, this suggests that permanent workers in such organizations may be more disaffected than those in perhaps more typical organizations where temporary workers are a much smaller minority.

Other aspects of the research methods seem less likely to have affected the results. The sample size allowed us to control for a large number of background variables. These included measures of age and family obligations so that we cannot explain the results as being a product of a large proportion of younger workers and students among the temporary sample. The implicit hypotheses that informed the study were based on the assumption that temporary workers would be disadvantaged and report lower well-being. We included a wide range of mediating variables, including factors such as job insecurity and employment contract of choice, which we assumed might help to explain this disadvantage. In the event, they did not have the influence we had expected. The analyses that we conducted were mainly conventional regressions, and it is possible that tests of interactions and use of structural equation modelling might have provided fuller insights; but we have no reason to believe that they would change the core finding.

The data were collected in a period around 2004 and 2005, a time of relative prosperity throughout Europe. It is possible that at the time, variables such as job insecurity that are strongly associated with temporary work were less salient. If the research had been conducted during an economic downturn, it is possible that temporary work would have appeared relatively less attractive. On the other hand, it can be argued that in times of high unemployment, temporary work attracts less of a stigma (Boyce et al., 2007), particularly if it can serve as a stepping stone to a permanent job. This supports the case for further research in a different economic climate where unemployment is higher.

A rather different explanation for the unexpected results might lie in an analysis of what has been happening to permanent jobs in recent years. There is evidence from some European countries that work has become more intense and demanding (Green, 2006). In some cases, such as Germany, this may be reflected in high levels of demand within constrained working hours; in others such as the United Kingdom, it can mean longer working hours. The evidence from this study is that permanent workers report a higher workload. An allied issue, noted above, is that organizations may be taking permanent workers for granted. Our analysis of tenure indicates that those who have spent longer in an organization are more likely to have experienced violation of the psychological contract and to report less fairness of treatment or trust in management. Interestingly, temporary workers who have been with an organization for a longer than average period begin to adopt the characteristics of permanent workers (Clinton and Guest, 2008); but unlike the claims of the research by Virtanen et al. (2005), this is manifested in greater disaffection rather than the opposite. By implication, it is not so much that temporary work has improved but that in buoyant economic times, permanent work has become more demanding and less attractive for many.

IMPLICATIONS FOR FUTURE RESEARCH AND FOR POLICY

Implications for future research

One of the implications of the preceding section is that the Psycones survey should be repeated in the context of economic recession. Allied to this, one of the limitations of the Psycones project is that it is cross-sectional. Future research needs to conduct longitudinal studies of temporary work in different economic and life cycles and with a longer time frame. The research reported by De Cuyper, Notelaers, and De Witte (2009) is a useful step in this direction. Although we found no major differences between types of temporary worker, future studies should also seek to incorporate more casual workers and those in jobs that would be described as highly precarious as well as covering other sectors of the economy. The similarities between participating countries were larger than the differences. Although we included participants from north, south, east (Germany), and west, we still feel that it would be valuable to replicate the study in some of the new Eastern European member states (Rigotti, Otto, and Mohr, 2007). Finally, while the Psycones research deliberately focused on subjective perceptions of health and well-being, future research of this type would be considerably strengthened by the use of independent outcome measures to reduce the potential impact of common method variance.

Future research on temporary work

Our results have several important implications for future research about temporary employment. First of all, our data do not really support notions about distinctions in attitudes between subgroups of temporary workers divided by qualifications or education. Results cannot confirm arguments about a distinction made by Marler, Barringer, and Milkovich (2002) between high skill, 'free workers' who voluntarily enter into temporary employment and low skill, 'precarious workers' who want more security. In the Psycones results, education level has almost no association in the regressions with outcomes. The professionals in our sample, mostly teachers, do not seem to be more positive towards temporary work than the sales personnel in retail or the blue-collar workers in manufacturing. Neither the free agent nor the precarious employment types seem to be sufficient to explain our findings.

Another issue of some importance concerns assumed differences related to objective and subjective characteristics of the temporary workers. The subjective preferences and motives for accepting a temporary contract seem far more important than objective criteria such as type of temporary contract, duration, or time remaining. As for preferences and volition, the most important factor appeared to be whether an individual felt that the present job was one that he or she preferred most (see also Bernhard-Oettel et al., 2008). This proved to be more important than being on a preferred contract, even though previous research had supported the assumption that this was of vital importance for the well-being of temporary workers (see e.g. Krausz, 2000a; Isaksson and Bellaagh, 2002). In the context of psychological contracts however, future research needs to aim at a clarification of the mechanisms behind these preferences and their consequences.

We have noted that temporary workers with longer contracts appear to develop attitudes that are closer to those of permanent workers. Previous research has suggested that this means they become more positive in various respects. Our research suggests that since permanent workers have more negative attitudes, it means the opposite. Further research is needed linking the tenure of temporary workers, as well as the overall time spent as a temporary worker, to their attitudes to determine whether tenure as a temporary worker has a positive or negative impact on outcomes.

Gender issues related to employment contracts merit further research. In our sample, we found very few gender-related effects. However, there do seem to be gender-related differences in the motives for accepting temporary work and in the meaning that it has for the individual.

Research on psychological contracts

The psychological contract, especially violation and fulfilment of promises and obligations helped to explain variations in attitudes and well-being. This study has reinforced the view that it is no longer enough to use fulfilment or non-fulfilment as a proxy for violation or breach. Instead, we have shown that fulfilment and violation should be treated as separate features of the psychological contract. Since it seems so important for outcomes, the further development of a robust measure of violation should be a priority.

Earlier research has to a very high degree concentrated on what the organization promises to its employees and how the psychological contract is perceived by employees. In this study, focusing on the employer's side has proved its value for the exchange and needs further exploration and inclusion in theoretical models. Future research should try to collect data from organizational agents to whom employees report directly. Mutuality and reciprocity, concepts assumed to be vital for the functioning of the psychological contract, clearly need further investigation. Although we only undertook a relatively limited exploration of these concepts, our results seem to contradict the belief that a balanced deal has positive effects. What we were able to show was that it is the fairness of the deal, reflected in both a general perception of fairness as well as any feeling that the contract has been violated, that has the stronger association with outcomes. This reinforces the need to take fuller account of fairness in assessing the psychological contract. Finally, the measurement and analysis of promises and commitments made by employees—the employee side of the psychological contract—is another of the dimensions of the psychological contract which has not been studied to a large extent. Yet, it had a strong association with some of the outcomes in this study, suggesting that its role should be incorporated in future studies aiming to investigate the employment relationship in an exchange framework. It can give clues to fairness in a context where fairness and trust seem to play an important role in our understanding of the state of the psychological contract and as guiding principles for the employment relationship in general.

We believe that one of the strengths of the Psycones study is the use of an elaborate model that makes assumptions about the nature, causes, and consequences of the psychological contract, and sets the psychological contract alongside other variables that have been shown in many studies to have an important impact on employee outcomes. We believe that this model, which incorporates an extensive array of measures of what we have termed the state of the psychological contract (Guest, 2004b), stands up well to scrutiny. In particular, we have found that some of the measures of the psychological contract appear to have stronger associations with outcomes than a number of more well-established measures. However, both the model and this finding in particular need further testing. They may also benefit from more rigorous forms of statistical analysis.

Much of the previous research on the psychological contract has drawn a distinction between transactional and relational psychological contracts. While this distinction has conceptual attractions, in practice the boundaries between them have proved difficult to draw, and previous research has not consistently supported an empirical distinction. Factor analysis in this study failed to support any distinction based on these dimensions and given the potentially idiosyncratic and dynamic nature of psychological contracts, we are not convinced that the pursuit of this distinction is likely to prove fruitful. On the same basis, in this study, with our large and wide-ranging sample, we used dimensions of the psychological contract that emerged both from previous research conducted by team members as well as from our extensive pilot study. We believe that the content of the psychological contract used in future research should be context-relevant and ideally derived from initial work in that context rather than based on standardized, but potentially inappropriate measures. We would also argue that the concept of breadth of the psychological contract is potentially more useful than the transactional–relational distinction and our research confirms that breadth brings challenges in terms of fulfilling a range of promises and obligations, as noted in the responses from the permanent workers. Finally, we believe there is a need to test new theoretical ideas about the structure and development of the psychological contract (e.g. Isaksson et al., 2010).

General implications for policy and practice

The changing nature of employment, and especially the increase of various forms of temporary employment contracts, has been the focus of discussions among researchers and in political debates among policy makers and social partners across Europe. The deviation from the standard employment contract, characterized as open-ended full-time employment, has been the topic of much concern, and the implications are important for all those involved in the shaping of future labour markets. European Council directives have supported various measures in favour of equal treatment of temporary and permanent workers building on agreements between social partners. One possible conclusion from the Psycones research is that striving towards equal treatment seems to have had some success, at least on the surface. For example, 53 per cent of employers describe no difference and 35 per cent only small differences in their treatment of workers on temporary and permanent contracts. Yet under the surface, in terms of the content of psychological contracts and the application of HR practices, differences remain. Despite this, when we turn to the well-being, satisfaction, and general health of temporary workers, they do not seem to be disadvantaged.

Implications for employers

Many of the policy issues already raised are relevant to employers. Employers need to ensure equal treatment and non-discrimination of temporary workers. Legislation increasingly requires this at the formal level. We are just as concerned about what goes on at the informal level. A critical issue for companies is the connection between strategies regarding staffing and use of temporary workers and their implementation in the organization. Does the strategy involve supplementation or substitution of permanent workers? Our results show that the reasons for using temporary workers have different consequences for turnover rates among temporary and permanent workers.

The main policy implications for employers concern their permanent workforces. There is evidence that permanent workers are taken for granted, often at some cost both to the workers and the organization. There needs to be careful management of their workloads; care needs to be taken to provide them with support; and promises must be kept by senior and local management. There is some acknowledgement among managers that they are neglecting the norm of reciprocity; indeed, our research almost challenges whether this remains a norm among managers. The failure to keep promises is resulting in perceptions of unfairness and reduced trust; in other words, the state of the psychological contract is often poor. This seems to be central to the evidence of some disaffection among permanent workers and managers must strive to address this issue. The simple recommendation is 'do not make promises you cannot keep'.

There are some questions about the accuracy of employer perceptions of temporary workers from our research. A majority of employers report high levels of equal treatment of temporary and permanent workers. At the same time, both parties report also that employer promises are less far-reaching for temporary compared to permanent employees. The impression is that there is a gap between ideals and policies in the organization and their practical implementation in the workplace. The most important way to deal with this gap and the main conclusion from our book is that the informal psychological contract, its content, state, and fulfilment need to be taken seriously and fully understood at all managerial levels of the organization. It is a matter of some concern that employers' representatives seem more ready than employees to admit that they do not always keep their promises and that this view is endorsed by the workforce. Given the important consequences of violation and non-fulfilment of the psychological contract, employers need to take this issue more seriously and ensure that they keep those promises that can be met.

One place where employers might start is with HR policies and practices. In line with much other research (Guest, 1999; Appelbaum et al., 2000), we find that workers who experience more of a set of progressive HR practices also report a range of positive outcomes that are likely to be of benefit to both the individual and the organization. At the same time, we found quite a marked disparity between the HR practices that managers claimed were in place and those reported as experienced by workers. Addressing this 'practice–implementation gap' should be a policy priority. As well as producing benefits for the organization, it is likely to result in a more fulfilled psychological contract and higher levels of well-being among workers.

Implications for unions

Our evidence suggests that strong hostility to temporary employment is misplaced. Also, from a union perspective, it seems important to strive for a combination of flexibility, security, and quality of jobs. In doing so, unions need to pay strong attention to the well-being of their core traditional membership in permanent jobs. The evidence suggests that unions should continue to support progressive HR practices in the interests of their members. Union membership is generally low among temporary workers in all countries. It seems important for the future of unions to increase their support for, and membership among temporary workers as well as other workers engaged in various kinds of flexible employment.

Implications for European policy makers

The research was conducted in the context of a European policy debate and a series of European legislative activities that have been based on the assumption that those on temporary contracts are significantly disadvantaged. Our research has failed to support this assumption. However, our findings, consistent across participating sectors and countries, have provided something of a paradox. A majority of the temporary workers, including those with relatively stable contracts, reported that they would prefer permanent work. This remains the ideal, despite the underlying costs that we have identified. Temporary workers also reported lower levels of job security than their permanent colleagues. There is an extensive body of research demonstrating the negative consequences of job insecurity (Cheng and Chan, 2008). Nevertheless, our findings indicate that temporary workers report higher levels of well-being than those on permanent contracts, after controlling for every possible confounding factor that we could think of. One of the clues to this paradox seems to lie in the psychological contract. If job security is not promised and is therefore not part of the psychological contract of temporary workers, it will have fewer negative effects since there is no perceived breach (De Cuyper and De Witte, 2006, 2008).

Because our results indicate that temporary workers report higher job satisfaction and well-being than those in permanent contracts, does this imply that policies should be redirected to encourage more temporary work? Our answer to this question would probably be 'Not in general'. This is because of the reasons noted above, namely that temporary employees in all countries report a higher level of job insecurity and only a minority state that a temporary contract is their employment contract of choice. Most temporary workers report 'push' motives (e.g. 'It was the only type of contract I could get') rather than positive 'pull' motives (e.g. 'It gives me more freedom') for accepting temporary employment. There is a negative association between perceptions of job insecurity and well-being, while expectation of contract extension was strongly associated with job satisfaction and well-being among temporary employees. Although workers in temporary employment may not be aware of the hidden costs that we have identified in this study, permanent employment, preferably in the job and profession of choice, is still the ideal for most workers.

There has been much concern in Europe and beyond about what is described as precarious employment. Rodgers and Rodgers (1989) and Cano (2000) define precarious employment as low-quality jobs, which are bad for the well-being and health of employees. The definition incorporates several dimensions:

- Temporal—for example, degree of stability or certainty of continuing the job
- Organizational—for example, control over working conditions, pace, income, etc.
- Protection by law—for example, collective agreements or practice against unfair treatment, dismissal, etc., or social protection in terms of access to social security benefits during illness, accidents, unemployment, etc.
- Economic in terms of, for example, low income and vulnerability

On an objective basis, and using this definition, many temporary jobs would be defined as precarious. What we can argue is that the relationship between temporary employment, precarious employment, and worker well-being needs rethinking. Our findings clearly indicate that despite potentially falling within an objective definition of precarious work, the temporary employees in our sample do not, in general, display low well-being and poor health. As already noted, some of the factors within the 'organizational' dimension of precarious employment may need to be more highly weighted if our main concern is with the well-being and health of workers. The violation of the psychological contract, the lack of organizational support, and an excessive workload fall within this category and these have more negative consequences for permanent workers. This implies that policy makers need to balance the concern for objective indicators reflected in the characterization of precarious employment, with a greater concern for the informal psychological contract and the associated issues of fairness and trust in the workplace.

One way round some of the contradictions in these findings may be found in the concept of 'flexicurity'. If employers can feel safe in promoting flexible employment, while workers can feel reasonably secure, then there is the potential for mutual benefits. This is likely to be more salient in times of economic downturn when employers have pressures on costs and workers are more anxious about their job security. The European policies designed to protect the rights of temporary workers go some way to promoting flexicurity. A recognition of the inevitability of flexible working and the growth of various forms of flexible employment, coupled with our evidence that temporary employment does not appear to have the negative consequences often ascribed to it, suggests that policy makers may need to rethink the traditional assumption that the standard against which to judge employment is the full-time permanent job.

There is now a focus in Europe on job quality and our findings reinforce the importance of giving priority to this area. Legislation trying to balance flexibility and security also needs to include job quality. Our research has highlighted three main areas where quality can be improved and where a

European policy emphasis may pay dividends. The first concerns the design of jobs and workloads. The well-established research of Karasek (1979) and others shows the importance of balancing autonomy and demand. The permanent workers in our sample seemed to be suffering from overly demanding workloads. Secondly, the permanent workers in our study reported lower levels of organizational and supervisory support, yet both our research and many previous studies have highlighted the importance for well-being and commitment of strong organizational support. Thirdly, more attention needs to be paid to meeting the promises and obligations in the psychological contract. Employers themselves admit that they are more likely than their workers to fail to keep their promises or, by implication, to provide fair treatment. As a result, permanent workers reported more violation and less fulfilment of the psychological contract. While these are issues for organizational policy implementers, they also have wider implications. In Europe, the concept of the standard full-time, permanent job continues to be promoted as the ideal. Attention has therefore been focused on the disadvantages of those who are in atypical employment arrangements. This focus appears to have resulted in a neglect of the traditional worker. It is an ironic conclusion to this study of temporary workers that we are calling for a stronger focus on the well-being of the traditional permanent worker.

Questionnaire on the perception of work: employees

I. Present job and employment contract

1. What is your job in this organization?
(e.g. teacher, headmaster, salesperson, secretary, accountant, plant/machine operator)

_____

2. How would you classify your current job?
Please focus only on the actual tasks and activities you are performing in your job (*not taking your educational level into account*)

❏ Unskilled blue-collar worker
    (e.g. plant/machine operator, assembly line worker,...)
❏ Skilled blue-collar worker or foremen
    (e.g. electrician, fitter, technician,...)
❏ Lower level white-collar worker
    (e.g. typist, secretary, telephone operator, computer operator, shop assistant,...)
❏ Intermediate white-collar worker or supervisor of white-collar workers
    (e.g. computer programmer, schoolteacher, sales representative,...)
❏ Upper white-collar worker, middle management/executive staff
    (e.g. store/shop/sales manager, office manager, engineer, university lecturer,...)
❏ Management or director
    (e.g. departmental/section manager, senior manager, headmaster, rector, etc.)

3(a) How many hours per week do you usually work at this job?

_____ hours/week

3(b) Do you work night shifts?   ❏ No   ❏ Yes

4. How long have you been working in this organization?

_____ years (if less than one year: _____ months or _____days)

5. Do you supervise other employees?   ❏ No   ❏ Yes

6. Are you a union member?   ❏ No   ❏ Yes

7. In addition to this job, do you have any other paid job(s)?   ❏ No   ❏ Yes → **How many hours per week do you work on average in this other job(s)?**
_____ hours

8. Please answer the following questions about your job in this organization.

	Strongly disagree	Somewhat disagree	Partly agree partly disagree	Somewhat agree	Strongly agree
(a) My current job is my preferred job.	1	2	3	4	5
(b) My current profession/occupation is my preferred one.	1	2	3	4	5

9. Do you have a permanent contract with *this organization*?

Please answer YES *or* NO and then follow instructions.

☐ **YES**, I do have a permanent contract with this organization

Please continue on page 6 with question 12.

☐ **NO,** I do *not* have a permanent contract with this organization

Please answer the questions below.

a) Which type of contract best describes your current employment situation?
(Please tick more than one box if appropriate)

- ☐ Fixed-term contract (e.g. replacement contract, project-based contract, etc.)
- ☐ Permanent contract with employment agency
- ☐ Temporary contract with employment agency
- ☐ Daily/on-call
- ☐ Probation
- ☐ Training
- ☐ Seasonal employment
- ☐ Job creation scheme
- ☐ Subcontractor
- ☐ Consultant
- ☐ Other (please specify): _____

b) In total, how long is the duration of your current contract/assignment in this organization?

_____Years; _____Months; _____Days

☐ Not specified/Don't know

c) How much time do you have left in your contract/assignment in this organization?

_____Years; _____Months; _____Days

☐ Not specified/Don't know

d) In total, how long have you worked on temporary contracts/assignments so far in your lifetime (including your current one)?

_____Years; _____Months; _____Days

☐ Not sure

Please continue on the next page with question 10.

10. Please state to what extent you agree with the following statements.

	Strongly disagree	Somewhat disagree	Partly agree partly disagree	Somewhat agree	Strongly agree
(a) I think I will be employed in this organization for longer than has been agreed in my employment contract.	1	2	3	4	5
(b) I expect that I will have to leave here once my present employment contract/assignment with this organization has run out.	1	2	3	4	5
(c) I think my present employment contract/assignment will be renewed when it expires.	1	2	3	4	5
(d) I have been promised that I will get a permanent contract with this organization when my present contract/assignment expires.	1	2	3	4	5

11. I have a non-permanent contract because

	Strongly disagree	Somewhat disagree	Partly agree partly disagree	Somewhat agree	Strongly agree
(a) it is difficult for me to find a permanent job.	1	2	3	4	5
(b) it suits my present needs/situation (e.g. family, study, leisure, etc.).	1	2	3	4	5
(c) it offers me a higher wage than other employment contracts.	1	2	3	4	5
(d) it gives me more freedom.	1	2	3	4	5
(e) this way, I hope to gain a permanent employment contract.	1	2	3	4	5
(f) it offers me a supplementary income.	1	2	3	4	5
(g) it allows me to gain experience and expertise with different tasks and jobs.	1	2	3	4	5
(h) the contract was offered with the job I wanted.	1	2	3	4	5
(i) it was the only type of contract I could get.	1	2	3	4	5

Please go to the next question on the following page.

To be answered by everyone from now on

12. Please state to what extent you agree with the following statements.	Strongly disagree	Somewhat disagree	Partly agree partly disagree	Somewhat agree	Strongly agree
(a) My present employment contract suits me for the time being.	1	2	3	4	5
(b) I would prefer a different kind of employment contract to the one I have now.	1	2	3	4	5
(c) My current employment contract is the one that I prefer.	1	2	3	4	5
(d) The employment contract I have today is the one I want to have in the future.	1	2	3	4	5

II. Job characteristics and performance in your present job

13. How would you describe your present job?	Rarely or never	Not often	Sometimes	Rather often	Very often or always
(a) I do *not* know what my responsibilities are in performing my job.	1	2	3	4	5
(b) I can plan my own work.	1	2	3	4	5
(c) My job requires me to be creative.	1	2	3	4	5
(d) I know exactly what is expected of me in my job.	1	2	3	4	5
(e) I can carry out my work in the way I think best.	1	2	3	4	5
(f) I can choose my job assignments.	1	2	3	4	5
(g) I have an opportunity to develop my own special abilities.	1	2	3	4	5
(h) I know how to get my job done.	1	2	3	4	5
(i) I can vary how I do my work.	1	2	3	4	5
(j) My job requires a high level of skills.	1	2	3	4	5
(k) My job requires me to learn new things.	1	2	3	4	5
(l) I can influence the way my section is organized	1	2	3	4	5

14. Regarding your present job, how often

	Rarely or never	Not often	Sometimes	Rather often	Very often or always
(a) are you pressed for time?	1	2	3	4	5
(b) do you miss all or part of a (lunch)break because of having too much work?	1	2	3	4	5
(c) do you go home late because of having too much work?	1	2	3	4	5
(d) is a fast pace required in your work?	1	2	3	4	5

15. We now list some questions concerning *your last working week*. In your own judgement, how well did you fulfil the following tasks?

	Very badly	Rather badly	Neither well nor badly	Rather well	Very well
(a) Make decisions?	1	2	3	4	5
(b) Perform without mistakes?	1	2	3	4	5
(c) Devote yourself to work?	1	2	3	4	5
(d) Achieve your objectives?	1	2	3	4	5
(e) Take initiatives?	1	2	3	4	5
(f) Take responsibility?	1	2	3	4	5

III. Attitudes towards the job and organization

16. Please answer the following questions.

	No	Yes	Don't know
(a) Does this organization provide you with sufficient opportunities to express your views on issues and concerns at work?	1	2	3
(b) During the past 12 months, have you been provided with any training and development – such as on-the-job training or some sort of course or planned activity – to update your skills?	1	2	3
(c) Is there any serious attempt in your organization to make the jobs of people like you as interesting and varied as possible?	1	2	3
(d) Have you received a formal performance appraisal during the past year?	1	2	3
(e) Does your organization provide any support with non-work responsibilities – for example, childcare facilities, flexible hours, financial planning, or legal services?	1	2	3
(f) Does your organization actively carry out equal opportunities practices in the workplace?	1	2	3
(g) Does your organization take active steps to prevent any kind of harassment or bullying for people like you?	1	2	3
(h) Is your pay related to your personal performance in any way through some sort of performance- or merit-related pay in this organization?	1	2	3

17. Employer obligations:

Next follows a list of some promises and commitments which organizations sometimes make to their employees. For each, I would like you to consider whether such a promise has been made *by this organization*, either formally or informally, and the extent to which it has been fulfilled.

	Has your organization promised or committed itself to	No	Yes, but promise not kept at all	Yes, but promise only kept a little	Yes, promise half-kept	Yes, and promise largely kept	Yes, and promise fully kept
(a)	provide you with interesting work?	0	1	2	3	4	5
(b)	provide you with a reasonably secure job?	0	1	2	3	4	5
(c)	provide you with good pay for the work you do?	0	1	2	3	4	5
(d)	provide you with a job that is challenging?	0	1	2	3	4	5
(e)	allow you to participate in decision making?	0	1	2	3	4	5
(f)	provide you with a career?	0	1	2	3	4	5
(g)	provide a good working atmosphere?	0	1	2	3	4	5
(h)	ensure fair treatment by managers and supervisors?	0	1	2	3	4	5
(i)	be flexible in matching demands of non-work roles with work?	0	1	2	3	4	5
(j)	provide possibilities to work together in a pleasant way?	0	1	2	3	4	5
(k)	provide you with opportunities to advance and grow?	0	1	2	3	4	5
(l)	provide you with a safe working environment?	0	1	2	3	4	5
(m)	improve your future employment prospects?	0	1	2	3	4	5
(n)	provide an environment free from violence and harassment?	0	1	2	3	4	5
(o)	help you deal with problems you encounter outside work?	0	1	2	3	4	5

18. Looking overall at how far this organization has or has not kept its promises and commitments, to what extent do you agree with the following statements? I feel

		Strongly disagree	Somewhat disagree	Partly agree partly disagree	Somewhat agree	Strongly agree
(a)	happy	1	2	3	4	5
(b)	angry	1	2	3	4	5
(c)	pleased	1	2	3	4	5
(d)	violated	1	2	3	4	5
(e)	disappointed	1	2	3	4	5
(f)	grateful	1	2	3	4	5

19(a) Your obligations. The following list consists of some promises and commitments that people sometimes make to their organization. For each, I would like you to consider whether you made such a promise *to this organization*, either formally or informally, and the extent to which it has been fulfilled.

Have you promised or committed yourself to	No	Yes, but not kept promise at all	Yes, but kept promise a little	Yes, half-kept promise	Yes, largely kept promise	Yes, fully kept promise
(a) go to work even if you don't feel particularly well?	0	1	2	3	4	5
(b) protect your company's image?	0	1	2	3	4	5
(c) show loyalty to the organization?	0	1	2	3	4	5
(d) work overtime or extra hours when required?	0	1	2	3	4	5
(e) be polite to customers or the public even when they are being rude and unpleasant to you?	0	1	2	3	4	5
(f) be a good team player?	0	1	2	3	4	5
(g) turn up for work on time?	0	1	2	3	4	5
(h) assist others with their work?	0	1	2	3	4	5
(i) volunteer to do tasks outside your job description?	0	1	2	3	4	5
(j) develop your skills to be able to perform well in this job?	0	1	2	3	4	5
(k) meet the performance expectations for your job?	0	1	2	3	4	5
(l) accept an internal transfer if necessary?	0	1	2	3	4	5
(m) provide the organization with innovative suggestions for improvement?	0	1	2	3	4	5
(n) develop new skills and improve your current skills?	0	1	2	3	4	5
(o) respect the rules and regulations of the company?	0	1	2	3	4	5
(p) work enthusiastically on jobs you would prefer not to be doing?	0	1	2	3	4	5
(q) take responsibility for your career development?	0	1	2	3	4	5

19(b) Please answer the following questions about your working life in general.

	Strongly disagree	Somewhat disagree	Partly agree partly disagree	Somewhat agree	Strongly agree
*(a) I'm not sure what I'm going to do work-wise ten years from now.	1	2	3	4	5
*(b) When I think of what I'm going to do career-wise in the longer-term, things become very unclear.	1	2	3	4	5
*(c) The kind of work I'll do in the future is obvious.	1	2	3	4	5
*(d) What happens next in my career at work is anybody's guess.	1	2	3	4	5

20. Please answer the following questions.

	Not at all				Totally
(a) Overall, do you feel you are rewarded fairly for the amount of effort you put into your job?	1	2	3	4	5
(b) To what extent do you trust senior management to look after your best interests?	1	2	3	4	5
(c) Do you feel that organizational changes are implemented fairly in your organization?	1	2	3	4	5
(d) In general, how much do you trust your organization to keep its promises or commitments to you and other employees?	1	2	3	4	5
(e) Do you feel you are fairly paid for the work you do?	1	2	3	4	5
(f) To what extent do you trust your immediate line manager to look after your best interests?	1	2	3	4	5
(g) Do you feel fairly treated by managers and supervisors?	1	2	3	4	5

21. Please state to what extent you agree with the following statements.

	Strongly disagree	Somewhat disagree	Partly agree partly disagree	Somewhat agree	Strongly agree
(a) To know that my own work had made a contribution to the good of the organization would please me.	1	2	3	4	5
(b) I am optimistic that I would find another job, if I looked for one.	1	2	3	4	5
(c) Work should only be a small part of one's life.	1	2	3	4	5
(d) Chances are, I will soon lose my job.	1	2	3	4	5
(e) I am *not* happy with my job.	1	2	3	4	5
(f) I will easily find another job if I lose this job.	1	2	3	4	5
(g) These days, I often feel like quitting.	1	2	3	4	5
(h) I am often bored with my job.	1	2	3	4	5
(i) I feel myself to be part of the organization.	1	2	3	4	5
(j) My supervisor is helpful in getting my job done.	1	2	3	4	5
(k) Whatever comes my way in my job, I can usually handle it.	1	2	3	4	5
*(l) The future of my job here is uncertain.	1	2	3	4	5
*(m) I can control whether I stay in this job or not.	1	2	3	4	5
*(n) My employment here is completely safe.	1	2	3	4	5
*(o) My future employment here will depend largely on the things I do.	1	2	3	4	5

22. Please state to what extent you agree with the following statements.	Strongly disagree	Somewhat disagree	Partly agree partly disagree	Somewhat agree	Strongly agree
(a) My supervisor pays attention to what I am saying.	1	2	3	4	5
(b) I am sure I can keep my job.	1	2	3	4	5
(c) In my view, an individual's personal life goals should be work-oriented.	1	2	3	4	5
(d) My organization really cares about my well-being.	1	2	3	4	5
(e) I could easily switch to another employer, if I wanted to.	1	2	3	4	5
(f) My supervisor is concerned about the welfare of those under him/her.	1	2	3	4	5
(g) When I am confronted with a problem in my job, I can usually find several solutions.	1	2	3	4	5
(h) Despite the obligations I have made to this organization, I want to quit my job as soon as possible.	1	2	3	4	5
(i) My organization shows very little concern for me.	1	2	3	4	5
(j) Even if this organization was not doing too well, I would be reluctant to change to another employer.	1	2	3	4	5
(k) Most days I am enthusiastic about my job.	1	2	3	4	5
(l) I can remain calm when facing difficulties in my job because I can rely on my abilities.	1	2	3	4	5
(m) My organization strongly considers my goals and values.	1	2	3	4	5
(n) In my work, I like to feel that I am making some effort, not just for myself but for the organization too.	1	2	3	4	5
(o) The most important things that happen to me involve work.	1	2	3	4	5
(p) At this moment, I would like to stay with this organization as long as possible.	1	2	3	4	5
*(q) My future employment with this organization is unsure.	1	2	3	4	5
*(r) It's entirely up to me whether I remain in this job or leave.	1	2	3	4	5

23(a) Please state to what extent you agree with the following statements.

	Strongly disagree	Somewhat disagree	Partly agree partly disagree	Somewhat agree	Strongly agree
(a) I am quite proud to be able to tell people who it is I work for.	1	2	3	4	5
(b) I feel appreciated by my supervisor.	1	2	3	4	5
(c) I am confident that I could quickly get a similar job.	1	2	3	4	5
(d) I feel insecure about the future of my job.	1	2	3	4	5
(e) Work should be considered central to life.	1	2	3	4	5
(f) My organization cares about my opinion.	1	2	3	4	5
(g) If I could, I would quit today.	1	2	3	4	5
(h) I think I might lose my job in the near future.	1	2	3	4	5
(i) I find enjoyment in my job.	1	2	3	4	5
*(j) I am certain of what is going to happen to my employment here.	1	2	3	4	5
*(k) What happens regarding the future of my job here is largely out of my control.	1	2	3	4	5
*(l) I am not sure if I will have a job here soon.	1	2	3	4	5
*(r) It's entirely up to me whether I remain in this job or leave.	1	2	3	4	5

23(b) Please state to what extent you agree with the following statements.

	Strongly disagree	Somewhat disagree	Partly agree partly disagree	Somewhat agree	Strongly agree
*(a) I would feel anxious if my employment here was changing.	1	2	3	4	5
*(b) I like to know exactly what I'm going to do next job-wise.	1	2	3	4	5
*(c) I like to think of a new job in terms of a challenge.	1	2	3	4	5
*(d) Uncertainty regarding my employment would frighten me.	1	2	3	4	5
*(e) I think having a variety of jobs is key to enjoying your working life.	1	2	3	4	5
*(f) I like career things to be planned out in detail.	1	2	3	4	5
*(g) I would get worried if my future employment became uncertain.	1	2	3	4	5
*(h) I find the prospect of employment changes exciting and stimulating.	1	2	3	4	5
*(i) I like my future employment being clearly mapped out.	1	2	3	4	5

24. In the past few weeks, how often have you felt each of the following regarding your work?

		Rarely or never	Not often	Sometimes	Rather often	Very often or always
(a)	Tense	1	2	3	4	5
(b)	Calm	1	2	3	4	5
(c)	Uneasy	1	2	3	4	5
(d)	Cheerful	1	2	3	4	5
(e)	Worried	1	2	3	4	5
(f)	Enthusiastic	1	2	3	4	5
(g)	Depressed	1	2	3	4	5
(h)	Contented	1	2	3	4	5
(i)	Gloomy	1	2	3	4	5
(j)	Relaxed	1	2	3	4	5
(k)	Miserable	1	2	3	4	5
(l)	Optimistic	1	2	3	4	5

25. Please indicate your agreement with each statement.

		Strongly Disagree	Quite strongly disagree	Somewhat disagree	Partly agree partly disagree	Somewhat agree	Quite strongly agree	Strongly agree
(a)	I have difficulty relaxing after work.	1	2	3	4	5	6	7
(b)	Even at home, I often think of my problems at work.	1	2	3	4	5	6	7
(c)	I get in a bad mood when I am disturbed by others.	1	2	3	4	5	6	7
(d)	Even on holiday I think about my problems at work.	1	2	3	4	5	6	7
(e)	From time to time I feel like a bundle of nerves.	1	2	3	4	5	6	7
(f)	I get angry quickly.	1	2	3	4	5	6	7
(g)	I get irritated easily, even when I don't want to.	1	2	3	4	5	6	7
(h)	When I come home tired after work, I feel irritable.	1	2	3	4	5	6	7

26. How often does it happen that

	Rarely or never	Not often	Sometimes	Rather often	Very often or always
(a) you come home cheerfully after a successful day at work, positively affecting the atmosphere at home?	1	2	3	4	5
(b) you fulfil your domestic obligations better because of the things you have experienced in your job?	1	2	3	4	5
(c) you manage your time at home more efficiently as a result of the way you do your job?	1	2	3	4	5
(d) you are better able to interact with your spouse/family/friends as a result of the things you have experienced at work?	1	2	3	4	5

27. How satisfied do you currently feel about

	Very dissatisfied						Very satisfied
(a) your life in general?	1	2	3	4	5	6	7
(b) your family life?	1	2	3	4	5	6	7
(c) your leisure time?	1	2	3	4	5	6	7
(d) your state of health and well-being?	1	2	3	4	5	6	7
(e) your work–life balance?	1	2	3	4	5	6	7
(f) the financial situation of your household?	1	2	3	4	5	6	7
(g) your career at work?	1	2	3	4	5	6	7

28. Please answer the following questions about your last year with this organization (or the period of time if less than a year).

	Never	Once	2–3 times	4–5 times	More than 5 times
(a) How often have you been absent from work due to your state of health over the *last 12 months*?	1	2	3	4	5
(b) How often have you *gone to work* despite feeling that you really should have stayed away due to your state of health over the *last 12 months*?	1	2	3	4	5
(c) Have you had an accident in the workplace over the *last 12 months*? (Please count all accidents, even when you have continued to work the same day).	1	2	3	4	5
(d) Have you personally experienced any incidents of harassment or violence at work in the *last 12 months*?	1	2	3	4	5

29. In general, would you say your health is?

	Poor	Fair	Good	Very good	Excellent
(a)	1	2	3	4	5

Please state to what extent you agree with the following statements.

	Definitely false	Mostly false	Not false, not true	Mostly true	Definitely true
(b) I seem to get sick a little easier than other people.	1	2	3	4	5
(c) I am as healthy as anybody I know.	1	2	3	4	5
(d) I expect my health to get worse in the near future.	1	2	3	4	5
(e) My health is excellent.	1	2	3	4	5

IV. Background information

30. What is your age?

_____ years

31. Are you

❑ Female
❑ Male

32. Do you live with a partner?

❑ Yes
❑ No, I live with parents/family/friends
❑ No, I live alone

33. What is your financial contribution to the household income?

❑ Sole earner (100%)
❑ Main earner (more than 50%)
❑ Joint earner (about 50%)
❑ Contributory earner (less than 50%)

34. How many people are largely dependent on the household income (including yourself)?

_____ persons

35. Are you in your household the person mainly responsible for ordinary shopping and looking after the home?

❑ Yes
❑ I am equally responsible with one or more other people
❑ No, someone else is mainly responsible

36(a) Educational level?

- ❏ Doctorate
- ❏ Masters degree or other postgraduate qualification
- ❏ Degree
- ❏ NVQ Level 4/5, HND, HNC, Diploma in HE
- ❏ A-Levels, GNVQ Advanced, NVQ Level 3, modern apprenticeship, or equivalent
- ❏ GCSEs, O-Levels, GNVQ Foundation/Intermediate, NVQ Level 1/2, or equivalent
- ❏ No formal qualifications
- ❏ Other

36(b) How many years of full-time education did you complete? _____ years

❏ I am currently a student (*please tick*)

* Questions marked with an asterisk were only asked in the British survey and address issues
of uncertainity at work.

Questionnaire on the perception of work:
HR Manager

Characteristics of the company/organization

1(a) How many employees are working for this organization (including those having an employment contract with another company as, for example, temporary agency workers or subcontractors)?

employees

1(b) How many permanent employees are employed by this organization?

employees

2(a) This organization is
❑ Public
❑ Private

2(b) This organization is
❑ a single independent establishment not belonging to another body (go to Q3)
❑ head office of different establishments (go to Q3)

❑ one of a number of different establishments within a larger UK-owned organization/institution (go to Q2c)
❑ the sole UK establishment of a foreign-owned organization (go to Q2c)
❑ one of a number of different establishments within a larger foreign-owned organization (go to Q2c)

2(c) Does this organization independently implement HR policies?
❑ Yes, HR policies and their implementation are the *full or the main* responsibility of this organization.
❑ Yes, HR policies and their implementation are a *joint* responsibility of the umbrella organization and this organization.
❑ No, almost all decisions on HR policies are implemented by the umbrella organization/government.

3. Please indicate for each type of contract whether or not it is present in this organization. If present, please indicate *either* the exact figure *or* the proportion of it as compared to the total group of non-permanent employees using the answer options.

	Not present	If present, how many?	Present, but small minority 0–25%	Present, but minority 26–45%	Present, about half of the non-permanent workforce 46–55%	Present, majority 56–75%	Present, large majority 76–100%
Fixed-term contract (e.g. replacement contract, project-based contract,...)	0	1	2	3	4	5
Contract with employment agency	0	1	2	3	4	5
Daily/on-call	0	1	2	3	4	5
Probation	0	1	2	3	4	5
Training	0	1	2	3	4	5
Seasonal employment	0	1	2	3	4	5
Job creation scheme	0	1	2	3	4	5
Subcontractor	0	1	2	3	4	5
Consultant	0	1	2	3	4	5
Other (please specify): --------	0	1	2	3	4	5

4. **To the best of your knowledge, what proportion of employees are members of a union?** None 10% 20% 30% 40% 50% 60% 70% 80% 90% 100% Don't know

5. **In the past three years, have there been any changes in**
   (a) the number of employees?
   - ❏ Yes, the number of employees *increased*
   - ❏ Yes, the number of employees *decreased*
   - ❏ No, there were no significant changes in the number of employees
   (b) the number of non-permanent employees?
   - ❏ Yes, the number of non-permanent employees *increased*
   - ❏ Yes, the number of non-permanent employees *decreased*
   - ❏ No, there were no significant changes in the number of non-permanent employees

6. **Over the next three years, do you expect the workforce of this organization to**
   - ❏ grow?
   - ❏ stay the same?
   - ❏ get smaller?

II. HR and practices

In the following, please refer to the most common group of non-permanent workers in your organization.

7. Please answer the following questions about provision of HR practices:		No	Yes, but mainly to permanent workers	Yes, to both permanent and non-permanent workers	I don't know
(a)	Does this organization provide employees with sufficient opportunities to express their views on issues and concerns at work?	1	2	3	4
(b)	Is there any serious attempt in this organization to make the jobs of its employees as interesting and varied as possible?	1	2	3	4
(c)	Does this organization provide to the employees any support with non-work responsibilities – for example, childcare facilities, flexible hours, financial planning, or legal services?	1	2	3	4
(d)	Does this organization actively carry out equal opportunities practices in the workplace?	1	2	3	4
(e)	Does this organization take active steps to prevent any kind of harassment or bullying of its employees?	1	2	3	4

7(f) If you compare permanent to non-permanent workers, would you say that both get the same treatment and opportunities in your organization (e.g. career opportunities, remuneration, etc.)?
- ❏ Yes, exactly the same
- ❏ No, small differences → What kind of differences?
- ❏ No, rather large differences

8. What percentage of permanent and temporary employees have been provided with any training and development—such as on-the-job training or some sort of course or planned activity (period January–December 2003)?

(a) permanent employees (%)	None	10	20	30	40	50	60	70	80	90	100	Don't know
(b) non-permanent employees (%)	None	10	20	30	40	50	60	70	80	90	100	Don't know

9. What percentage of permanent and temporary employees have their performance regularly (e.g. quarterly or annually) formally appraised?

(a) permanent employees (%)	None	10	20	30	40	50	60	70	80	90	100	Don't know
(b) non-permanent employees (%)	None	10	20	30	40	50	60	70	80	90	100	Don't know

10. What percentage of permanent and temporary employees are covered by a system of pay related to their performance?

(a) permanent employees (%)	None	10	20	30	40	50	60	70	80	90	100	Don't know
(b) non-permanent employees (%)	None	10	20	30	40	50	60	70	80	90	100	Don't know

11. How often are the following factors instrumental in the use of non-permanent contracts by this organization?

In our organization, we use non-permanent contracts, because	Never	Not often	Sometimes	Rather often	Very often
(a) it helps to match staff to peaks in demand.	1	2	3	4	5
(b) it covers staff short-term absence/vacancies.	1	2	3	4	5
(c) it covers maternity or longer periods of staff absence.	1	2	3	4	5
(d) we are otherwise unable to fill vacancies.	1	2	3	4	5
(e) we can bring in specialist skills.	1	2	3	4	5
(f) we need a freeze on permanent staff numbers.	1	2	3	4	5
(g) it can improve our performance.	1	2	3	4	5
(h) we offer trial periods before employing a permanent employee.	1	2	3	4	5
(i) we would like to have personnel for unusual working hours (e.g. night-time, evening, and weekend).	1	2	3	4	5
(j) it saves wage-costs.	1	2	3	4	5
(k) it saves training-costs	1	2	3	4	5
(l) it saves fringe-benefit costs.	1	2	3	4	5

12. To what extent are you satisfied with

	Very dissatisfied						Very satisfied

(a)	the performance of employees on non-permanent contracts?	1	2	3	4	5	6	7
(b)	the performance of employees on permanent contracts?	1	2	3	4	5	6	7

13. How much influence do union/work council representatives have on the following aspects?

	No influence	Little influence	Moderate influence	Much influence	Very much influence
(a) Employment contracts	1	2	3	4	5
(b) HR practices	1	2	3	4	5
(c) Working conditions	1	2	3	4	5

14. How easy or difficult is it to fill vacancies?

Very easy	Easy	So-so	Difficult	Very difficult
1	2	3	4	5

III. Performance indicators

Please answer the following questions regarding performance indicators of your company for the year 2003 (1 January 2003 to 31 December 2003):

15. For permanent employees:

(a) How many permanent employees left this organization voluntarily?

(b) How many permanent employees were dismissed?

(c) What percentage of working time was lost due to sick leave of permanent employees?

(d) How many accidents involving permanent workers were reported?

16. For non-permanent employees:

(a) How many non-permanent employees left this organization voluntarily (quit before the contract ran out)?

(b) How many non-permanent employees got a renewal of contract or a permanent contract?

(c) What percentage of working time was lost due to sick leave of non-permanent employees?

(d) How many accidents involving non-permanent workers were reported?

IV. Employer–employee relations

Next follows a list of some promises and commitments which organizations sometimes make to their employees. For each, I would like you to let me know if such a promise has been made by your organization separately for permanent workers and then temporary workers. If yes, then please give me an answer from 1 to 5, where 1 means that your organization has not kept its promise or commitment to the employees and 5 means that it has totally kept its promise or commitment.

17. Employer obligations towards employees

Permanent Employees

Has your organization promised or committed itself to	No	Yes, but promise not kept at all	Yes, but promise only kept a little	Yes, promise half-kept	Yes, and promise largely kept	Yes, and promise fully kept
(a) provide employees with interesting work?	0	1	2	3	4	5
(b) provide employees with a reasonably secure job?	0	1	2	3	4	5
(c) provide employees with good pay for the work they do?	0	1	2	3	4	5
(d) provide employees with a job that is challenging?	0	1	2	3	4	5
(e) allow employees to participate in decision making?	0	1	2	3	4	5
(f) provide employees with a career?	0	1	2	3	4	5
(g) provide employees with a good working atmosphere?	0	1	2	3	4	5
(h) ensure fair treatment by managers and supervisors?	0	1	2	3	4	5
(i) be flexible in matching demands of non-work roles with work?	0	1	2	3	4	5
(j) provide possibilities of working together in a pleasant way?	0	1	2	3	4	5
(k) provide employees with opportunities to advance and grow?	0	1	2	3	4	5
(l) provide employees with a safe working environment?	0	1	2	3	4	5
(m) improve future employment prospects of employees?	0	1	2	3	4	5
(n) provide an environment free from violence and harassment?	0	1	2	3	4	5
(o) help in dealing with problems encountered outside work?	0	1	2	3	4	5

18. Employer obligations towards employees

Non-Permanent Employees

Has your organization promised or committed itself to	No	Yes, but promise not kept at all	Yes, but promise only kept a little	Yes, promise half-kept	Yes, and promise largely kept	Yes, and promise fully kept
(a) provide employees with interesting work?	0	1	2	3	4	5
(b) provide employees with a reasonably secure job?	0	1	2	3	4	5
(c) provide employees with good pay for the work they do?	0	1	2	3	4	5
(d) provide employees with a job that is challenging?	0	1	2	3	4	5
(e) allow employees to participate in decision-making?	0	1	2	3	4	5
(f) provide employees with a career?	0	1	2	3	4	5
(g) provide employees with a good working atmosphere?	0	1	2	3	4	5
(h) ensure fair treatment by managers and supervisors?	0	1	2	3	4	5
(i) be flexible in matching demands of non-work roles with work?	0	1	2	3	4	5
(j) provide possibilities of working together in a pleasant way?	0	1	2	3	4	5
(k) provide employees with opportunities to advance and grow?	0	1	2	3	4	5
(l) provide employees with a safe working environment?	0	1	2	3	4	5
(m) improve future employment prospects of employees?	0	1	2	3	4	5
(n) provide an environment free from violence and harassment?	0	1	2	3	4	5
(o) help in dealing with problems encountered outside work?	0	1	2	3	4	5

Next follows a list of some promises and commitments which employees sometimes make to their employers. For each, I would like you to let me know if you think such a promise has been made by the employees. If yes, then please give me an answer from 1 to 5, where 1 means that the employees have not kept their promises or commitments to the employer at all and 5 means that they have totally kept their promise or commitment. Similarly to the last question, you will be asked this first of permanent employees and then of non-permanent employees.

19. Employee obligations

Permanent Employees

As far as your organization is concerned, what do you think do permanent employees promise or commit themselves to?	No	Yes, but not kept promise at all	Yes, but kept promise only a little	Yes, half-kept promise	Yes, and largely kept promise	Yes, and fully kept promise
(a) go to work even if they don't feel particularly well?	0	1	2	3	4	5
(b) protect your company's image?	0	1	2	3	4	5
(c) show loyalty to the organization?	0	1	2	3	4	5
(d) work overtime or extra hours when required?	0	1	2	3	4	5
(e) be polite to customers or the public even when they are being rude and unpleasant?	0	1	2	3	4	5
(f) be a good team player?	0	1	2	3	4	5
(g) be punctual (prompt)?	0	1	2	3	4	5
(h) assist others with their work?	0	1	2	3	4	5
(i) volunteer to do tasks outside their job description?	0	1	2	3	4	5
(j) develop their competencies to be able to perform efficiently in their job?	0	1	2	3	4	5
(k) meet the performance expectations for their job?	0	1	2	3	4	5
(l) accept an internal transfer if necessary?	0	1	2	3	4	5
(m) provide the organization with innovative suggestions for improvement?	0	1	2	3	4	5
(n) develop new skills and improve their current skills?	0	1	2	3	4	5
(o) respect the norms and regulations of the company?	0	1	2	3	4	5
(p) work enthusiastically on jobs they would prefer not doing?	0	1	2	3	4	5
(q) be responsible for their career?	0	1	2	3	4	5

20. Employee obligations

Non-Permanent Employees

As far as your organization is concerned, what do you think do non-permanent employees promise or commit themselves to?	No	Yes, but not kept promise at all	Yes, but kept promise only a little	Yes, half-kept promise	Yes, and largely kept promise	Yes, and fully kept promise
(a) go to work even if they don't feel particularly well?	0	1	2	3	4	5
(b) protect your company's image?	0	1	2	3	4	5
(c) show loyalty to the organization?	0	1	2	3	4	5
(d) work overtime or extra hours when required?	0	1	2	3	4	5
(e) be polite to customers or the public even when they are being rude and unpleasant?	0	1	2	3	4	5
(f) be a good team player?	0	1	2	3	4	5
(g) be punctual (prompt)?	0	1	2	3	4	5
(h) assist others with their work?	0	1	2	3	4	5
(i) volunteer to do tasks outside their job description?	0	1	2	3	4	5
(j) develop their competencies to be able to perform efficiently in their job?	0	1	2	3	4	5
(k) meet the performance expectations for their job?	0	1	2	3	4	5
(l) accept an internal transfer if necessary?	0	1	2	3	4	5
(m) provide the organization with innovative suggestions for improvement?	0	1	2	3	4	5
(n) develop new skills and improve their current skills?	0	1	2	3	4	5
(o) respect the norms and regulations of the company?	0	1	2	3	4	5
(p) work enthusiastically on jobs they would prefer not doing?	0	1	2	3	4	5
(q) be responsible for their career?	0	1	2	3	4	5

Technical Appendix

In this appendix, we present the information about the various measures used in the study, together with their psychometric properties. These measures are all contained in the employee and employer questionnaires presented in Appendix 1.

Employee questionnaire

In this section, we describe the derivation and use of the items in the employee questionnaire and the psychometric properties of each scale. These are based on the statistics produced by both exploratory and confirmatory analyses [1] to assess the factorial validity of scales for the overall sample, and equivalence testing across countries and between the temporary and permanent workers. Equivalence testing is used to assess whether the measures are appropriate in each country and in the two categories of temporary and permanent workers. Additionally, we present measures of internal consistencies across country samples, and separately for temporary and permanent workers using Cronbach's alphas. Table A2.1 presents the psychometric data for the total sample, and Table A2.2 presents the comparative data for each of the subgroups. Unless otherwise stated, the findings of these analyses supported the validity and reliability of each of the measures we used in the questionnaire and the equivalence of the measurements in each country and contract type at acceptable or very close to acceptable levels.

Independent variable—employment contract

Participants were asked to indicate their employment contract from a list of eleven possible contract types that were observed during the pilot stage. The eleven types of contract were as follows: permanent contract, fixed-term contract, permanent contract with employment agency, temporary contract with employment agency, daily or on-call, probation, training, seasonal employment, job creation scheme, subcontractor, and consultant. Respondents were also given the chance to give an alternative contract type if required. In all cases these could be reclassified into one of the other categories. From this measure it was possible to distinguish between permanent and temporary workers in general and also identify types of temporary contract.

Table A2.1 FIT-statistics of CFA for total sample, skewness, kurtosis of variables, means, standard deviations, t-tests for temporary and permanent workers

	CFA for total sample					Skew	Kurt	Temps		Perms		t	p	d
	χ^2	df	CFI	AGFI	RMSEA			M	SD	M	SD			
Employers' obligations														
Content	2,680.18	90	78	1.00	.07	−0.26	−1.05	7.78	4.51	9.21	4.52	−11.03	**	.32
Fulfilment						−0.73	0.45	3.78	0.86	3.64	0.82	5.88	**	.17
Employees' obligations														
Content	1,653.96	119	.63	.99	.05	−1.47	1.57	12.73	4.39	13.78	3.98	−8.66	**	.25
Fulfilment						−0.97	2.07	4.36	0.52	4.29	0.50	4.80	**	.14
Violation	109.70	8	.99	.98	.05	0.64	0.13	2.15	0.84	2.38	0.86	−9.03	**	.27
Trust	11.28	4	.99	.99	.02	−0.29	−0.52	3.29	1.01	3.10	0.99	6.74	**	.19
Fairness								3.18	1.21	2.97	1.15	6.27	**	.18
Job insecurity	52.36	2	.99	.98	.07	0.70	−0.06	2.67	1.01	1.93	0.82	27.28	**	.80
Employability	50.36	2	.99	.98	.07	−0.18	−0.64	3.19	1.01	3.16	1.08	1.03	.301	.03
Employee expectations						−0.55	−0.38	3.51	1.12					
Volition	63.15	2	.99	.97	.08	−0.26	−1.13	2.32	1.07	3.93	1.01	−53.43	**	1.55
Motives	68.47	5	.97	.95	.09	0.54	−0.40	2.32	1.03					
Work involvement	79.06	2	.98	.96	.09	0.21	−0.14	2.75	0.87	2.75	0.88	0.12	.905	.00
Role clarity	75.09	5	.99	.98	.05	−1.39	2.38	4.25	0.85	4.33	0.81	−3.48	.001	.10
Autonomy	146.76	2	.98	.93	.12	−0.46	−0.20	3.23	0.91	3.51	0.87	−10.94	**	.31
Skill utilization	613.30	2	.90	.72	.24	−0.63	−0.08	3.46	1.02	3.62	0.89	−5.58	**	.17
Work load	28.02	2	.99	.99	.05	0.06	−0.44	2.83	0.89	3.20	0.85	−14.43	**	.43
POS						−0.24	−0.24	3.33	0.88	3.24	0.89	3.64	**	.10

(*Continued*)

Table A2.1 Continued

	CFA for total sample							Temps		Perms				
	χ^2	df	CFI	AGFI	RMSEA	Skew	Kurt	M	SD	M	SD	t	p	d
PSS	16.33	2	.99	.99	.04	−0.52	−0.11	3.65	0.91	3.49	0.95	5.79	**	.17
Job satisfaction	74.48	2	.99	.96	.08	−0.95	0.74	4.03	0.85	3.95	0.85	3.31	.001	.09
Life satisfaction	597.28	9	.95	.91	.11	−0.70	0.61	5.23	1.11	5.22	1.04	0.39	.693	.01
Positive work–home	37.11	2	.99	.98	.06	0.06	−0.41	2.93	0.92	2.91	0.91	0.74	.458	.02
Cognitive irritation	408.79	8	.97	.93	.10	0.31	−0.81	3.04	1.54	3.42	1.56	−8.69	**	.25
Emotional irritation						0.72	0.08	2.53	1.22	2.81	1.27	−7.82	**	.22
Occupational self-efficacy						−0.31	−0.04	3.94	0.66	3.98	0.63	−2.54	.011	.06
General health	119.28	5	.98	.97	.07	−0.63	0.13	4.03	0.71	3.93	0.73	4.91	**	.14
Anxiety	1,216.14	38	.96	.92	.08	0.35	0.00	2.40	0.73	2.52	0.74	−5.78	**	.16
Depression						0.86	0.73	2.00	0.71	2.12	0.73	−5.93	**	.17
Performance	703.96	9	.91	.89	.12	−0.44	0.71	4.00	0.53	4.07	0.51	−4.76	**	.13
Intention to quit	23.19	2	.99	.99	.05	1.24	1.10	1.76	0.87	1.90	0.93	−5.30	**	.16
Commitment	35.28	2	.99	.98	.06	−0.67	0.59	3.89	0.76	4.00	0.70	−5.20	**	.15

CFI = comparative fit index, AGFI = adjusted goodness of fit index, RMSEA: root mean square error of approximation
**$p < .0003$ (Bonferroni correction)

Control variables

On the basis of our literature review and pilot study, we identified a range of background variables, at different levels of analysis, that we considered it necessary to control for when exploring the effects of type of employment contract. At the same time, it is recognized that many of these control variables are of interest in their own right. We can distinguish between macro-level control variables, for example differences between countries; meso-level control variables, for example differences between sectors or organizations; and micro-level control variables, for example differences between individuals. Variables at each level were controlled for in our research models and are presented below.

Country differences (macro-level) were controlled by six dummies for the country samples, using Israel as reference category. To control for possible confounding effects on the meso-level, we used two dummies for the manufacturing and education sectors with the retail services sector as reference category, a measure of size of organization, whether the organization was in the public or private sector, the percentage of non-permanent employees in the organization and whether the organization was independent or the headquarters or part of a larger umbrella organization.

On the micro level, we collected information about both work-related variables and personal information. Regarding work-related variables we collected information about average hours worked per week, length of organizational tenure, union membership, any supervisory role, night-shift working, and any additional jobs. More complex questions ascertained the position or level of job using the Goldthorpe's Class Schema. The scale's validity has been endorsed on a number of occasions (e.g. Evans, 1992). We distinguish between (a) unskilled blue-collar worker, (b) skilled blue-collar worker or foreman, (c) lower-level white collar worker, (d) intermediate white-collar worker or supervisor of white-collar workers, (e) upper white-collar worker, middle management/executive staff, and (f) management or director. We also used a measure developed by Guest and Conway (1998) to assess the experience of eight core HR policies or practices, such as performance appraisal, training and development, and performance-related pay. The final work-related control variable was a three-item measure of work involvement taken from a scale developed by Kanungo (1982). The psychometric properties of this scale were a little below what had been expected

Personal or background information collected included age, gender, domestic circumstances (whether living alone or with others), financial contribution to the household, the number of dependants and level of responsibility for domestic tasks. In addition, educational achievement was measured using the ISCED scale (OECD, 1999b), which provides a classification of six educational levels that are comparable across countries (see Table A.2.3): 'The basic concept and definitions of ISCED have therefore been designed to be universally valid and invariant to the particular circumstances of a national education system' (UNESCO, 2003, p. 196).

Intervening variables

In our research model, we propose that any differences between permanent and temporary contract workers in well-being and other dependent variables might be explained (i.e. mediated) or might differ in the strength of relationship (i.e. moderated) by a set of individual perceptions. According to Baron and Kenny (1986, p. 1173), mediation is 'the...function of a third variable, which represents the generative mechanism through which the focal independent variable is able to influence the dependent variable of interest'. A moderating variable on the other hand, 'affects the direction and /or strength of the relation between an independent or predictor variable and a dependent or criterion variable' (Baron and Kenny, 1986, p. 1174).

Psychological contract

We used several measures of the psychological contract and the associated concept of the state of the psychological contract.

Perceived employers' obligations and promises

To assess perceived employers' promises and obligations, a set of fifteen items was constructed, based on factor analyses of earlier studies and on a literature review of the content of the psychological contract (e.g. De Jong, 2001; Huiskamp and Schalk, 2002; Robinson, Kraatz, and Rousseau, 1994). We asked our respondents to answer the items by using the instruction 'Has your organization promised or committed itself to...' (e.g.) 'provide you with a reasonably secure job?'. Answers could range from 'no' (0) if employees perceived that no promise had been given, and 'yes, but promise not kept at all' (1) to 'yes, and promise fully kept' (5) to rate the fulfilment of the promise.

The content measure indicates the number of promises made and reflects the breadth of the deal. Thus, the scale values can range from 0 to 15. Fulfilment or delivery of the deal is operationalized by computing the mean level of fulfilment of all promises indicated as being part of the deal, with values ranging from 1 to 5. A comparable measurement approach has been used by Kickul, Lester, and Finkl (2002).

Measures of content and fulfilment of both sides of the psychological contract do not lend themselves to standard factor analysis or reliability testing. Content is based on dichotomous variables and is therefore different to the ordinal data produced from scales. Due to the conditional nature of the delivery of the deal there is a large amount of legitimately missing data in relation to these items. As a result, psychometric analyses are carried out only on content data. However, even these analyses must be viewed as limited due to the dichotomous data.

Employees' obligations and promises to the organization

For employee obligations and promises a set of seventeen items was developed. The response format mirrored that of the employer obligations and promises discussed previously. Following the instruction 'Have you promised or committed yourself to...', respondents could indicate 'no' (0) to an item, if employees perceived

Table A2.2 Cronbach's alphas across country samples, and results of CFA for multiple group testing of measurement invariance for job characteristics

Variable/sample	Cronbach's alphas across countries and contract types										Model constraints	CFA across countries						CFA between temps and perms					
	Sw	G	N	B	UK	Sp	I	Total	T	P		χ^2	df	CFI	ΔCFI	AGFI	RMSEA	χ^2	df	CFI	ΔCFI	AGFI	RMSEA
Employers obligations*																							
Content	.91	.90	.89	.91	.89	.90	.89	.90	.89	.90	Unconst												
Employees' obligations*																							
Content	.90	.90	.92	.92	.88	.91	.92	.91	.91	.91	Facload												
Violation	.86	.79	.82	.88	.85	.89	.83	.85	.85	.85	Unconst	22.96	14	.99	—	.98	.01	13.83	4	.99	—	.99	.02
											Facload	170.86	68	.99	.006	.97	.02	15.09	13	1.00	.000	.99	.01
Trust	.75	.80	.72	.83	.86	.82	.82	.81	.82	.80	Unconst	279.19	39	.98	—	.95	.04	13.70	8	.99	—	.99	.01
											Facload	331.49	54	.98	.003	.95	.03	20.55	11	.99	.000	.99	.01
Fairness	.67	.88	.86	.87	.80	.82	.88	.81	.82	.80													
Job insecurity	.87	.83	.82	.38	.88	.81	.84	.83	.71	.81	Unconst	76.21	14	.99	—	.96	.03	57.10	4	.99	—	.97	.05
											Facload	333.17	32	.96	.029	.93	.04	109.32	7	.98	.008	.97	.05
Employability	.89	.88	.92	.90	.84	.88	.86	.89	.87	.90	Unconst	77.07	14	.99	—	.96	.03	54.29	4	.99	—	.97	.05
											Facload	197.35	32	.99	.009	.96	.03	84.95	7	.99	.003	.98	.05
Employee expectations	.85	.90	.83	.80	.74	.86	.74	.91	—	—	Unconst	28.14	12	.99	—	.96	.03	Question for temps only					
											Facload	—											
Volition	.90	.83	.93	.92	.81	.91	.87	.89	.82	.84	Unconst	142.98	14	.99	—	.93	.04	57.00	4	.99	—	.97	.05
											Facload	309.75	32	.98	.012	.94	.04	310.40	7	.96	.031	.91	.09
Motives	.75	.66	.75	.78	.63	.78	.75	.74	—	—	Unconst	154.57	35	.94	—	.89	.05	Question for temps only					
											Facload	203.53	59	.92	.014	.92	.04						
Work involvement	.68	.59	.74	.72	.73	.72	.70	.71	.69	.73	Unconst	61.91	12	.98	—	.97	.03	5.06	2	.99	—	.99	.02
											Facload	—						—					
Role clarity*	.54	.47	.59	.48	.38	.47	.37	.47	.53	.44	—												
Autonomy	.82	.84	.80	.74	.80	.82	.74	.80	.79	.79	Unconst	202.14	35	.98	—	.95	.03	71.71	10	.99	—	.98	.04
											Facload	402.31	59	.95	.024	.95	.03	100.28	14	.99	.003	.98	.04
Skill utilization	.81	.80	.79	.76	.86	.80	.85	.81	.84	.80	Unconst	195.52	14	.97	—	.91	.05	146.33	4	.98	—	.93	.08
											Facload	277.82	32	.97	.009	.94	.04	168.11	7	.98	.003	.96	.07
Workload	.82	.76	.76	.73	.79	.83	.68	.77	.76	.77	Unconst	665.24	14	.90	—	.70	.10	608.67	4	.89	—	.72	.17
											Facload	772.14	32	.88	.014	.85	.07	612.42	7	.89	.000	.84	.13

(*Continued*)

Table A2.2 Continued

Variable/sample	Cronbach's alphas across countries and contract types										Model constraints	CFA across countries						CFA between temps and perms					
	Sw	G	N	B	UK	Sp	I	Total	T	P		χ^2	df	CFI	ΔCFI	AGFI	RMSEA	χ^2	df	CFI	ΔCFI	AGFI	RMSEA
Perceived organizational support	.86	.79	.83	.83	.85	.83	.80	.82	.81	.83	Unconst	46.56	14	.99	—	.98	.02	30.35	4	.99	—	.99	.03
											Facload	132.36	32	.99	.009	.97	.03	33.89	7	.99	.001	.99	.03
Perceived supervisor support	.81	.80	.83	.82	.90	.89	.81	.84	.82	.85	Unconst	40.29	14	.99	—	.98	.02	17.67	4	.99	—	.99	.03
											Facload	78.99	32	.99	.002	.98	.02	25.63	7	.99	.000	.99	.02
Job satisfaction	.84	.75	.83	.83	.83	.82	.78	.82	.83	.81	Unconst	97.11	14	.99	—	.95	.03	75.03	4	.99	—	.96	.06
											Facload	245.91	32	.97	.018	.95	.04	87.69	7	.99	.001	.98	.05
Life satisfaction	.82	.81	.80	.85	.86	.84	.84	.84	.85	.83	Unconst	845.94	63	.93	—	.87	.05	634.85	18	.95	—	.90	.08
											Facload	919.24	93	.93	.004	.91	.04	642.28	23	.95	.000	.92	.07
Positive work–home	.78	.77	.80	.80	.86	.85	.85	.83	.83	.83	Unconst	98.15	14	.99	—	.95	.03	44.43	4	.99	—	.98	.04
											Facload	200.19	32	.98	.011	.96	.03	50.30	7	.99	.000	.99	.04
Cognitive irritation	.82	.86	.81	.83	.81	.86	.74	.81	.81	.81	Unconst	520.28	56	.97	—	.92	.04	414.60	16	.97	—	.93	.07
											Facload	690.26	80	.96	.010	.92	.04	420.78	20	.97	.000	.95	.06
Emotional irritation	.89	.85	.85	.88	.84	.86	.76	.83	.85	.85	Facload	40.19	12	.99	.015	.98	.02	5.99	2	.99	.002	.99	.02
Occupational self-efficacy	.67	.54	.62	.60	.68	.68	.59	.66	.66	.65													
General health	.76	.68	.76	.79	.80	.78	.77	.77	.77	.77	Unconst	184.36	35	.98	—	.95	.03	126.24	10	.98	—	.97	.05
											Facload	258.22	59	.97	.008	.96	.03	134.50	14	.98	.001	.97	.05
Anxiety	.81	.84	.81	.83	.84	.81	.79	.82	.80	.82	Unconst	1,788.12	266	.95	—	.88	.03	1,960.06	92	.93	—	.89	.06
											Facload	2,106.59	326	.94	.009	.89	.03	2,051.29	102	.93	.003	.90	.06
Depression	.83	.79	.85	.88	.87	.85	.75	.83	.82	.83	Unconst	894.72	63	.90	—	.86	.05	707.01	18	.91	—	.89	.09
											Facload	1,037.92	93	.88	.014	.89	.05	718.68	23	.91	.001	.91	.08
Performance	.78	.76	.77	.79	.82	.79	.78	.79	.78	.79													
Intention to quit	.84	.79	.79	.82	.82	.85	.79	.82	.81	.83	Unconst	61.01	14	.99	—	.97	.03	25.97	4	.99	—	.99	.03
											Facload	167.75	32	.98	.012	.97	.03	33.88	7	.99	.000	.99	.03
Commitment	.67	.67	.69	.73	.69	.78	.69	.72	.73	.71	Unconst	46.94	14	.99	—	.98	.02	39.65	4	.99	—	.98	.04
											Facload	138.71	32	.97	.020	.97	.03	44.91	7	.99	.001	.99	.03

Sw = Sweden, G = Germany, N = Netherlands, B = Belgium, UK = United Kingdom, Sp = Spain, I = Israel, T = Temporary, P = Permanent workers; CFI = comparative fit index, AGFI = adjusted goodness of fit index, RMSEA: root mean square error of approximation

POS = Perceived organizational support, PSS = Perceived supervisory support

* Presented are alphas for three items, we will use a single item for role clarity

Table A2.3 Educational levels according to ISCED-97

0	Pre-primary level of education
1	Primary level of education
2	Lower secondary level of education
3	Upper secondary level of education
4	Post-secondary, non-tertiary education
5	First stage of tertiary education
6	Second stage of tertiary education (leading to an advanced research qualification)

Source: OECD, 1999

that no promise was made or a range from 'yes, but promise not kept at all' (1) to 'yes, and promise fully kept' (5) to rate the fulfilment of the promise. Measures of content and fulfilment could be computed from these responses.

Violation

A conceptual distinction has been made between breach (non-fulfilment) and violation of the psychological contract. Whereas breach only covers the cognitive awareness of an unfulfilled deal, violation involves the emotional reaction (cf. Robinson and Morrison, 2000). A measure of violation was developed for this study to reflect this conceptual difference. It asked 'Looking overall at how far this organization has or has not kept its promises and commitments, to what extent do you agree with the following statements? I feel ... happy, angry, pleased, violated, disappointed, and grateful'. These were rated on a five-point scale ranging from 'strongly disagree' (1) to 'strongly agree' (5).

While in the German, Dutch, and Israeli samples we found evidence for a wording effect of positively and negatively worded items which produced different factors, in the total sample, in the other national samples, and in the employment contract subgroups, the items were found to form a single factor. Thus, Cronbach's alphas are reported for a six-item composite scale (Table A2.2). The alpha for this measure of contract violation in the total sample is 0.85.

Trust and Fairness

Organizational 'trust' was measured using a subset of three items from Guest and Conway (1998). An example item is 'To what extent do you trust your immediate line manager to look after your best interests?' Answers could be given on a five-point scale ranging from 'not at all' (1) to 'totally' (5). For organizational 'fairness', a four-item measure also from Guest and Conway (1998) was used. An example item for this measure is 'Overall, do you feel fairly rewarded for the amount of effort you put into your job?' The response format was again 'not at all' (1) to 'totally' (5). A two-factor solution (one for trust, one for fairness) showed good fit in all country samples. Alphas across countries for the subscales are good and alphas for the total sample are 0.81 for trust and 0.78 for fairness.

Employment prospects

Respondents completed measures of job insecurity, employability, and contract and work of choice. In addition, temporary workers were asked about their expectations regarding the continuation of their current contract and motives for temporary working.

Job insecurity

A four-item measure developed by De Witte (2000) was used to assess perceived job insecurity. An example item for this measure is 'Chances are I will soon lose my job'. Responses were given on a five-point scale, ranging from 'strongly disagree' (1) to 'strongly agree' (5). The items fitted one latent variable in all country samples and the alpha reliabilities are above 0.80 throughout and 0.83 for the total sample.

Employability

Employability refers to individuals' perceptions of their opportunities in the labour market and was assessed using a four-item scale also developed by De Witte (1992). An example is 'I am optimistic that I would find another job if I looked for one'. Answers could be given on a five-point scale, ranging from 'strongly disagree' (1) to 'strongly agree' (5). The analysis supports a single latent construct. Alpha reliabilities are high across all country samples and there is an alpha score of 0.89 in the total sample.

Employee expectations

Temporary employee expectations regarding the likely continuation of their contract with their current employer were measured. We formulated three items in the pilot study (e.g. 'I think I will be employed in this organization for longer than has been agreed in my employment contract') with responses provided on a five-point scale from 'strongly disagree' (1) to 'strongly agree' (5). We also measured perceived prospects of getting a permanent contract through a single item: 'I have been promised that I will get a permanent contract with this organisation when my present contract/assignment expires'. The findings from exploratory factor analyses and reliability analyses of the three-item scale show that the items load highly onto a single factor (>.80) and that they have an alpha reliability of 0.91 in the total sample.

Contract of choice–volition

Contract of choice refers to whether one would choose the present type of employment contract, whether permanent or temporary (Krausz, 2000a). We developed and tested four items in the pilot survey (e.g. 'My present employment contract suits me for the time being'), with responses on a range from 'strongly disagree' (1) to 'strongly agree' (5). The analysis confirms that the items support one latent factor (see Table A2.1). The test of equivalence across countries is acceptable, but temporary workers and permanent workers seem to differ in their interpretation of the items, as measurement invariance is not supported by the delta comparative fit index (Δ CFI).

Alpha is above 0.80 for both groups but this potential constraint should be borne in mind when interpreting findings derived from this measure.

Work and occupational choice

In addition to contract of choice, we wanted to measure whether respondents had the kind of job and profession or occupation that they wanted. Two items, adapted from research reported by Aronsson and Goransson (1999) measured the extent to which respondents had the 'job' and 'profession or occupation' of choice. These could be combined or looked at separately.

Motives for accepting temporary work

A measure was developed to tap the motives for being a temporary worker. Items from measures developed by Ellingson, Gruys, and Sackett (1998), Tan and Tan (2002), and Galais (2003) were used to develop our own nine-item measure. When the items are analysed using exploratory factor analyses three factors emerge that can be interpreted for the whole sample. The first factor, including items such as 'It gives me more freedom', seems to represent 'pull factors' or aspects of non-permanent employment that may be viewed as attractive or beneficial in some way. The second factor, including items such as 'It is difficult for me to find a permanent job' appears to represent 'push factors' or factors which indicate that they would prefer permanent employment but are pressured into temporary work. The final factor is made up of a single item ('It was the contract offered with the job I wanted'), which represents a more ambivalent or pragmatic motivation towards non-permanent employment (see also Chapter 4). However, these three factors are not universally supported across the national datasets, which questions the equivalency of this factor structure and the validity of progressing with these three factors. Indeed, analyses of the reliability of each of the factors also question the utility of progressing with three factors. Only items within the first factor are consistently tapping the underlying construct ($a = 0.74$) and the one factor 'pull' model has an acceptable fit across samples.

Job characteristics

Four job characteristics were measured using standardized scales: role clarity, autonomy, skill utilization, and workload.

Role clarity

We used a three-item measure of role clarity presented by Price (1997). Responses could be given on a five point scale, ranging from 'rarely or never' (1) to 'often or always' (5). A sample item is 'I know exactly what is expected of me in my job'. The items did not work well as a scale with Cronbach's alphas below 0.70 in most of the country samples and 0.47 in the full sample. We therefore decided to use a single item 'I know exactly what is expected of me in my job' for role clarity, acknowledging the limitations of proceeding in this way.

Autonomy

Autonomy may be defined as amount of decision-making latitude in the job. We used a scale previously used by Rosenthal, Guest, and Peccei (1996). The scale consists of five items and an example item is 'I can plan my own work'. The same word anchors have been used as for role clarity. Both the fit statistics for a one-factor model and internal consistencies are good ($a = 0.80$ in the full sample). While measurement invariance across country samples is not supported, the comparison of temporary workers and permanent workers supports measurement invariance. However, this is not the case for cross-country comparisons. This should be borne in mind when considering the results.

Skill utilization
To assess skill utilization four items were taken from the Leiden quality of work questionnaire (Van Der Doef and Maes, 1999). A sample item from this measure is 'My job requires a high level of skills'. Although the root mean square error of approximation (RMSEA; .12) points towards redundancies in the scale, there is support for a one-factor solution, which is also reflected in high internal consistencies across countries ($a = 0.81$ in the full sample).

Workload
A four-item measure developed by Semmer, Zapf, and Dunckel (1999) was used to measure workload on a five-point scale ranging from 'rarely or never' (1) to 'very often or always' (5). An example item is 'Is a fast pace required in your job?'. The one-factor model shows poor fit (Adjusted Goodness of Fit Index (AGFI) = 0.72, RMSEA = 0.24), but no improvements could be observed by shortening the scale. However, internal consistencies range from acceptable to good across countries and the alpha reliability for the full sample is 0.77.

Support
Two aspects of support were measured: perceived support from the organization and then more specifically from a supervisor.

Organizational support
We used a five-item version of the thirty-six-item scale for Perceived Organizational Support (POS) (Eisenberger, Fasolo, and Davis-LaMastro, 1990). An example item is 'My organisation really cares about my well-being' and response categories ranged from 'strongly disagree' (1) to 'strongly agree' (5). Analysis supports a single factor and the alpha for this measure was 0.82 in the full sample.

Social support by supervisor
To measure supervisory support we used the subscale 'Social Support Supervisor' from the Leiden quality of work questionnaire (Van Der Doef and Maes, 1999), consisting of four items. An example item is 'I feel appreciated by my supervisor'. Ratings could be given, ranging from 'strongly disagree' (1) to 'strongly agree' (5). Analysis supports a single factor and the alpha reliability for this measure was 0.84 in the full sample.

Outcome variables

A broad range of reports of well-being, work attitudes, and behaviours were assessed. The measure tapping each is presented in the following section.

Job satisfaction

To measure job satisfaction we used a four-item measure reported by Price (1997), modified from Brayfield and Rothe (1951) with a five-point response format ranging from 'strongly disagree' (1) to 'strongly agree' (5). An example item from this measure is 'I find enjoyment in my job'. A one-factor model is supported by the data. The four items provide a consistent scale in all countries ($\alpha = 0.82$ in the total sample).

Life satisfaction

Though it is common to employ a single item to measure life satisfaction, we preferred to utilize a fuller measure taken from Guest and Conway (1998), which we tested in the pilot study. Six items (e.g. 'How satisfied do you currently feel about... your life in general?') were used with seven Kunin-face gradations from 'very dissatisfied' (1) to 'very satisfied' (7). There is support for one factor based on the analysis, although the RMSEA (.11) points towards some redundancy in the item pool. Measurement invariance across countries and types of contract is supported. Alpha for this measure was found to be 0.82 in the full sample.

Sick leave and sick presence
To measure sickness absence and sickness presence we asked two questions: 'How often have you been absent from work due to your state of health over the last 12 months?' and 'How often have you *gone to work* despite feeling that you really should have stayed away due to your state of health over the last 12 months?' Responses were recorded as a count of occasions ranging from 'never' (1) to 'more than five times' (5).

Accidents and incidents
We measured the number of accidents respondents had been involved in and any incidents of harassment and violence at work by asking two questions: 'Have you had an accident in the work place over the last 12 months (Please count all accidents, even when you have continued to work the same day)?' and 'Have you personally experienced any incidents of harassment or violence at work in the last 12 months?' Answers could range from 'never' (1) to 'more than five times' (5).

Irritation
According to Müller, Mohr, and Rigotti (2004, p. 223), irritation can be defined as 'a state of psychological impairment caused by perceived thwarting of goals'. An eight-item measure was used to capture the concept of work-related irritation that serves as an indicator of mental strain related to work. A two-factor model with eight items as reported in the German literature (cognitive and emotional dimensions; Müller, Mohr and Rigotti, 2004) was not supported across country samples. Instead a

unidimensional structure was supported and was used in analyses. The alpha for this measure was 0.83 in the full sample.

Positive work–home interference

Since some of the possible negative aspects of work–home interference are covered by the measure of irritation, we used a subscale from the SWING (Survey Werk-thuis Interferentie-Nijmegen; Geurts et al., 2005; Wagena and Geurts, 2000) to measure what can be termed 'positive work–home interference'. This consisted of four items (e. g. 'you come home cheerfully after a successful day at work, positively affecting the atmosphere at home'), and rated from 'rarely or never' (1) to 'often or always' (5). Analysis supports a one-factor model and good internal consistencies ($a = 0.83$ in the full sample).

Occupational self-efficacy

Self-efficacy is the belief in one's ability to successfully fulfil a task (Bandura, 1977). The measure developed by Schyns and von Collani (2002) covers a broader concept of self-efficacy and refers to the competence a person feels concerning the ability to successfully fulfil the tasks involved in his or her job. Due to space considerations, we limited this measure to three items assessed on a five-point scale from 'strongly disagree' (1) to 'strongly agree' (5). An example of the items is 'Whatever comes my way in my job I can usually handle it'. This three-item measure showed borderline evidence of internal consistency across countries. In the full sample, the alpha is found to be 0.66, which is a little below the conventionally accepted threshold of 0.70. This measure should therefore be viewed with some caution in the analysis.

General Health

To assess general health, we used the subscale of the SF–12 questionnaire (Ware, 1999) assessing general health, consisting of five items. Answers could be given on a five-point scale, ranging from 'definitely false' (1) to 'definitely true' (5). An example item is 'I am as healthy as anyone I know'. Translations in all Psycones languages were already available. This five-item measure of general health worked well, showing acceptable to good internal consistencies ($a = 0.77$ in the full sample).

Affective well-being

The dimensions of anxiety–contentment and depression–enthusiasm from the Warr (1990) scale of work-related affective well-being were used. Each dimension lists six adjectives (e.g. tense and calm for anxiety and miserable and enthusiastic for depression) and asks respondents to rate them on the following basis: 'In the past few weeks, how often have you felt each of the following regarding your work?' Answers are given on a five-point scale from 'rarely or never' (1) to 'often or always' (5). The two-factor conceptualization of affective well-being was supported in confirmatory factor analysis, but only when wording effects were taken into account. For the full sample, an alpha of 0.82 was found for anxiety and 0.83 for depression.

Self-rated performance

Six items from the scale developed by Abramis (1994) were selected after testing in the pilot study. Typical items included 'In your own judgement, how well did you fulfil the following tasks . . . Achieve your objectives?' These items were rated on a five-point scale from 'very badly' (1) to 'very well' (5). There was only partial support for a single latent construct (AGFI = 0.89, RMSEA = 0.12), although internal consistencies are satisfactory ($\alpha = 0.79$ in the full sample).

Intention to quit

Standard measures of intention to quit cannot sensibly be used with temporary workers for a number of reasons related to their temporary status. We therefore had to develop an adapted measure for this study. Using items from Price (1997) and Sjöberg and Sverke (2000) we developed a new scale, consisting of four items that would be appropriate for both permanent and temporary workers (e.g. 'Despite the obligations I have made to this organization, I want to quit my job as soon as possible'), to be answered on a five-point scale, ranging from 'strongly disagree' (1) to 'strongly agree' (5). The four items cluster well into one construct and internal reliabilities are high across country samples ($\alpha = 0.82$ in the full sample).

Organizational commitment

Four items from the Cook and Wall (1980) organizational commitment scale were used (e.g. 'I feel myself to be part of the organization'; those items more closely linked with plans to stay or leave the organization were not used). The answer format ranged from 'strongly disagree' (1) to 'strongly agree' (5). Analysis confirmed that the four items represent one dimension. Internal consistencies are acceptable for group statistics and the alpha in the full sample is 0.72.

Employers' (HR managers') questionnaire

The employers' questionnaire covered characteristics of the company or organization, human resource policies and practices, performance indicators, and the psychological contract.

Characteristics of company or organization

We were interested in those characteristics that may affect the experience of working in a particular organization. These could be used as controls in the employee-level analysis and as possible explanatory variables in the multilevel analysis. We therefore collected information on organizational size, sector, level of unionization, the proportion of different types of temporary employees in the organization, and whether the organization was independent, a headquarters, or part of a larger umbrella organization. Data were also collected on changes in the size of both permanent and temporary workforces, both in the past and anticipated for the future.

Human resource policies and practices

The HR managers were asked for information about the same eight HR policies and practices as in the employee questionnaire. They were asked whether each practice was applied to both permanent and temporary workers and, if so, the proportion of temporary and permanent workers to which each practice was applied. An additional question asked whether there was equal treatment of permanent and temporary workers, with an open question to describe any differences that existed.

Two further questions explored the extent to which unions or work councils have an influence over HR decisions and also characteristics of the labour market in which the organization is operating. The first asked about the level of influence unions or work council representatives have over employment contracts, HR practices, and working conditions. The response format ranged from 'no influence' (1) to 'very much influence' (5). The second question asked 'How easy or difficult is it to fill vacancies?' The response format ranged from 'very easy' (1) to 'very difficult' (5).

Motives for hiring temporary workers

We measured the motives for using temporary workers in each organization. Twelve possible motives or reasons for hiring temporary workers were developed from the literature, (e.g. matching staff to peaks in demand, cost-savings, or to bring in specialist skills). Answer options are presented on a five-point scale from 'never' (1) to 'very often' (5).

Performance indicators

While there is a wide range of indicators of organizational performance, those that are valid across sectors are more limited. For example, financial performance is not relevant in most parts of the education sector. Therefore, we chose to measure aspects of the workforce performance that could be comparable. Two single-item measures rated management satisfaction with performance of permanent employees and temporary employees. Ratings could be given on a seven-point scale using Kunin-faces.

To complement these subjective assessments, information was also collected on the voluntary turnover and dismissal rates for both permanent and temporary workers. In addition, data on the percentage of time lost to sick leave and the number of accidents reported by each group was recorded. The previous calendar year was given as a reference point for these questions so as to make information comparable. As these performance indicators are included in annual reports in some countries, we felt this might be relatively unproblematic information for HR managers both to find and disclose.

Psychological contract

We decided that as a key 'agent' of the organization, the HR manager was an appropriate source from whom to collect information about the employer's side of the deal. The same items as those in the employee questionnaire were used to ask HR managers about the employer promises and obligations and their perceptions of employee promises and obligations to the organization. The introduction and some of the questions were rephrased to make sense from an employer perspective. The same response format and computation of the content and fulfilment of the psychological contract was used. An important aspect of the questionnaire was that the HR manager was asked first about their psychological contract with permanent workers and then again about their psychological contract with temporary workers. This enabled us to compare any differences between the two groups.

Summary and conclusion

This appendix has reported the source of the measures used in the study and, where appropriate, the statistical properties of the scales. In most cases, the measures display acceptable reliabilities across the different contexts and samples and can therefore be used with confidence.

Intercorrelations of all variables in the employee survey

	1	2	3	4	5	6	7	8	9	10	11	12	13	14	15	16	17	18	19	20	21	22	23	24	25	26	27	28	29	30	31	32	33	34	35	36	37	38	39	40	41	42	43	44	45	46	47	48	49	50	51	52	53	54	55	56	57	58	59	60	61	62
1 Sweden dummy																																																														
2 Germany dummy	.15																																																													
3 Netherlands dummy	.17	.15																																																													
4 Belgium dummy	.15	.13	.16																																																											
5 UK dummy	.15	.14	.16	.14																																																										
6 Spain dummy	.18	.17	.19	.17	.17																																																									
7 Israel dummy	.19	.17	.20	.17	.17	.22																																																								
8 Manufacturing dummy	.12	.13	.15	.14	.16	.01	.01																																																							
9 Education dummy	.12	.10	.09	.08	.12	.02	.03	.56																																																						
10 Number of employees	.34	.33	.10	.30	.39	.04	.15	.09	.16																																																					
11 % of 'non-perm' employees	.10	.07	.04	.07	.10	.08	.06	.04	.14	.16																																																			
12 Private-sector org'	.09	.16	.19	.14	.23	.35	.13	.43	.03	.12																																																			
13 Independent/HQ org'	.39	.01	.09	.11	.01	.09	.11	.16	.10	.16	.06	.02																																																
14 Age	.01	.01	.02	.04	.02	.11	.13	.05	.25	.01	.06	.26	.04																																																
15 Gender	.04	.05	.08	.02	.05	.03	.03	.23	.14	.05	.01	.07	.06	.02																																															
16 ISCED	.01	.09	.00	.05	.19	.01	.11	.02	.03	.01	.01	.02	.01	.05	.01																																													
17 Domestic situation	.11	.03	.00	.01	.02	.08	.09	.03	.02	.01	.03	.01	.08	.03	.01	.00																																											
18 Domestic contribution	.06	.03	.04	.03	.01	.09	.02	.11	.03	.00	.02	.01	.06	.15	.27	.01	.51																																									
19 Dependency on income	.04	.01	.03	.04	.05	.06	.23	.06	.03	.03	.04	.10	.02	.20	.05	.03	.37	.20																																						
20 Domestic responsibility	.03	.05	.09	.00	.06	.15	.03	.07	.11	.03	.01	.12	.05	.14	.32	.02	.39	.20	.13																																				
21 Work involvement	.02	.17	.01	.06	.14	.03	.30	.01	.00	.13	.04	.04	.01	.15	.02	.01	.04	.07	.09	.00																																		
22 Occupational level	.02	.02	.09	.00	.05	.15	.02	.51	.52	.05	.06	.22	.19	.19	.10	.04	.01	.01	.00	.04	.03																																	
23 Work hours	.07	.05	.11	.10	.07	.14	.01	.34	.26	.05	.02	.01	.06	.03	.24	.00	.17	.01	.10	.05	.04																																
24 Night shifts	.03	.04	.12	.04	.05	.10	.19	.39	.26	.03	.04	.20	.06	.18	.04	.00	.11	.07	.01	.11	.39	.14																															
25 Tenure	.02	.02	.01	.10	.08	.00	.16	.03	.11	.07	.04	.17	.01	.60	.04	.04	.08	.11	.20	.04	.12	.15	.07	.03																											
26 Supervision	.12	.10	.07	.12	.11	.02	.05	.01	.05	.03	.01	.02	.04	.13	.09	.00	.03	.09	.08	.02	.06	.29	.22	.03	.17																									
27 Union membership	.29	.00	.02	.16	.14	.19	.23	.03	.11	.10	.04	.15	.21	.23	.04	.03	.05	.10	.11	.08	.05	.01	.08	.25	.03																								
28 Additional job(s)	.00	.02	.02	.06	.07	.07	.05	.05	.06	.00	.03	.02	.01	.00	.03	.00	.00	.04	.07	.02	.02	.02	.03																								
29 Core HR-practices	.09	.07	.05	.03	.06	.07	.02	.08	.00	.08	.03	.00	.01	.05	.01	.04	.01	.12	.19	.08	.04	.05	.18	.01	.00																						
30 Permanent contract	.01	.11	.07	.11	.10	.02	.01	.06	.06	.01	.09	.05	.04	.33	.03	.04	.03	.11	.12	.05	.00	.10	.15	.01	.46	.25	.15	.05	.12															

Correlation matrix (lower triangle; continuation, items 31–63). Column headers (item numbers) are not printed on this page.

Item	Correlations
31 Content employer obs'	.12 .12 .05 .10 .12 .08 .08 01 .09 .10 .06 .04 .00 .01 .07 .02 .02 .03 .02 .04 .14 .12 .13 .01 .03 .20 .04 .00 .44 .15
32 Fulfilment employer obs'	.07 .10 .02 .02 .01 .00 .05 .11 .09 .02 .04 .04 .07 .01 .04 .00 .03 .02 .00 .05 .12 .12 .06 .05 .06 .03 .01 .32 .08 .08
33 Violation of PC	.02 .09 .09 .09 .06 .08 .14 .09 .03 .01 .06 .13 .05 .07 .00 .01 .03 .04 .02 .07 .12 .10 .08 .36 .12 .01 .13 .0. .37 .13 .25 .58
34 Trust	.04 .11 .09 .06 .04 .10 .09 .03 .01 .06 .11 .07 .04 .01 .01 .02 .02 .01 .04 .18 .11 .05 .07 .10 .02 .10 .01 .42 .09 .31 .53 .64
35 Fairness	.05 .10 .12 .09 .06 .02 .12 .09 .03 .03 .04 .10 .06 .02 .00 .01 .01 .01 .05 .15 .12 .07 .05 .07 .02 .12 .06 .39 .11 .27 .56 .65 .76
36 Content employee obs'	.17 .08 .18 .18 .13 .10 .01 .05 .15 .04 .02 .03 .03 .00 .01 .04 .02 .03 .02 .17 .01 .13 .06 .07 .14 .02 .01 .22 .12 .50 .51 .07 .14 .08
37 Fulfilment employee obs'	.09 .06 .09 .06 .03 .01 .12 .01 .01 .01 .02 .08 .06 .06 .02 .03 .01 .03 .02 .15 .02 .34 .03 .04 .05 .02 .02 .08 .07 .04 .36 .19 .19 .18 .00
38 Job insecurity	.08 .03 .03 .07 .06 .12 .11 .07 .10 .01 .05 .01 .14 .01 .00 .03 .03 .07 .00 .08 .03 .01 2. .16 .05 .01 .20 .35 .17 .15 .19 .20 .14 .07 .08
39 Employability	.08 .25 .09 .16 .14 .12 .05 .07 .02 .08 .00 .06 .03 .01 .03 .08 .04 .02 .01 .29 .01 .05 .19 .13 .13 .06 .02 .05 .02 .07 .01 .05 .02 .06 .20
40 Contract of choice	.01 .03 .00 .01 .03 .06 .02 .08 .00 .06 .04 .20 .01 .01 .02 .04 .03 .01 .08 .04 .17 .01 .05 .19 .13 C3 .04 .35 .15 .06 .01 .20 .60 .16 .13 .14 .12 .16 .06 .01 .38 .02
41 Job of choice	.09 .05 .02 .06 .05 .02 .12 .12 .20 .04 .05 .14 .07 .23 .05 .01 .07 .00 .11 .03 .22 .27 .02 .06 .19 .13 .03 .00 .15 .29 .33 .29 .31 .08 .13 .19 .01 .24
42 Profession of choice	.08 .04 .01 .03 .05 .06 .13 .19 .30 .00 .07 .17 .11 .24 .04 .00 .05 .01 .08 .03 .21 .38 .01 .11 .18 .12 .03 .01 .21 .07 .14 .24 .26 .25 .25 .07 .15 .18 .03 .19 .67
43 Role clarity	.02 .08 .02 .03 .01 .16 .13 .02 .04 .07 .00 .01 .01 .12 .05 .03 .02 .02 .06 .05 .15 .07 .04 .07 .09 .03 .07 .00 .14 .05 .05 .22 .20 .19 .18 .05 .24 .11 .03 .10 .21 .14
44 Autonomy	.01 .04 .03 .02 .04 .04 .20 .22 .30 .06 .03 .03 .03 .06 .10 .02 .23 .42 .0. .08 .18 .27 .07 .03 .30 .15 .22 .22 .20 .20 .18 .10 .13 .27 .16 .20 .38 .40 .24
45 Skill utilization	.08 .09 .10 .05 .13 .02 .12 .27 .40 .03 .07 .22 .03 .21 .00 .06 .09 .04 .23 .49 .00 .11 .17 .22 .10 .05 .30 .08 .23 .21 .21 .23 .20 .10 .14 .22 .10 .14 .43 .43 .14 .66
46 Workload	.07 .01 .09 .08 .01 .03 .12 .09 .12 .00 .01 .14 .02 .14 .01 .01 .05 .04 .06 .04 .28 .18 .04 .14 .27 .11 .01 .01 .20 .05 .14 .20 .15 .21 .08 .04 .09 .13 .07 .04 .10 .04 .7 .26
47 Organizational support	.03 .03 .06 .08 .09 .03 .07 .09 .04 .08 .03 .04 .02 .00 .01 .03 .01 .06 .04 .29 .13 .01 .03 .08 .01 .00 .47 .05 .34 .48 .60 .67 .60 .16 .20 .28 .04 .14 .33 .29 .22 .33 .33 .10
48 Supervisory support	.08 .03 .03 .02 .11 .08 .07 .00 .01 .01 .04 .08 .03 .02 .02 .03 .01 .05 .19 .11 .00 .03 .05 .09 .05 .00 .35 .07 .22 .41 .52 .59 .50 .13 .21 .19 .06 .07 .25 .21 .18 .23 .23 .06 .59
49 Occ' self-efficacy	.08 .15 .05 .12 .07 .02 .25 .04 .04 .01 .01 .10 .02 .12 .04 .04 .04 .03 .04 .08 .01 .17 .11 .01 .05 .06 .24 .04 .02 .15 .03 .09 .20 .14 .15 .12 .11 .36 .23 .27 .06 .17 .18 .24 .33 .24 .07 .27 .25
50 Pos' work–home int'	.07 .06 .05 .08 .05 .04 .17 .07 .04 .03 .06 .03 .10 .04 .03 .06 .01 .08 .01 .34 .11 .03 .00 .09 .08 .01 .34 .11 .23 .19 .26 .26 .26 .19 .12 .10 .05 .09 .29 .27 .13 .30 .29 .02 .35 .27 .21
51 Work anxiety	.12 .01 .15 .07 .09 .08 .01 .03 .04 .02 .02 .03 .09 .02 .01 .03 .00 .03 .01 .03 .05 .03 .13 .03 .04 .06 .01 .02 .31 .08 .32 .43 .35 .36 .02 .14 .22 .06 .07 .20 .16 .21 .17 .09 .31 .38 .28 .29 .22
52 Work depression	.05 .01 .17 .10 .11 .04 .00 .12 .09 .00 .03 .00 .00 .04 .03 .01 .04 .05 .05 .04 .14 .17 .09 .35 .02 .05 .35 .01 .30 .08 .16 .40 .54 .44 .45 .04 .22 .26 .11 .08 .35 .30 .20 .29 .29 .12 .49 .38 .33 .35 .69
53 Irritation	.02 .03 .08 .01 .01 .07 .13 .08 .14 .06 .02 .13 .05 .07 .08 .01 .01 .02 .01 .06 .05 .11 .18 .09 .97 .13 .12 .08 .00 .08 .13 .01 .18 .28 .19 .22 .04 .09 .06 .01 .02 .07 .14 .35 .16 .13 .16 .01 .56 .42
54 Sick leave	.02 .09 .06 .07 .07 .08 .03 .01 .01 .01 .02 .03 .05 .10 .12 .02 .06 .07 .02 .05 .00 .12 .05 .00 .06 .02 .03 .01 .36 .07 .08 .00 .14 .16 .13 .16 .01 .13 .02 .02 .11 .11 .00 .07 .09 .00 .10 .09 .07 .09 .13 .20 .12
55 Sick presence	.02 .03 .13 .07 .03 .06 .16 .02 .01 .06 .02 .07 .00 .02 .06 .08 .01 .02 .06 .02 .07 .02 .11 .09 .08 .01 .07 .14 .02 .16 .23 .17 .22 .14 .04 .03 .06 .01 .05 .02 .00 .03 .22 .10 .09 .05 .01 .24 .20 .28 .32
56 Accidents	.04 .03 .07 .03 .03 .01 .02 .10 .12 .03 .02 .05 .05 .10 .08 .01 .04 .03 .04 .02 .19 .14 .03 .01 .04 .01 .01 .07 .01 .00 .08 .14 .14 .14 .04 .04 .04 .04 .10 .14 .02 .08 .08 .04 .08 .09 .02 .08 .12 .15 .09 .17 .17
57 Incidents	.00 .06 .05 .04 .05 .00 .01 .01 .01 .04 .04 .01 .01 .04 .04 .01 .01 .05 .03 .02 .05 .03 .02 .05 .01 .06 .02 .01 .06 .01 .01 .01 .12 .04 .03 .21 .23 .18 .20 .03 .06 .06 .04 .03 .09 .07 .04 .06 .04 .10 .16 .17 .03 .05 .17 .20 .16 .12 .13 .21
58 General health	.03 .01 .03 .02 .04 .09 .01 .04 .05 .00 .01 .01 .05 .01 .02 .03 .02 .07 .04 .17 .20 .15 .15 .03 .18 .14 .12 .02 .11 .10 .10 .12 .08 .07 .19 .15 .23 .16 .30 .33 .30 .28 .21 .10 .12
59 Life satisfaction	.04 .02 .11 .05 .06 .04 .06 .02 .03 .00 .05 .00 .00 .01 .03 .02 .16 .13 .07 .09 .10 .01 .05 .11 .18 .00 .13 .23 .30 .26 .29 .07 .15 .17 .11 .11 .18 .31 .22 .25 .27 .42 .45 .35 .13 .17 .09 .12 .42
60 Job satisfaction	.01 .14 .17 .13 .16 .01 .07 .21 .20 .03 .04 .06 .07 .14 .07 .00 .08 .01 .02 .00 .28 .06 .09 .07 .12 .02 .32 .05 .19 .44 .52 .47 .46 .11 .27 .22 .01 .14 .56 .52 .24 .42 .39 .01 .53 .42 .30 .40 .41 .62 .17 .20 .12 .16 .17 .24 .34
61 Org' commitment	.10 .02 .00 .02 .02 .08 .18 .04 .01 .02 .01 .03 .12 .14 .00 .03 .09 .00 .11 .02 .37 .21 .06 .00 .11 .17 .00 .34 .07 .27 .38 .41 .45 .42 .24 .35 .29 .09 .18 .41 .38 .38 .08 .56 .48 .38 .41 .25 .45 .04 .13 .01 .08 .13 .21 .27 .58
62 Intention to quit	.03 .22 .13 .14 .17 .07 .06 .06 .05 .04 .04 .03 .09 .08 .01 .00 .08 .01 .08 .03 .24 .11 .01 .0C .03 .04 .03 .00 .27 .07 .15 .40 .52 .46 .45 .11 .23 .20 .12 .12 .46 .40 .24 .23 .29 .09 .48 .40 .17 .29 .36 .54 .22 .20 .13 .14 .20 .18 .30 .70 .51
63 Self-rated performance	.01 .02 .00 .01 .14 .18 .02 .02 .00 .07 .00 .13 .01 .05 .04 .04 .10 .04 .23 .06 .01 .10 .09 .13 .08 .01 .17 .07 .11 .19 .17 .16 .11 .11 .38 .18 .09 .09 .25 .25 .35 .39 .33 .10 .26 .18 .44 .23 .23 .32 .08 .09 .05 .01 .02 .18 .22 .36 .37 .25

Correlations in excess of 0.03 are significant at the 5% level

References

Abramis, D. (1994). 'Relationship of Job Stressors to Job Performance: Linear or Inverted-U?', *Psychological Reports*, 75: 547–58.

Adams, J. (1965). 'Inequity in Social Exchange', in L. Berkowitz (ed.), *Advances in Experimental Social Psychology* (Vol. 2), New York: Academic Press, 267–99.

Anderson, N. and Schalk, R. (1998). 'The Psychological Contract in Retrospect and Prospect', *Journal of Organizational Behaviour*, 19: 637–47.

Appelbaum, E., Bailey, T., Berg, P., and Kalleberg, A. (2000). *Manufacturing Advantage*, Ithaca, NY: Cornell University Press.

Arbuckle, J. (2003). *AMOS (Version 5)*, Chicago, IL: Small Waters.

Argyris, C. (1960). *Understanding Organizational Behavior*, Homewood, IL: Dorsey Press.

Arnold, J. (1996). 'The Psychological Contract: A Concept in Need of Closer Scrutiny?', *European Journal of Work and Organizational Psychology*, 5: 511–20.

Aronsson, G. and Goransson, S. (1999). 'Permanent Employment but Not in a Preferred Occupation: Psychological and Health Aspects, Research Implications', *Journal of Occupational Health Psychology*, 4: 152–63.

—— Gustafsson, K., and Dallner, M. (2002). 'Work Environment and Health in Different Types of Temporary Jobs', *European Journal of Work and Organizational Psychology*, 11: 151–75.

Arthur, M. and Rousseau, D. (eds.) (1996). *The Boundaryless Career: A New Employment Principle for a New Employment Era*, Oxford, UK: Oxford University Press.

Atkinson, J. (1984). 'Manpower Strategies for Flexible Organisations', *Personnel Management*, 28–31 August.

Bandura, A. (1977). 'Self-Efficacy: Toward a Unifying Theory of Behavioral Change', *Psychological Review*, 84: 191–215.

Bardasi, E. and Francesconi, M. (2004). 'The Impact of Atypical Employment on Individual Well-Being: Evidence from a Panel of British Workers', *Social Science and Medicine*, 58: 1671–88.

Barley, S. and Kunda, G. (2004). *Gurus, Hired Guns, and Warm Bodies*, Princeton, NJ: Princeton University Press.

Barling, J. and Gallagher, D. (1996). 'Part-time Working', in C. Cooper and I. Robertson (eds.), *International Review of Industrial and Organizational Psychology*, 11: 243–77.

Baron, R. and Kenny, D. (1986). 'The Moderator–Mediator Variable Distinction in Social Psychological Research: Conceptual, Strategic, and Statistical Considerations', *Journal of Personality and Social Psychology*, 51: 1173–82.

Beard, K. and Edwards, J. (1995). 'Employees at Risk: Contingent Work and the Psychological Experience of Contingent Workers', in C. Cooper and D. Rousseau (eds.), *Trends in Organizational Behaviour* (Vol. 2), Oxford, UK: Wiley, 109–20.

Beck, U. (2000). *The Brave New World of Work*, Cambridge, UK: Polity Press.

Becker, G. (1993). *Human Capital: A Theoretical and Empirical Analysis with Special Reference to Education*, Chicago, IL: University of Chicago Press.

Behling, O. and Law, K. (2000). 'Translating Questionnaires and Other Research Instruments: Problems and Solutions', in *Paper Series on Qualitative Applications in the Social Sciences, 07–131*, Thousand Oaks, CA: Sage.

Benach, J., Gimeno, D., Benavides, F. G., Martinez, J. M., and Torne, M. D. (2002). 'Types of Employment and Health in the European Union', *European Journal of Public Health*, 14: 314–21.

Bentler, P. (1990). 'Comparative Fix Indexes in Structural Models', *Psychological Bulletin*, 107: 238–46.

Bergström, O. (2003). *New Understanding of European Work Organization* (Final report EU-project HPSE-CT-1999–00009), Brussels: European Commission. Web site: http://ec.europa.eu/research/social-sciences/knowledge/projects/article_3522_en.htm

Bernhard-Oettel, C. and Isaksson, K. (2005). 'Work-Related Well-Being and Job Characteristics Among Temporary Workers in Sweden', in N. De Cuyper, K. Isaksson, and H. De Witte (eds.), *Employment Contracts and Well-Being Among European Workers*, Hampshire, UK: Ashgate, 177–200.

—— Sverke, M., and De Witte, H. (2005). 'Comparing Three Alternative Types of Employment with Permanent Full-time Work: How Do Employment Contract and Perceived Job Conditions Relate to Health Complaints?', *Work and Stress*, 19: 301–18.

—— De Cuyper, N., Berntson, E., and Isaksson, K. (2008). 'Well-Being and Organizational Attitudes in Alternative Employment: The Role of Contract and Job Preferences', *International Journal of Stress Management*, 15: 345–63.

Blau, P. (1964). *Exchange and Power in Social Life*, New York: Wiley.

Bocchino, C., Hartman, B., and Foley, P. (2003). 'The Relationship Between Person–Organization Congruence, Perceived Violations of the Psychological Contract, and Occupational Stress Symptoms', *Consulting Psychology Journal*, 55: 203–14.

Booth, A., Francesconi, M., and Frank, J. (2002). 'Temporary Jobs: Stepping Stones or Dead Ends?', *Economic Journal*, 112: 189–213.

Boxall, P. and Purcell, J. (2008). *Strategy and Human Resource Management*, 2nd edn., London: Palgrave Macmillan.

Boyce, S., Ryan, A., Imus, A., and Morgeson, F. (2007). '"Temporary Worker, Permanent Loser?" A Model of the Stigmatization of Temporary Workers', *Journal of Management*, 33: 5–29.

Brayfield, A. and Rothe, H. (1951). 'An Index of Job Satisfaction', *Journal of Applied Psychology*, 35: 307–11.

Bridges, W. (1995). *Job Shift: How to Prosper in a Workplace Without Jobs*, New York: Addison-Wesley.

Brough, P. and Pears, J. (2004). 'Evaluating the Influence of the Type of Support on Job Satisfaction and Work-Related Psychological Well-Being', *International Journal of Organizational Behavior*, 8: 472–85.

Browne, M. and Cudeck, R. (1992). 'Alternative Ways of Assessing Model Fit', *Sociological Methods and Research*, 21: 230–58.

Burchell, B., Lapido, D., and Wilkinson, F. (2002). *Job Insecurity and Work Intensification*, London: Routledge.

Burgess, G. and Connell, J. (2006). 'Temporary Work and Human Resources Management: Issues, Challenges and Responses', *Personnel Review*, 35: 129–40.

Caballer, A., Silla, I., Gracia, F., and Ramos, J. (2005). 'Current Evidence Concerning Employment Contracts and Employee/Organizational Well-Being in Spain', in N. De Cuyper, K. Isaksson, and H. De Witte (eds.), *Employment Contracts and Well-Being Among European Workers*, Hampshire, UK: Ashgate, 153–76.

Cano, E. (2000). 'Analisis de los Procesos Socioeconomicos de Precarizacion Laboral' ('Analysis of Socioeconomic Processes of Labour Precariousisation'), in E. Cano, A. Bilbao, and G. Standing (eds.), *Precariedad Laboral, Flexibilidad y Desregulacion*, Valencia, Spain: Germania.

Cappelli, P. (1999). *The New Deal at Work*, Cambridge, MA: Harvard Business School Press.

Chambel, M. and Castanheira, F. (2005). 'Different Temporary Work Status, Different Behaviors in Organization', *Journal of Business and Psychology*, 30: 351–67.

Cheng, G. and Chan, D. (2008). 'Who Suffers More from Job Insecurity? A Meta-Analytic Review', *Applied Psychology: An International Review*, 57: 272–303.

Cheung, G. and Rensvold, R. (2002). 'Evaluating Goodness-of-Fit Indexes for Testing Measurement Invariance', *Structural Equation Modeling*, 9: 233–55.

Claes, R., De Witte, H., Schalk, R., Guest, D., Isaksson, K., Krausz, M., et al. (2002). 'Het Psychologisch Contract van Vaste en Tijdelijke Werknemers' ('The psychological contract of permanent and temporary workers'), *Gedrag en Organisatie*, 14: 436–55.

Clinton, M. and Guest, D. (2008). 'Familiarity Breeds Contempt? An Exploration of the Unanticipated Consequences of Job Tenure', Paper presented to the Institute of Work Psychology Conference, Sheffield. June, 2008.

Connelly, C. and Gallagher, D. (2004). 'Emerging Trends in Contingent Work Research', *Journal of Management*, 30: 959–83.

Conway, N. and Briner, R. (2002a). 'Full-Time Versus Part-Time Employees: Understanding the Links Between Work Status, the Psychological Contract and Attitudes', *Journal of Vocational Behavior*, 61: 279–301.

————(2002b). 'A Daily Diary Study of Affective Responses to Psychological Contract Breach and Exceeded Promises', *Journal of Organizational Behavior*, 23: 287–302.

————(2005). *Understanding Psychological Contracts at Work*, Oxford, UK: Oxford University Press.

Cook, J. and Wall, T. (1980). 'New Work Attitude Measures of Trust, Organizational Commitment and Personal Need Non-fulfilment', *Journal of Occupational Psychology*, 53: 39–52.

Coyle-Shapiro, J. (2002). 'A Psychological Contract Perspective on Organizational Citizenship Behaviour', *Journal of Organizational Behaviour*, 23: 927–46.

—— and Kessler, I. (2000). 'Consequences of the Psychological Contract for the Employment Relationship: A Large-Scale Survey', *Journal of Management Studies*, 37: 903–30.

—— —— (2002*a*). 'Contingent and Non-Contingent Working in Local Government: Contrasting Psychological Contracts', *Public Administration*, 80: 77–101.

—— —— (2002*b*). 'Exploring Reciprocity Through the Lens of the Psychological Contract: Employee and Employer Perspectives', *European Journal of Work and Organizational Psychology*, 11: 69–86.

—— and Neuman, J. (2004). 'The Psychological Contract and Individual Differences: The Role of Exchange and Creditor Ideologies', *Journal of Vocational Behavior*, 64: 150–64.

Dabos, G. and Rousseau, D. (2004). 'Mutuality and Reciprocity in the Psychological Contracts of Employees and Employers', *Journal of Applied Psychology*, 89: 52–72.

Danna, K. and Griffin, R. (1999). 'Health and Well-Being in the Workplace: A Review and Synthesis of the Literature', *Journal of Management*, 25: 357–84.

Davis-Blake, A. and Uzzi, B. (1993). 'Determinants of Employment Externalization: A Study of Temporary Workers and Independent Contractors', *Administrative Science Quarterly*, 38: 195–223.

—— Broschak, J., and George, E. (2003). 'Happy Together. How Using Non-Standard Workers Affects Exit, Voice, and Loyalty Among Standard Employees', *Academy of Management Journal*, 46: 475–85.

De Cuyper, N. and De Witte, H. (2005*a*). 'Temporary Employment in Belgium: Is It Really Precarious?', in N. De Cuyper, K. Isaksson, and H. De Witte (eds.), *Employment Contracts and Well-Being Among European Workers*, Hampshire, UK: Ashgate, 51–74.

—— —— (2005*b*). 'Job Insecurity: Mediator or Moderator of the Relationship Between Type of Contract and Various Outcomes?', *SA Journal of Industrial Psychology*, 31: 79–86.

—— —— (2006). 'The Impact of Job Insecurity and Contract Type on Attitudes, Well-Being and Behavioural Reports: A Psychological Contract Perspective', *Journal of Occupational and Organizational Psychology*, 79: 395–409.

—— —— (2007). 'Job Insecurity in Temporary Versus Permanent Workers: Associations with Attitudes, Well-Being and Behaviour', *Work and Stress*, 21: 65–84.

—— —— (2008). 'Volition and Reasons for Accepting Temporary Employment: Associations with Attitudes, Well-being and Behavioural Intentions', *European Journal of Work and Organizational Psychology*, 17: 363–87.

—— Isaksson, K., and De Witte, H. (eds.) (2005). *Employment Contracts and Well-Being Among European Workers*, Hampshire, UK: Ashgate.

—— De Jong, J., De Witte, H., Isaksson, K., Rigotti, T., and Schalk, R. (2008). 'Literature Review of Theory and Research on the Psychological Impact of Temporary Employment: Towards a Conceptual Model', *International Journal of Management Reviews*, 10: 25–51.

——— Notelaers, G., and De Witte, H. (2009). 'Transitioning Between Temporary and Permanent Employment: A Two-Wave Study on the Entrapment, the Stepping Stone and the Selection Hypothesis', *Journal of Occupational and Organizational Psychology*, 82: 67–88.

——— Sora, N., De Witte, H., Caballer, A., and Peiró, J. M. (2009). '"Organizations", Use of Temporary Employment and Job Insecurity Climate Among Belgian and Spanish Permanent Workers', *Economic and Industrial Democracy*, 30: 1–28.

De Jong, J. (2001). *Alvast Flexibel?* (*Already Flexible?*), Nijmegen, The Netherlands: University of Nijmegen.

——— and Schalk, R. (2005a). 'Employment Strategy, the Psychological Contract, and Perceptions of Trust, Fairness, and Equity Among Temporary Workers', in F. Avallone, H. Sinangil, and A. Caetano (eds.), *Convivence in Organizations and Society*, Milan, Italy: Studio Guerini, 81–9.

——— ——— (2005b). 'Temporary Employment in The Netherlands: Between Flexibility and Security', in N. De Cuyper, K. Isaksson, and H. De Witte (eds.), *Employment Contracts and Well-Being Among European Workers*, Hampshire, UK: Ashgate, 119–52.

De Vos, A. (2002). 'The Individual Antecedents and the Development of Newcomers' Psychological Contracts During the Socialization Process: A Longitudinal Study.' Unpublished Dissertation, Ghent, Belgium: Universiteit Gent.

——— Buyens, D., and Schalk, R. (2003). 'Psychological Contract Development During Organizational Socialization: Adaptation to Reality and the Role of Reciprocity', *Journal of Organizational Behavior*, 24: 537–59.

De Witte, H. (1992). 'Tussen Optimisten en Teruggetrokkenen. Een Empirisch Onderzoek Naar Het Psychosocial Profiel van Langdurig Werklozen en Deelnemers aan de Weer-Werkactie in Vlaanderen' ('Between Optimism and Withdrawal. An Empirical Analysis of the Long-term Unemployed in Flanders, Belgium'). Leuven, Belgium: Hoger Instituut voor de Arbeid-K. U. Leuven.

——— (1999). 'Job Insecurity and Psychological Well-Being: Review of the Literature and Exploration of Some Unresolved Issues', *European Journal of Work and Organizational Psychology*, 8: 155–77.

——— (2000). 'Arbeidsethos en Jobonzekerheid: Meting en Gevolgen voor Welzijn, Tevredenheid en Inzet op het Werk' ('Work Ethic and Job Insecurity: Measurement and Consequences for Well-Being, Satisfaction and Work Performance'), in R. Bouwen, K. De Witte, H. De Witte, and T. Taillieu (eds.), *Van Groep naar Gemeenschap* (*Liber Amicorum Prof. Dr. Leo Lagrou*), Leuven, Belgium: Garant, 325–50.

——— (ed.) (2005). *Job Insecurity, Union Involvement and Union Activism*, Aldershot, UK: Ashgate.

——— and Näswall, K. (2003). '"Objective" Versus "Subjective" Job Insecurity: Consequences of Temporary Work for Satisfaction and Organizational Commitment in Four European Countries', *Economic and Industrial Democracy*, 24: 149–88.

Deery, S. and Kinnie, N. (eds.) (2004). *Call Centres and Human Resource Management*, London: Palgrave Macmillan.

DePaulo, B., Bittingham, G., and Kaiser, M. (1983). 'Receiving Competence-relevant Help: Effects of Reciprocity, Affect, and Sensitivity to the Helper's Nonverbally Expressed Needs', *Journal of Personality and Social Psychology*, 45: 1045–60.

Dick, P. (2006). 'The Psychological Contract and the Transition from Full to Part-time Police Work', *Journal of Organizational Behavior*, 27: 37–58.

DiNatale, M. (2001). 'Characteristics of and Preference for Alternative Work Arrangements', *Monthly Labor Review*, 124: 28–49.

Easterlin, R. (2001). 'Income and Happiness: Towards a Unified Theory', *Economic Journal*, 111: 465–84.

Eisenberger, R., Cummings, J., Armeli, S., and Lynch, P. (1997). 'Perceived Organizational Support, Discretionary Treatment, and Job Satisfaction', *Journal of Applied Psychology*, 82: 812–20.

—— Huntington, R., Hutchison, S., and Sowa, D. (1986). 'Perceived Organizational Support', *Journal of Applied Psychology*, 71: 500–7.

—— Fasolo, P., and Davis-LaMastro, V. (1990). 'Perceived Organizational Support and Employee Diligence, Commitment and Innovation', *Journal of Applied Psychology*, 75: 51–9.

Ellingson, J., Gruys, M., and Sackett, P. (1998). 'Factors Related to the Satisfaction and Performance of Temporary Employees', *Journal of Applied Psychology*, 83: 913–21.

Engellandt, A. and Riphahn, R. (2005). 'Temporary Contracts and Employee Efforts', *Labour Economics*, 12: 281–99.

Engle, E. and Lord, R. (1997). 'Implicit Theories, Self-schemas, and Leader–Member Exchange', *Academy of Management Journal*, 40: 988–1010.

Eurostat (1996). *Labour Force Survey: Methods and Definition*, Luxembourg: Statistical Office of the European Commission.

Evans, G. (1992). 'Testing the Validity of the Goldthorpe Class Schema', *European Sociological Review*, 8: 211–32.

Feather, N. and Rauter, K. (2004). 'Organizational Citizenship Behaviours in Relation to Job Status, Job Insecurity, Organizational Commitment and Identification, Job Satisfaction and Work Values', *Journal of Occupational and Organizational Psychology*, 77: 81–94.

Feldman, D., Doerpinghaus, H., and Turnley, W. (1994). 'Managing Temporary Workers: A Permanent HRM Challenge', *Organizational Dynamics*, 23: 49–63.

Ford, C. and Slater, G. (2006). 'The Nature and Experience of Agency Working in Britain. What are the Challenges for HRM?', *Personnel Review*, 35: 141–57.

Forrier, A. and Sels, L. (2003). 'Temporary Employment and Employability: Training Opportunities and Efforts of Temporary and Permanent Employees in Belgium', *Work, Employment and Society*, 17: 641–66.

Gagliarducci, S. (2005). 'The Dynamics of Repeated Temporary Jobs', *Labour Economics*, 12: 429–48.

Gakovic, A. and Tetrick, L. (2003). 'Psychological Contract Breach as a Source of Strain for Employees', *Journal of Business and Psychology*, 18: 235–46.

Galais, N. (2003). *Anpassung bei Zeitarbeitnehmern—Eine Längsschnittstudie zu Individuellen Determinanten der Übernahme und des Wohlbefindens*, Unpublished Dissertation, Friedrich-Alexander-Universität, Erlangen-Nürnberg, Germany.

Galunic, C. and Anderson, E. (2000). 'From Security to Mobility: Generalized Investments in Human Capital', *Organization Science*, 11: 1–20.

George, E. (2003). 'External Solutions and Internal Problems: The Effects of Employment Externalization on Internal Workers' Attitudes', *Organization Science*, 14: 386–402.

Geurts, S., Taris, T., Kompier, M., Dikkers, J., Van Hooff, M., Kinnunen, U., et al. (2005). 'Work-Home Interaction from a Work Psychological Perspective: Development and Validation of a New Questionnaire, the SWING', *Work and Stress*, 19: 319–39.

Goudswaard, A. and Andries, F. (2002). *Employment Status and Working Conditions*, Dublin, Ireland: European Foundation for the Improvement of Living and Working Conditions.

——Kraan, K., and Dhondt, S. (2000). *Flexibiliteit in Balans. Flexibilisering en de Gevolgen voor Werkgever en Werknemer* (*Flexibility in Balance. Flexibility of Labour and the Consequences for Employer and Employee*), Hoofddorp, The Netherlands: TNO Arbeid.

Gouldner, A. W. (1960). 'The Norm of Reciprocity: A Preliminary Statement', *American Sociological Review*, 25: 161–78.

Green, F. (2006). *Demanding Work*, Princeton, NJ: Princeton University Press.

Greenberg, M. S. (1980). 'A Theory of Indebtedness', in K. Gergen, M. Greenberg, and R. Willis (eds.), *Social Exchange: Advances in Theory and Research*, New York: Plenum, 3–26.

Griffeth, R., Hom, P., and Gaertner, S. (2000). 'A Meta-analysis of Antecedents and Correlates of Employee Turnover: Update, Moderator Tests and Research Implications for the Next Millennium', *Journal of Management*, 26: 463–88.

Guest, D. (1998). 'Is the Psychological Contract Worth Taking Seriously?', *Journal of Organizational Behaviour*, 19: 649–64.

—— (1999). 'Human Resource Management: The Workers' Verdict', *Human Resource Management Journal*, 9 (3): 5–25.

—— (2004a). 'Flexible Employment Contracts, the Psychological Contract and Employee Outcomes: An Analysis and Review of the Evidence', *International Journal of Management Reviews*, 5: 1–19.

—— (2004b). 'The Psychology of the Employment Relationship: An Analysis Based on the Psychological Contract', *Applied Psychology: An International Review*, 53: 541–55.

——and Clinton, M. (2005). 'Contracting in the UK: Current Research Evidence on the Impact of Flexible Employment and the Nature of Psychological Contracts', in N. De Cuyper, K. Isaksson, and H. De Witte (eds.), *Employment Contracts and Well-Being Among European Workers*, Hampshire, UK: Ashgate, 201–24.

——and Conway, N. (1998). *Fairness at Work and the Psychological Contract*, London: IPD.

Guest, D. and Conway, N. (2002a). *Pressure at Work and the Psychological Contract*, London: CIPD.

—— —— (2002b). 'Communicating the Psychological Contract: An Employer's Perspective', *Human Resource Management Journal*, 12 (2): 22–38.

—— and Sturges, J. (2007). 'Living to Work: Working to Live: Conceptualizations of Careers Among Contemporary Workers', in H. Gunz and M. Peiperl (eds.), *Handbook of Career Studies*, Thousand Oaks, CA: Sage, 310–26.

Guzzo, R. and Noonan, K. (1994). 'Human Resource Practices as Communicators and the Psychological Contract', *Human Resource Management*, 33: 447–62.

Handy, C. (1989). *The Age of Unreason*, London: Random House.

Helliwell, J. (2003). 'How's Life? Combining Individual and National Variables to Explain Subjective Well-Being', *Economic Modelling*, 20: 331–60.

Herriot, P., Manning, W., and Kidd, J. (1997). 'The Content of the Psychological Contract', *British Journal of Management*, 8: 151–62.

Hesselink, D. and van Vuuren, T. (1999). 'Job Flexibility and Job Insecurity: The Dutch Case', *European Journal of Work and Organizational Psychology*, 8: 273–93.

Ho, V. (2005). 'Social Influence on Evaluations of Psychological Contract Fulfilment', *Academy of Management Review*, 30: 113–28.

—— Weingart, L., and Rousseau, D. (2004). 'Responses to Broken Promises: Does Personality Matter?', *Journal of Vocational Behavior*, 65: 276–93.

Hofstede, G. (2001). *Culture's Consequences*, 2nd edn., Thousand Oaks, CA: Sage.

Hui, C., Lee, C., and Rousseau, D. (2004). 'Psychological Contract and Organizational Citizenship Behavior in China: Investigating Generalizability and Instrumentality', *Journal of Applied Psychology*, 89: 311–21.

Huiskamp, R. and Schalk, R. (2002). 'Psychologische Contracten in Arbeidsrelaties: De Stand van Zaken in Nederland' ('Psychological Contracts in Labour Relations: A State of the Art of the Netherlands'), *Gedrag en Organisatie*, 14: 370–85.

Ichino, A. and Riphahn, R. (2001). *The Effect of Employment Protection on Worker Effort: A Comparison of Absenteeism During and After Probation*, IZA Discussion Paper 385, Bonn, Germany: IZA.

Isaksson, K. and Bellaagh, K. (2002). 'Health Problems and Quitting Among Female "Temps"', *European Journal of Work and Organizational Psychology*, 11: 27–45.

—— Bernhard, C., Claes, R., De Witte, H., Guest, D., and Krausz, M. (2003a). *Employment Contracts and Psychological Contracts in Europe: Results from a Pilot Study*, Stockholm, Sweden: SALTSA.

—— —— Mohr, G., Peiró, J. M., et al. (2003b). Psychological Contracts Across Employment Situations (PSYCONES). Results from the Pilot Study, http://www.uv.es/~psycon.

—— De Cuyper, N., and De Witte, H. (2005). 'Employment Contracts and Well-Being Among European Workers. Introduction', in N. De Cuyper, K. Isaksson, and H. De Witte (eds.), *Employments Contracts and Well-Being Among European Workers*, Hampshire, UK: Ashgate, 1–14.

—— —— Bernhard-Oettel, C., and De Witte, H. (2010 in press). 'The Role of the Formal Employment Contract in the Range and Fulfilment of the Psychological

Contract: Testing a Layered Model', *European Journal of Work and Organizational Psychology.*

Jones, J., Huxtable, C., Hodgson, J., and Price, M. (2003). *Self-Reported Work Related Illness in 2001/02: Results from a Household Survey.* Sudbury, UK: HSE Books.

Kanungo, R. N. (1982). 'Measurement of Job and Work Involvement', *Journal of Applied Psychology,* 67: 341–9.

Karasek, R. (1979). 'Job Demands, Job Decision Latitude, and Mental Strain: Implications for Job Design', *Administrative Science Quarterly,* 24: 285–308.

Kickul, J. (2001). 'When Organizations Break Their Promises: Employee Reactions to Unfair Processes and Treatment', *Journal of Business Ethics,* 29: 289–307.

——and Lester, S. (2001). 'Broken Promises: Equity Sensitivity as a Moderator Between Psychological Contract Breach and Employee Attitudes and Behavior', *Journal of Business and Psychology,* 16: 191–216.

——Neuman, G., Parker, C., and Finkl, J. (2001). 'Settling the Score: The Role of Organizational Justice in the Relationship Between Psychological Contract Breach and Anticitizenship Behavior', *Employee Responsibilities and Rights Journal,* 13: 77–93.

——Lester, S., and Finkl, J. (2002). 'Promise Breaking During Radical Organizational Change: Do Justice Interventions Make a Difference?', *Journal of Organizational Behavior,* 23: 469–88.

Kinnunen, U. and Nätti, J. (1994). 'Job Insecurity in Finland: Antecedents and Consequences', *European Journal of Work and Organizational Psychology,* 4: 297–321.

Knell, J. (2000). *Most Wanted: The Quiet Birth of the Free Worker,* London: The Work Institute.

Koene, B., Pauuwe, J., and Groenwegen, J. (2004). 'Understanding the Development of Temporary Agency Work in Europe', *Human Resource Management Journal,* 14 (3): 53–73.

——and van Riemsdijk, M. (2005). 'Managing Temporary Workers: Work Identity, Diversity and Operational HR Choices', *Human Resource Management Journal,* 15 (1): 76–92.

Korpi, T. and Levin, H. (2001). 'Precarious Footing: Temporary Employment as a Stepping Stone Out of Unemployment in Sweden', *Work, Employment and Society,* 15: 127–48.

Kotter, J. (1973). 'The Psychological Contract: Managing the Joining up Process', *California Management Review,* 15: 91–9.

Kottke, J. and Sharafinski, C. (1988). 'Measuring Perceived Supervisory and Organizational Support', *Educational and Psychological Measurement,* 48: 1075–9.

Kraimer, M., Wayne, S., Liden, R., and Sparrowe, R. (2005). 'The Role of Job Insecurity in Understanding the Relationship Between Employees' Perception of Temporary Workers and Employees' Performance', *Journal of Applied Psychology,* 90: 389–98.

Krausz, M. (2000a). 'Effects of Short and Long Term Preferences for Temporary Work on Psychological Outcomes', *International Journal of Manpower,* 21: 635–47.

Krausz, M. (2000*b*). 'Psychological Contracts in Israel', in D. Rousseau, and R. Schalk (eds.), *Psychological Contracts in Employment: Cross-National Perspectives*, Thousand Oaks, CA: Sage, 125–40.

—— Brandwein, T., and Fox, S. (1995). 'Work Attitudes and Emotional Responses of Permanent, Voluntary and Involuntary Temporary-Help Employees: An Exploratory Study', *Applied Psychology: An International Review*, 44: 217–32.

Layard, R. (2005). *Happiness*, London: Penguin Books.

Lepak, D. and Snell, S. (1999). 'The Human Resource Architecture: Toward a Theory of Human Capital Allocation and Development', *Academy of Management Review*, 24: 31–48.

—— Taylor, S., Tekleab, A., Marrone, J., and Cohen, D. (2002). 'Understanding the Use and Performance Implications of High Investment HR Systems for Different Employee Groups', Paper presented at the Strategic HRM conference at the University of Bath, England.

Levinson, H., Price, C., Munden, K., Mandl, H., and Solley, C. (1962). *Men, Management and Mental Health*, Cambridge, MA: Harvard University Press.

Lewicki, R., McAllister, D., and Bies, R. (1998). 'Trust and Distrust: New Relationships and Realities', *Academy of Management Review*, 23: 438–58.

Lidwall, U., Marklund, S., and Skogman Thoursie, P. (2005). 'Sickness Absence in Sweden', in R. Gustafsson and I. Lundberg (eds.), *Worklife and Health in Sweden*, Stockholm: National Institute for Working Life, 183–204.

Lievens, F. and Anseel, F. (2004). 'Confirmatory Factor Analysis and Invariance of an Organizational Citizenship Behaviour Measure Across Samples in a Dutch Speaking Context', *Journal of Occupational and Organizational Psychology*, 77: 299–306.

McDonald, D. and Makin, P. (2000). 'The Psychological Contract, Organisational Commitment and Job Satisfaction of Temporary Staff', *Leadership & Organization Development Journal*, 21: 84–91.

McLean Parks, J. and Kidder, D. (1994). 'Till Death Us Do Part. Changing Work Relationships in the 1990s', in C. Cooper and D. Rousseau (eds.), *Trends in Organizational Behaviour* (Vol. 1), New York: Wiley, 111–36.

—— —— and Gallagher, D. (1998). 'Fitting Square Pegs into Round Holes: Mapping the Domain of Contingent Work Arrangements onto the Psychological Contract', *Journal of Organizational Behavior*, 19: 697–730.

Marler, J., Barringer, M., and Milkovich, G. (2002). 'Boundaryless and Traditional Contingent Employees: Worlds Apart', *Journal of Organizational Behavior*, 23: 425–53.

Mauno, S., Kinnunen, U., Mäkikangas, A., and Nätti, J. (2005). 'Psychological Consequences of Fixed-Term Employment and Perceived Job Insecurity Among Health Care Staff', *European Journal of Work and Organizational Psychology*, 14: 209–38.

Mayer, R., Davis, J., and Schoorman, F. (1995). 'An Integrative Model of Organizational Trust', *Academy of Management Review*, 20: 709–34.

MacNeil, I. (1985). 'Relational Contract: What We Do and Do Not Know', *Wisconsin Law Review*, 3: 483–525.

Meckler, M., Drake, B., and Levinson, H. (2003). 'Putting Psychology Back into Psychological Contracts', *Journal of Management Inquiry*, 12: 217–28.

Millward, L. and Brewerton, P. (1999). 'Contractors and Their Psychological Contracts', *British Journal of Management*, 10: 253–74.

Millward-Purvis, L. and Cropley, M. (2003). 'Psychological Contracting: Processes of Contract Formation During Interviews Between Nannies and Their "Employers"', *Journal of Occupational and Organizational Psychology*, 76: 213–41.

Morrison, E. and Robinson, S. (1997). 'When Employees Feel Betrayed: A Model of How Psychological Contract Violation Develops', *Academy of Management Review*, 22: 226–56.

Müller, A., Mohr, G., and Rigotti, T. (2004). 'Differentielle Aspekte Psychischer Beanspruchung aus Sicht der Zielorientierung. Die Faktorstruktur der Irritations-Skala' ('Differential Aspects of Psychological Strain with Respect to Goal Orientation: The Factor-Structure of the Irritation Scale'), *Zeitschrift für Differentielle und Diagnostische Psychologie*, 25: 213–25.

Nollen, S. and Axel, H. (1998). 'Benefits and Costs to Employers', in K. Barker and K. Christensen (eds.), *Contingent Work: American Employment Relations in Transition*, Ithaca, NY: Cornell University Press, 126–43.

OECD (1999a). *Employment Outlook 1999*, Paris: OECD Publications.

—— (1999b). *Classifying Educational Programme, Manual for ISCED-97 Implementation in OECD Countries*, 1999 edition, Paris: OECD Publications.

—— (2002). *Employment Outlook 2002, Organization for Economic Co-operation and Development*, Paris: OECD Publications.

—— (2006). http://stats.oecd.org/wbos/Index.aspx.

—— (2008). http://stats.oecd.org/wbos.

Parker, S., Griffin, M., Sprigg, C., and Wall, T. (2002). 'Effect of Temporary Contracts on Perceived Work Characteristics and Job Strain: A Longitudinal Study', *Personnel Psychology*, 55: 689–717.

—— and Wall, T. (1998). *Job and Work Design*, Thousand Oaks, CA: Sage.

Pate, J., Martin, G., and McGoldrick, J. (2003). 'The Impact of Psychological Contract Violation on Employee Attitudes and Behaviour', *Employee Relations*, 25: 557–73.

Pearce, J. and Randel, A. (1998). 'The Actual Job Insecurity of Contingent Workers: Effects of Trust and Social Capital', Paper presented to the Academy of Management Conference, San Diego, August.

Peel, S. and Boxall, P. (2005). 'When Is Contracting Preferable to Employment? An Exploration of Management and Worker Perspectives', *Journal of Management Studies*, 42: 1675–97.

Peters, T. (1987). *Thriving on Chaos*, New York: Alfred A Knopf.

Pettinger, R. (2000). *The Future of Industrial Relations*. London: Continuum.

Pfeffer, J. and Baron, J. (1988). 'Taking Workers Back Out: Recent Trends in the Structuring of Employment', in B. Staw and L. Cummings (eds.), *Research in Organizational Behavior* (Vol. 10), Greenwich, CT: JAI Press 257–303.

Pollert, A. (ed.) (1991). *Farewell to Flexibility*, Oxford, UK: Blackwell.

Porter, L., Pearce, J., Tripoli, A., and Lewis, K. (1998). 'Differential Perceptions of Employers' Inducements: Implications for Psychological Contracts', *Journal of Organizational Behavior*, 19: 769–82.

Price, J. L. (1997). 'Handbook of Organizational Measurement', *International Journal of Manpower*, 18 (4_5_6), 305–558.

PSYCONES (2004). *Societal Dimensions: Context of the Psychological Contract*, Brussels: European Commission, HPSE-CT-2002–00121. Deliverable 4.1. Available at www.uv.es/~psychon.

—— (2005). *Exploring National and Sector Differences and Similarities*, Brussels: European Commission, HPSE-CT-2002–00121. Deliverables 7.1a, 7.1b. Available at www.uv.es/~psychon.

Purcell, J. (1999). 'Best Practice and Best Fit: Chimera or Cul-de-sac?', *Human Resource Management Journal*, 9 (3): 26–41.

Reilly, P. (1998). 'Balancing Flexibility: Meeting the Interests of the Employer and Employee', *European Journal of Work and Organizational Psychology*, 7: 7–22.

Rhoades, L. and Eisenberger, R. (2002). 'Perceived Organizational Support: A Review of the Literature', *Journal of Applied Psychology*, 87: 698–714.

Rigotti, T. and Mohr, G. (2005). 'German Flexibility: Loosening the Reins Without Losing Control', in N. De Cuyper, K. Isaksson, and H. De Witte (eds.), *Employment Contracts and Well-Being Among European Workers*, Hampshire, UK: Ashgate, 75–102.

—— Otto, K., and Mohr, G. (2007). 'East–West Differences in Employment Relations, Organizational Justice and Trust: Possible Reasons and Consequences', *Economic and Industrial Democracy*, 28: 212–38.

Robinson, S. (2003). 'Monkey See, Monkey Do: Dissatisfaction Behavior from a Social Information Processing Perspective'. Paper presented at the Eighth Annual Conference of the Society for Industrial and Organizational Psychology, San Francisco.

—— (1996). 'Trust and Breach of the Psychological Contract', *Administrative Science Quarterly*, 41: 574–99.

—— —— and Morrison, E. (2000). 'The Development of Psychological Contract Breach and Violation: A Longitudinal Study', *Journal of Organizational Behavior*, 21: 525–46.

—— and Rousseau, D. (1994). 'Violating the Psychological Contract: Not the Exception but the Norm', *Journal of Organizational Behaviour*, 15: 245–59.

—— Kraatz, M., and Rousseau, D. (1994). 'Changing Obligations and the Psychological Contract: A Longitudinal Study', *Academy of Management Journal*, 37: 137–52.

Rodgers, G. and Rogers, J. (eds.) (1989). *Precarious Jobs in Labour Market Regulation: The Growth of Atypical Employment in Western Europe*, ILO (International Institute of Labour Studies), Brussels, Belgium: Free University of Brussels.

Rosenthal, P., Guest, D., and Peccei, R. (1996). 'Gender Difference in Managers' Explanations for their Work Performance: A Study in Two Organizations', *Journal of Occupational and Organizational Psychology*, 69: 145–51.

Rousseau, D. (1989). 'Psychological and Implied Contracts in Organizations', *Employee Responsibilities and Rights Journal*, 2: 121–39.

—— (1990). 'New Hire Perceptions of Their Own and Employer's Obligations: A Study of Psychological Contracts', *Journal of Organizational Behavior*, 11: 389–400.

—— (1995). *Psychological Contracts in Organizations: Understanding Written and Unwritten Agreements*, Thousand Oaks, CA: Sage.

—— (2001). 'Schema, Promise, and Mutuality: The Building Blocks of the Psychological Contract', *Journal of Occupational and Organizational Psychology*, 74: 511–41.

—— (2005). *I-deals: Idiosyncratic Deals Employees Bargain for Themselves*, Armonk, NY: Sharpe.

—— and Greller, M. (1994). 'Human Resource Practices: Administrative Contract Makers', *Human Resource Management*, 33: 385–401.

—— and Schalk, R. (2000*a*). 'Introduction', in D. Rousseau and R. Schalk (eds.), *Psychological Contracts in Employment: Cross-National Perspectives*, Thousand Oaks, CA: Sage, 1–28.

—— —— (2000*b*). 'Learning from Cross-National Perspectives on Psychological Contracts', in D. Rousseau and R. Schalk (eds.), *Psychological Contracts in Employment: Cross-National Perspectives*, Thousand Oaks, CA: Sage, 283–304.

—— and Tijoriwala, S. (1998). 'Assessing Psychological Contracts: Issues, Alternatives and Measures', *Journal of Organizational Behavior*, 19: 679–95.

—— and Wade-Benzoni, K. (1994). 'Linking Strategy and Human Resources Practices: How Employee and Customer Contracts Are Created', *Human Resource Management*, 33: 463–89.

—— Sitkin, S., Burt, R., and Camerer, C. (1998). 'Not So Different After All: A Cross-Discipline View of Trust', *Academy of Management Review*, 23: 393–404.

Roxburgh, S. (1996). 'Gender Differences in Work and Well-Being: Effects of Exposure and Vulnerability', *Journal of Health and Social Behavior*, 37: 265–77.

Rupp, D. and Cropanzano, R. (2002). 'The Mediating Effect of Social Exchange Relationships in Predicting Workplace Outcomes from Multifoci Organizational Justice', *Organizational Behaviour and Human Decision Processes*, 89: 925–46.

Saloniemi, A., Virtanen, P., and Vahtera, J. (2004). 'The Work Environment in Fixed-Term Jobs: Are Poor Psychosocial Conditions Inevitable?', *Work, Employment and Society*, 18: 193–208.

Salzberger, T., Sinkovics, R., and Schlegelmilch, B. (1999). 'Data Equivalence in Cross-Cultural Research: A Comparison of Classical Test Theory and Latent Trait Theory-Based Approaches', *Australasian Marketing Journal*, 7: 23–38.

Saxenian, A. (1990). 'Regional Networks and the Resurgence of Silicon Valley', *California Management Review*, 33: 89–112.

Schalk, R. (2004). 'Changes in the Employment Relation Across Time', in J. Coyle-Shapiro, L. Shore, S. Taylor, and L. Tetrick (eds.), *The Employment Relationship: Examining Psychological and Contextual Perspectives*, Oxford, UK: Oxford University Press, 284–311.

Schalk, R. and Freese, C. (1997). 'New Facets of Commitment in Response to Organizational Change: Research Trends and the Dutch Experience', in C. Cooper and D. Rousseau (eds.), *Trends in Organizational Behaviour*, New York: Wiley, 107–23.

—— and Rousseau, D. (2001). 'Psychological Contracts in Employment', in N. Anderson, D. Ones, H. Sinangil, and C. Viswesvaran (eds.), *Handbook of Industrial, Work and Organizational Psychology. Volume 2. Organizational Psychology*, Thousand Oaks, CA: Sage, 134–42.

—— and Soeters, J. (2009). 'Psychological Contracts Around the Globe', in P. Smith, M. Peterson, and D. Thomas (eds.), *Handbook of Cross-Cultural Management Research*, Thousand Oaks: Sage.

Schein, E. A. (1965). *Organizational Psychology*, Englewood Cliffs, NJ: Prentice-Hall.

—— (1978). *Career Dynamics: Matching Individual and Organizational Needs*, Reading, MA: Addison-Wesley.

Scherer, S. (2004). 'Stepping-Stones or Traps? The Consequences of Labour Market Entry Positions on Future Careers in West Germany, Great Britain and Italy', *Work, Employment and Society*, 18: 369–94.

Schneider, B., Hanges, P., Smith, B., and Salvaggio, A. (2003). 'Which Comes First: Employee Attitudes or Organizational Financial Market Performance?', *Journal of Applied Psychology*, 88: 836–51.

Schwartz, S. (1994*a*). 'Cultural Differences Across Nations: A Value Perspective'. Paper presented at the Symposium 'Values and Work—A Comparative Perspective', WORC paper 94.11.050/6, The Netherlands: Tilburg University, 9–12 November (33p.).

—— (1994*b*). 'Beyond Individualism and Collectivism: New Cultural Dimensions of Values', in U. Kim, H. Triandis, C. Kagicibasi, S. Choi, and G. Yoon (eds.), *Individualism and Collectivism: Theory, Methods and Application*, Thousand Oaks, CA: Sage, 58–119.

—— (1999). 'A Theory of Cultural Values and Some Implications for Work', *Applied Psychology: An International Review*, 48: 23–47.

Schyns, B. and von Collani, G. (2002). 'A New Occupational Self-Efficacy Scale and Its Relation to Personality Constructs and Organizational Variables', *European Journal of Work and Organizational Psychology*, 11: 219–41.

Sels, L., Janssens, M., and Van den Brande, I. (2004). 'Assessing the Nature of Psychological Contracts: A Validation of Six Dimensions', *Journal of Organizational Behavior*, 25: 461–88.

Semmer, N., Zapf, D., and Dunckel, H. (1999). 'Instrument zur Stressbezogenen Tätigkeitsanalyse (Instrument for Stress-related Job Analysis (ISTA)', in H. Dunckel (ed.), *Handbuch Psychologischer Arbeitsanalyseverfahren*, Zurich, Switzerland: vdf Hochschulverlag, 179–204.

Sherer, P. and Leblebici, H. (2001). 'Bringing Variety and Change into Strategic Human Resource Management Research', in G. Ferris (ed.), *Research in Personnel and Human Resource Management* (Vol. 20), Greenwich, CT: JAI Press, 199–230.

Shore, L. and Barksdale, K. (1998). 'Examining Degree of Balance and Level of Obligation in the Employment Relationship: A Social Exchange Approach', *Journal of Organizational Behavior*, 19: 731–44.

——and Tetrick, L. (1994). 'The Psychological Contract as an Explanatory Framework in the Employment Relationship', in C. Cooper and D. Rousseau (eds.), *Trends in Organizational Behaviour*. New York: Wiley, 91–109.

Siegrist, J. (1996). 'Adverse Health Effects of High-Effort/Low-Reward Conditions', *Journal of Occupational Health Psychology*, 1: 27–41.

Silla, I., Gracia, F., and Peiró, J. M. (2005). 'Job Insecurity and Health-Related Outcomes Among Different Types of Temporary Workers', *Economic and Industrial Democracy*, 26: 89–117.

Sjoberg, A. and Sverke, M. (2000). 'The Interactive Effect of Job Involvement and Organizational Commitment on Job Turnover Revisited: A Note on the Mediating Role of Turnover Intention', *Scandinavian Journal of Psychology*, 41: 247–52.

Stanworth, C. and Druker, J. (2006). 'Human Resource Solutions? Dimensions of Employers' Use of Temporary Agency Labour in the UK', *Personnel Review*, 35: 175–90.

Staw, B. (1986). 'Organizational Psychology and the Pursuit of the Happy/Productive Worker', *California Management Review*, 28: 40–53.

Steiger, J. (1990). 'Structural Model Evaluation and Modification: An Interval Estimation Approach', *Multivariate Behavioral Research*, 25: 173–80.

Stjernberg, T. and Bergstrom, O. (2003). *New Understanding of European Work Organization (NUEWO): Final Report*, Brussels, Belgium: European Commission.

Storrie, D. (2003). 'The Flexibility–Security Trade-off in Europe', in O. Bergström and D. Storrie (eds.), *Contingent Employment in Europe and the United States*, Cheltenham, UK: Edward Elgar, 224–48.

Sutton, G. and Griffin, M. (2004). 'Integrating Expectations, Experiences, and Psychological Contract Violations: A Longitudinal Study of New Professionals', *Journal of Occupational and Organizational Psychology*, 77: 493–514.

Sverke, M., Gallagher, D., and Hellgren, J. (2000). 'Alternative Work Arrangements: Job Stress, Well-Being and Work Attitudes Among Employees with Different Employment Contracts', in K. Isaksson, C. Hogstedt, C. Eriksson, and T. Theorell (eds.), *Health Effects of the New Labour Market*, New York: Kluwer, 145–67.

——Hellgren, J., and Näswall, K. (2002). 'No Security: A Meta Analysis and Review of Job Insecurity and its Consequences', *Journal of Occupational Health Psychology*, 7: 242–64.

Tan, H. and Tan, C. (2002). 'Temporary Employees in Singapore: What Drives Them?', *Journal of Psychology*, 136: 83–102.

Tekleab, A. and Taylor, S. (2003). 'Aren't There Two Parties in an Employment Relationship? Antecedents and Consequences of Organization–Employee Agreement on Contract Obligations and Violations', *Journal of Organizational Behavior*, 24: 585–608.

Thomas, D., Au, K., and Ravlin, E. (2003). 'Cultural Variation and the Psychological Contract', *Journal of Organizational Behavior*, 24: 451–71.

Thomas, H. and Anderson, N. (1998). 'Changes in Newcomers' Psychological Contracts During Organizational Socialization: A Study of Recruits Entering the British Army', *Journal of Organizational Behavior*, 19: 745–67.

Tsui, A., Pearce, J., Porter, L., and Tripoli, A. (1997). 'Employee–Organisation Relationship: Does Investment in Employees Pay Off?', *Academy of Management Journal*, 40: 1089–121.

Tunny, G. and Mangan, J. (2004). 'Stepping Stones to Permanent Employment in the Public Service', *Labour*, 18: 591–614.

Turnley, W. and Feldman, D. (1999*a*). 'The Impact of Psychological Contract Violations on Exit, Voice, Loyalty, and Neglect', *Human Relations*, 52: 895–922.

———— (1999*b*). 'A Discrepancy Model of Psychological Contract Violations', *Human Resource Management Review*, 9: 367–86.

———— (2000). 'Re-examining the Effects of Psychological Contract Violations: Unmet Expectations and Job Dissatisfaction as Mediators', *Journal of Organizational Behaviour*, 21: 25–42.

UNESCO (2003). 'International Standard Classification of Education, ISCED 1997', in J. Hoffmeyer-Zlotnik and C. Wolf (eds.), *Advances in Cross-National Comparison. A European Working Book for Demographic and Socio-Economic Variables*, New York: Kluwer Academic/Plenum Publishers, 195–220.

Van der Doef, M. and Maes, S. (1999). 'The Leiden Quality of Work Questionnaire: Its Construction, Factor Structure and Psychometric Qualities', *Psychological Reports*, 85: 954–62.

Van Dyne, L. and Ang, S. (1998). 'Organizational Citizenship Behaviour of Contingent Workers in Singapore', *Academy of Management Journal*, 41: 692–703.

Vigneau, C., Ahlberg, K., Bercusson, B., and Bruun, N. (1999). *Fixed-Term Work in the EU: A European Agreement Against Discrimination and Abuse*, Stockholm, Sweden: National Institute for Working Life.

Virtanen, M., Kivimäki, M., Elovainio, M., Vahtera, J., and Cooper, C. (2001). 'Temporary Employment, Health and Sickness Absence', *Scandinavian Journal of Work, Environment and Health*, 27: 365–72.

—— Vahtera, J., Kivimäki, M., Pentii, J., and Ferrie, J. (2002). 'Employment Security and Health', *Journal of Epidemiological Community Health*, 56: 569–74.

—— Liukkonen, V., Vahtera, J., Kivimäki, M., and Koskenvuo, M. (2003). 'Health Inequalities in the Workforce: The Labour Market Core–Periphery Structure', *International Journal of Epidemiology*, 32: 1015–21.

—— Kivimäki, M., Joensuu, M., Virtanen, M., Elovainio, M., and Vahtera, J. (2005). 'Temporary Employment and Health: A Review', *International Journal of Epidemiology*, 34: 610–22.

von Hippel, C., Mangum, S., Greenberger, R., Heneman, R., and Skoglind, J. (1997). 'Temporary Employment: Can Organizations and Employees Both Win?', *The Academy of Management Executive*, 11: 93–104.

Wagena, E. and Geurts, S. (2000). 'SWING. Ontwikkeling en Validering van de "Survey Werk-thuis Interferentie-Nijmegen"' ('SWING. Development and Validation of the "Survey Work-Home Interference-Nijmegen"'), *Gedrag en Organisatie*, 28: 138–58.

Ware, J. (1999). 'SF-36 Health Survey', in M. Maruish (ed.), *The Use of Psychological Testing for Treatment Planning and Outcomes Assessment*, 2nd edn., Mahwah, NJ: Lawrence Erlbaum Associates, 1227–46.

Warr, P. (1987). *Work, Unemployment and Mental Health*, Oxford, UK: Clarendon Press.

—— (1990). 'The Measurement of Well-Being and Other Aspects of Mental Health', *Journal of Occupational Psychology*, 63: 193–210.

—— (2002). 'The Study of Well-Being, Behaviour and Attitudes', in P. Warr (ed.), *Psychology at Work*, 5th edn., London: Penguin, 1–25.

—— (2007). *Work, Happiness and Unhappiness*, Mahwah, NJ: Lawrence Erlbaum Associates.

Wayne, S., Shore, L., and Liden, R. (1997). 'Perceived Organizational Support and Leader–Member Exchange: A Social Exchange Perspective', *Academy of Management Journal*, 40: 82–111.

Werner, O. and Campbell, D. (1970). 'Translating, Working through Interpreters, and the Problem of Decentering', in R. Naroll and R. Cohen (eds.), *A Handbook of Method in Cultural Anthropology*, New York: American Museum of Natural History, 398–420.

Westwood, R., Sparrow, P., and Leung, A. (2001). 'Challenges to the Psychological Contract in Hong Kong', *International Journal of Human Resource Management*, 12: 621–51.

Whitley, R. (1999). *Divergent Capitalisms: The Social Structuring and Change of Business Systems*, Oxford, UK: Oxford University Press.

Wikman, A., Andersson, A., and Bastin, M. (1998). *Nya Relationer i Arbetslivet (New Relations in Working Life)*, Stockholm, Sweden: National Institute for Working.

Williamson, O. (1979). 'Transaction Cost Economics: The Governance of Contractual Relations', *Journal of Law and Economics*, 22: 233–61.

—— (1985). *The Economic Institutions of Capitalism*, New York: Free Press.

World Health Organization (1998). 'Definition of Health'. http://www.who.ch/about-who/definition.htm.

Index